Rhetoric

Rhetoric

A USER'S GUIDE

John D. Ramage
Arizona State University

PEARSON
Longman

New York   San Francisco   Boston
London   Toronto   Sydney   Tokyo   Singapore   Madrid
Mexico City   Munich   Paris   Cape Town   Hong Kong   Montreal

Publisher: Joseph Opiela
Acquisitions Editor: Lauren Finn
Marketing Manager: Alexandra Rivas-Smith
Production Manager: Donna DeBenedictis
Project Coordination, Text Design, and Electronic Page Makeup:
  Elm Street Publishing Services, Inc.
Cover Designer/Manager: Wendy Ann Fredericks
Cover Art: ©Jose Ortega/Images.com/CORBIS
Senior Manufacturing Buyer: Dennis J. Para
Printer and Binder: RR Donnelley & Sons Company/Harrisonburg
Cover Printer: Coral Graphic Services

Library of Congress Cataloging-in-Publication Data
Ramage, John D.
  Rhetoric : a user's guide / John D. Ramage.
    p. cm.
  Includes bibliographical references and index.
  ISBN 0-321-20212-0 (alk. paper)
  1. Rhetoric.   I. Title.

PN187.R36 2006
808—dc22
                                    2005020784

Please visit us at http://www.ablongman.com

ISBN 0-321-20212-0

1 2 3 4 5 6 7 8 9 10—DOH—08 07 06 05

CONTENTS

To the Instructor
ೕಀನಀ

A Slightly Polemical Introduction

In the process of communicating back and forth about *Rhetoric: A User's Guide*, my editor, reviewers, and I converted its obligatorily cumbersome title to a more manageable acronym, *RUG*. Happily, "*RUG*" turned out to be a suggestively ironic metaphor for the project. As was soon apparent to all and distressing to some, *RUG* is singularly unconcerned with "coverage" of the field. Many of the terms it uses are drawn from a fairly narrow range of sources, some are invented, and exhaustive definitions of standard terms are seldom offered. Names and dates are in short supply, and little effort is made to construct a master narrative tracking the great rhetorical debates through the centuries. When all is said and done, *RUG*, *qua* rugs, is more of a sisal welcome mat than a room-sized Persian.

And because of *RUG*'s economic scale—if 1 may be permitted a more eulogistic descriptor—it looks alarmingly slight in the company of other texts commonly used to introduce students to rhetoric. Placing *RUG* next to Bizzell and Herzberg's voluminous *The Rhetorical Tradition* is like placing a spiral-bound carb counter next to *The Joy of Cooking*. And certainly there is much to like about *The Rhetorical Tradition* beyond mere bulk. It combines generous and representative samples of primary works from all the major figures in the field with intelligent introductions that analyze and interconnect the material. Despite its great length, few would wish it briefer. And even when placed beside *The Rhetorical Tradition*'s slimmer cousins, the handful of introductory texts that attempt to replicate its admirable scope minus its formidable scale by glossing many of the works Bizzell and Herzberg anthologize, *RUG* looks undersized.

So what is lost and what is gained by offering so terse an introduction to the field? Certainly *RUG* is ill-suited to serve as the sole text in a survey course. While most other introductions offer one a comprehensive view of rhetoric and invite one to traverse the field at various paces, *RUG* offers a synthesis of rhetorical thinking and invites one to apply it immediately. (Among the notable exceptions to this generalization about introductory texts I would include a handful of useful anthologies and a pair of admirable little books—David Blakesley's *Elements of Dramatism* and William Covino's *Elements of Persuasion*—that use a somewhat narrower lens than *RUG's* to encapsulate the whole of rhetoric.) And while there are certainly costs associated with *RUG's* failure to offer a comprehensive view of our twenty-five-hundred-year-old discipline, its ready usefulness and applicability represent compensatory benefits.

Which brings us to a second irony implicit in its title. *RUG* is not a user's guide in the ordinary sense of the term. There are no schematic drawings of enthymemes here, no elaborate descriptions of rhetorical mechanisms, no troubleshooting charts to consult when one's arguments go astray or one's interpretations break down, no brisk instructions about how to set up the rhetorical apparatus in the comfort of one's own home. *RUG* serves as a user's guide in the same tongue-in-cheek way that a work entitled, say, *Philosophy: A User's Guide* might be one. (And if such a title seems outlandish, consider the even more unlikely title of a supplemental text in my intro to philosophy course many years ago: *Philosophy Made Simple.*) *RUG* promises to help one apply some of the lessons of the field without necessarily implying that it will teach one all, or even all the important, lessons to be learned from the field.

RUG's narrowness, its emphasis on focus over scope, is a necessary condition of its usefulness. And this preference for dealing with representative bits of larger wholes, what Kenneth Burke calls "representative anecdotes," or what Clifford Geertz has called "thick descriptions," is an element of the rhetorical way discussed in Chapter 1. What rhetoric invites one always to keep in mind is that "a way of seeing is also a way of not seeing," that insight requires blindness, that reflection requires deflection. In trying to see everything, you'll end up seeing nothing. In attempting to present things absolutely objectively, you end up simply replicating the thing you set out to represent. What rhetoric teaches one is that meaning must be *made*, that it can't simply be found whole or transmitted unfiltered. And one makes meaning by extracting "gists" from texts, events, and experiences through a process of selection and exclusion and then understanding those gists "in terms of" other gists, themselves the product of the same process of selection and exclusion. The process may be highly routinized and purposive; it may be intuitive and quirky. It all depends on how conscious we are of the lens, terministic screen, ideology, theory, position, or heuristic that focuses our inquiry.

Most of the time, the process of meaning making falls somewhere between the extremes of algorithm and accident. No matter how rational our instruments of knowing may be, the process of meaning making is so open ended, the possible permutations of gists and pairings are so numerous, that some element of the unforeseen inevitably creeps into the equation. By the same token, no matter how determined we are to exclude rationality from the process, no matter how Dadaist our designs or incongruous our perspectives, our culturally determined predilections and preoccupations—our "occupational psychoses"—will shape our choices. As a consequence of all this, our "ratios"—the products or "third things" that we derive from seeing one thing in terms of another—serve mostly to "round out" rather than to disambiguate our understanding of the original term. They are sufficiently rational to be seen as plausible extensions of our first term, but sufficiently magical to be seen as transformations of the original.

At this point in the proceedings some among you may be wondering when I'm going to get around to mentioning Aristotle or revealing what advice I might have about finding the available means of persuasion in a given circumstance. Others may more pointedly wonder why I persist in using the term "rhetoric" to describe views that should properly be ascribed to Kenneth Burke. Even casual students of Burke may recognize in the previous two paragraphs the traces of an outline for Burke's dramatistic method. All that's needed to bring those traces into clearer relief is a discussion of the pentad and an explanation of how one can use act, agent, agency, scene, and purpose as grammatical terms to form twenty sets of master ratios (ten pairs of reversible terms) into which one can substitute everything under the sun and be rewarded with an incongruous perspective and a novel understanding. One would be correct to assume that the logic of dramatism and Burkean dialectic underlies the thinking in these two paragraphs. Indeed, Kenneth Burke could be deemed the tutelary spirit for this entire little book, an admission that will require justification for those, and there are more than a few, who consider Burke too abstruse, too monolithic, too dated . . . take your pick—whatever excess he might be charged with, he has been charged with. So how does one justify so close an identification of rhetoric with Burke?

Let me begin my justification with a confession. My inclination to privilege Burke over Aristotle is in part an accident of personal history. I read Burke's *Grammar of Motives* and *Rhetoric of Motives* before I read Aristotle's *Rhetoric* and so tend to understand Aristotle "in terms of" Burke. Insofar as the second term in a Burkean ratio is the position from which one understands the first term, it serves as the "essence" of the pair. While that relationship is not invariant, while I am welcome to reverse their positions within the ratio and on occasion have found myself doing so, I never fully recovered from that first experience of understanding Aristotle through the terministic screen of Burke. And the particulars of how I came to read Burke before Aristotle render my narrative of discovery even more suspiciously random than I've so far let on. Indeed, if this were a different sort of book, I would be busily erasing all such signs of contingency from my narrative and imbuing it with a reassuring sense of necessity or inevitability. But since rhetoric allows, indeed requires, that contingency be acknowledged and granted its place in our accounts, even when it disrupts those accounts, I'll offer up my own anecdote about my introduction to the field and the difficulties that anecdote poses for any sort of necessitarian origin myth I might wish to create from it.

As it turns out, I came across Burke not in some graduate seminar or university library—I don't recall Burke ever being mentioned during my time in graduate school—but in a newly opened, decidedly odd little bookstore that I chanced upon many years ago while passing through the seedy "lower" end of Portland's Burnside Street en route to several more respectable bookstores a few blocks farther up. I almost didn't stop. This was no place for casual shoppers or flaneurs. More of the neighborhood's business was conducted in its doorways than inside its stores. And from the sidewalk I could see that the store's freshly cut bookshelves were only half full of what appeared to be mostly romances, mysteries, and Chilton car manuals. But on a whim, I went in. Once inside, I was elaborately ignored by the only other person in the store, a slight, sallow fellow behind the counter wearing inch-thick glasses and smiling dreamily into a space only he could penetrate. I tried browsing, but finding no apparent order to the shelves and getting no help from Mr. Dreamy, I decided to leave. At which point, the store's proprietor, Walt Powell, a stout, sixtyish man wearing a flannel shirt and baggy wool pants held loosely in place with suspenders, came bustling up to me from the back room, speaking rapidly in an accent I couldn't place, asking me questions I couldn't understand. He was simultaneously a very ordinary and a very mysterious fellow whose pronounced overbite and aureole of frizzy white hair lent him an air of rabbity wisdom. Put Walt in a velvet cloak and he would have looked right at home in a *Harry Potter* film.

He turned out to be an affable, utterly unpretentious man, pleased and excited to have found a customer, even an inadvertent one, in his store. Almost the first thing he told me was that he knew nothing about books (except for Chilton car manuals, about which he was extremely keen). If I did happen to know a thing or two, and I looked to him like someone who did, he'd hire me on the spot to clean up his literature and philosophy sections and to sort through the dozens of boxes in the back that he'd bought off book scouts. Because I was on break from grad school, broke, and charmed, I accepted his offer. And so it was there, while culling literary wheat from boxes of New Age chaff that I came across Burke. And it was there during my lunch hours that I tried, with little initial success, to read Burke. All of which makes my eventual infatuation with Burke either a totally predestined or a totally random event, depending, I suppose, on whether one sees the upshot of the infatuation to be ironic in the tragic or in the comic sense. And by the same token, the fact that the seedy little shop on the corner where I fished Burke out of a box of literary dreck, the scene of my drama, would eventually become the colossus across the street, Powell's Books, largest used bookstore in the world, may be seen as either enlarging or dwarfing my primal act.

So much for the context of discovery. What about the context of justification? How can I justify such a heavy reliance on Kenneth Burke while presuming to introduce people to so august and diverse a discipline as rhetoric? First, Burke, for all his reputation as a singular thinker, is a respectful student of the rhetorical tradition. He draws on that tradition constantly, incorporating many notions from rhetoric through the ages in the process of developing his own thinking. And as has often been remarked—perhaps, alas, too often—Burke anticipates many of the ideas that have animated recent and current debates over the relationship between language and being. While he may not be a typical rhetorical figure in the quantitative sense of typicality, he is, I would argue, in his own sense of representation a representative rhetorical figure: a part of the whole that is particularly helpful in identifying that whole without ever being identical to it.

Moreover, I would argue that Burke's view of rhetoric—echoing a not-altogether-sanguine reviewer's comments—constitutes the only comprehensive view of the subject offering something more than "footnotes on Aristotle." Burke allows us at once to understand Aristotle from a modern perspective, a perspective better anticipated by his Sophist predecessors than by Aristotle, and to extend the reach of rhetoric beyond the narrow bounds set for it by Aristotle. Without suggesting that Burke is all one needs to know about rhetoric, I would argue that he is *primus inter pares* in relation to other rhetorical figures. If one must choose a single thinker as one's entry point into the field of rhetoric, Burke, by virtue of his theory's scope, reflexiveness, and usefulness, is, I'm convinced, the most defensible choice. But that still leaves open crucial questions of pedagogy: Is this focus on a single figure the best way to introduce students to a field? Shouldn't they jog, trot, or dash across the entire territory in anticipation of a later, more leisurely examination of its individual sites?

My answer to the second question is a reasonably firm, "No," while my answer to the first is a more tentative, "Yes, if one selects one's figure with great care." My modest certitude in this matter emboldens me to cajole, but not to debunk, those who champion introductory surveys. (Many years ago I wrote an article in the *Journal of Aesthetic Education* that did its best to debunk the reigning rationale for the introductory survey, and that experience has, with every passing year, left me increasingly convinced of the rightness of Burke's dictum that we cannot debunk others without subverting ourselves.) In the matter of introducing students to a subject, the perplexities are so numerous and so apparent that humility should come easily. Above all, where does one start? How can students understand one part—a thinker, a theory, an epoch, an idea—unless they understand another part and so on *ad infinitum*. They need to know the whole before they can properly understand any part, but how do they acquire the whole except part by part?

Burke touches on this conundrum in his discussion of "efficiency." Because one cannot say everything one wishes or needs to say at one go, one must "efficiently" put matters one at a time, a process that entails an emphasis or overemphasis on those matters one puts before other matters. One can't avoid efficiency, one can only mitigate its effects by maintaining an "ecological balance" among the parts as one proceeds. By maintaining that balance and relying on one's audience to exercise the "counterefficiency" of "discounting" what one says in terms of what one has not said, or not yet said, one can minimize, but never eliminate, the distortions. But of course an audience's ability to discount terms is a function of its familiarity with the domain within which the terms are used. Novices, including students in introductory courses, are less capable of predicting what's to come and of understanding the larger context when they are dealing with an unfamiliar vocabulary.

E. D. Hirsch, in *Cultural Literacy*, famously finesses this problem by calling for both "intensive" and "extensive" curricula, with the former charged to look intensively at local problems or questions in a field, while the latter looks broadly at myriad pieces of "background information" that for Hirsch comprise literacy. (Hirsch's focus, of course, is K–12 education with an emphasis on early education. But the assumptions underlying his model have been readily adapted to college education, most notably by counterinsurgents during the Great Canon debates.) While Hirsch says the two are complementary and necessary to each other, he leaves little doubt that the extensive curriculum needs to come first and is far more likely to yield reliable results. From my position—which is closer to that of Burke, and Hirsch's favorite whipping boy, John Dewey—Hirsch's solution represents a contrived binary that privileges the wrong term. While it appears perfectly reasonable, thus, that one could acquire extensive knowledge of a discipline through the serial application of disciplinary methods to multiple problems, it's less clear that one could acquire intensive knowledge of a discipline by memorizing heaps of isolated factoids, no matter how vast the heaps. Moreover, what any given factoid may mean is a function of the circumstances in which it is used, and if students learn them in isolation prior to using them in any given circumstance, they may well find that their "background information" does not travel well when summoned to any particular foreground.

The matter of scope, which bears significantly on the usefulness of any informational unit, gets short shrift from Hirsch. For the most part, he appears to have in mind the names of people, places, events, and phrases. And when more general information is deemed worthy of assimilation, only a superficial understanding of its import is required. Burke, meanwhile, gives extended attention to the matter of scope. The representative anecdote, which is his primary analytical instrument, "itself so dramatistic a conception that we might call it the dramatistic approach to dramatism" (GOM, 60), must have sufficient scope to be representative of a larger whole, yet be simple enough to allow one to contemplate it fully. It is not simply one unit of information in an ensemble of informational units that collectively form a larger context, it is part of the whole through which one can come to a clear understanding of the workings of the whole. It's a microcosm of the macrocosm to which it belongs. Which is how I use Burke—as a representative anecdote for rhetoric. To the extent that other approaches to rhetoric can be identified with Burke's approach, to the extent that in learning how to use Burke one develops a sense for how to go about using rhetoric, our anecdote turns out to be properly representative.

But before going on to offer some fairly specific and practical advice about *RUG*'s intended audience and its possible classroom uses, I need to make explicit what's implied by the above analysis. By the lights of the very approach I'm using, I can't simply use it without altering it. It is not, after all, "Burke" who appears on the following pages, it is my particular gist of Burke in combination with my particular gist of numerous other people—Richard Lanham, John Dewey, Hans Blumenberg, Timothy Crusius, Ann Berthoff, Wayne Booth, Susan Jarrett, Aristotle, and so forth—whose ideas have influenced me directly or influenced my reading of Burke. As always, my responsibility is not so much to remain faithful to some originary Burke, but to maintain an ecological balance among the various readings of Burke that comprise my own version of him.

A Few Words about *RUG*'s Possible Uses

If one writes a book about rhetoric, one should be prepared to identify its intended audience. After all, even people who know little about rhetoric know that a concern for audience is a distinguishing characteristic of rhetorical understanding. To put the matter somewhat reductively: Arguments are efficacious if they have the desired effect on the intended audience, inefficacious if they fail that test. And while I mostly subscribe to that view, I also subscribe to a couple of other views that complicate matters a bit.

First there is the view, put forth most famously by Walter Ong, and in a different form by Lisa Ede and Andrea Lunsford, that writers also create their audiences, or at least positions for their audiences to occupy. Second, there is Burke's view that some arguments rightfully ignore their audiences in order to realize the unforeseen possibilities arising from the complications of their own unfolding; in such cases the text becomes, in a sense, self-authorizing. Most of the books I enjoy the most and learn the most from show signs of these last two complications. They appear to have no designs on me (the more insistent those designs, the more "cunning" the rhetoric, according to Burke), and often speak to me not as they take me to be, but as they challenge me to become. In keeping with my own reading predilections, I've tried to write a book that various audiences might find readable but also challenging. To the extent that teachers comprise my primary audience, I hope *RUG* persuades you to entertain an unconventional notion of how students might be introduced to rhetoric and a correspondingly unorthodox notion of what a textbook might look like. To the extent that students comprise my primary audience, I hope *RUG* persuades them that nothing is more complex, interesting, and chockablock with meaning than the everyday, the routine, the taken-for-granted, and the commonsensical, when looked at systematically from incongruous rhetorical perspectives.

Assuming that *RUG* wins some converts, how might one actually use it in the classroom and with what sorts of students? When I initially conceived of *RUG*, I had in mind using it in somewhat the way I've used Terry Eagleton's fine little book *Literary Theory* over the years. I have used Eagleton's book in graduate seminars and undergraduate courses on theory, both rhetorical and literary, basically to introduce the subject to students. I generally have students read the book independently over a week or so and then spend several class periods discussing key issues and questions raised in the book. I spend little time worrying about historical sequences and distinctions among the various schools of thought; I spend considerable time reflecting on what people over the years have imagined literature to be and consequently what they might *do* with it. Eagelton makes no bones about the position from which he views his subject and I try to make clear where I agree (mostly) and where I disagree with his positions. I then proceed to an examination of primary works by several theorists using our discussions of Eagleton to inform our later discussions and to help students keep some of the larger questions in mind as they try to sort their way through the sometimes labyrinthine inner workings of individual arguments.

My conception of the book evolved over the years as my teaching assignments and the curriculum I operated within changed. For several years, for example, I cotaught the orientation and the seminar for new TA's preparing to work in our first-year composition program. Typically, 90 percent of the grad students in the course were not rhetoric and composition students. They were a combination of MFA, literature, linguistics, and English-education students. Our composition program was at the time using a cultural studies approach. It soon became clear that many of our grad students would benefit from a brief introduction to rhetoric with an emphasis on actual application. We needed something more sophisticated than the rhetoric supplied by the textbook—the cultural studies text we were using offered scant rhetorical advice and in fact little help on how to "do" cultural studies—but something less survey-like than the earlier discussed introductory texts or the various reading packets we put together. We needed a little book that did not assume those using it would necessarily go on in the discipline, a book of praxis that was self-reflective about its underlying theory but that spent more time exploring the implications of the theory for users than it did defending itself against other theories or taking issue with other theorists.

Beyond its use with nonspecialist graduate students, I could foresee *RUG* being used in an English department "gateway" course that introduced students, usually sophomores and juniors, to different aspects of English studies including rhetoric. It might be used in an undergraduate introduction to rhetorical studies course in somewhat the same way I've used Eagleton down through the years. And I'm increasingly convinced that *RUG* could be useful in upper-division writing courses focused on, say, public policy issues, argument, or cultural studies. Particularly when such courses are taught by nonspecialists, the resources of rhetoric may not always be fully exploited. Its implications for identity and its usefulness in interpretation are often ignored in favor of its persuasive focus and its concern for audience. There tends to be a disconnect, subsequently, between teaching students how to construct essays and arguments and teaching them how to construe situations and texts. And for those of us who learned long ago from Ann Berthoff that "How you construe is how you construct," and vice versa, that rupture results in a decided loss. If we offer students a systematic approach to meaning making, as opposed to a more piecemeal approach through the use of heuristics, they should be better prepared to construct more complex and more developed arguments, and better able to connect those arguments to larger contexts that matter to them.

And finally there is one further audience issue that requires comment. In thinking of students as the primary audience for *RUG*, a priority was given to its readability. I would like to think that the book could be read through independently in several sittings without causing students undue hardship. Consequently, the extensive scholarly apparatus and documentation that might otherwise accompany a text that is so allusive, so indebted to Burke and others for the main lines of its argument, has been considerably reduced.

Acknowledgments

First of all, to the nearly 2,500 students I calculate that I've taught over the years, many thanks for "beta testing" my ideas and refining my methods. Of the many colleagues, friends, and teachers who did what they could to help me get where I needed to go and to help me figure out just where "where" might be, a number deserve special thanks. My old philosophy professor, Bill Soper, first introduced me to the idea that education was above all conversation in basement seminars featuring lots of German philosophy and execrable home brew. My fellow seminarians and I continued these conversations with great relish over "Switches" in the SUB, on stools at the Green Lantern, and in Jerry

Cederblom's cozy upstairs apartment. Years later, in Ann Berthoff's NEH seminar on philosophy and composition, I engaged in another conversation so interesting and provocative that it caused me to redirect my whole career. Much of this book has its roots in the reading I did and the conversations I had with the very special people of that seminar. I'd like to acknowledge the reviewers of this manuscript: John C. Bean, Seattle University; David Blakesley, Purdue University; Timothy W. Crusius, Southern Methodist University; Susanmarie Harrington, Indiana University Purdue University Indianapolis; and Donna Strickland, University of Missouri. And finally to the TAs I've worked with over the years in the TA seminar and my most excellent coteacher of that seminar, Jeanne Dugan, thank you for your wisdom and your patience.

JOHN D. RAMAGE

1

❧

Introduction

THE WAY OF RHETORIC

Anyone who presumes to offer a fully rounded view of rhetoric must sooner or later address the perplexing two-part mystery of its existence, a mystery that goes something like this. Part One: Why do so many people view rhetoric as such a dubious—make that "odious"—undertaking? Part Two: How, given these widespread misgivings about rhetoric, has it managed to endure for two-and-a-half millennia and to enjoy something of a renaissance over the past several decades? In the following introduction, each of these two questions will be addressed in turn. In the first part, we will don the mask of the Anti-Rhetoric Spokesperson and consider four major objections to rhetoric; in the second part, we will examine the appeal of rhetoric as a "way," a distinctly and robustly Western version of the Chinese "Tao," or the Navajo "Dine." And in the process of enumerating its features and virtues, the aforementioned objections will be addressed. What we won't be doing in this introductory chapter is telling you flat out what rhetoric is in fifty words or less—other than to say it always has to do with the production/interpretation of symbolic acts and usually has to do with persuasion. We will, to be sure, say a good deal about what rhetoric is like, what it does, and what it means "in terms of" other things, just not what it *is*. In response to which, rhetoric's many critics will doubtless Hrmph! (the anti-rhetorical faction is big on Hrmphing) and grumble, "Typical rhetorical evasion!" Rhetoric's few but plucky supporters, meanwhile, will likely smile and

1

murmur, "Exactly." The Great Rhetoric Mystery. It is, as reggae artist Jimmie Cliff might say, "a perfect ponder."

A Word from the Anti-Rhetoric Spokesperson: Four Reasons for Abolishing Rhetoric

1. *Rhetoric is a low-budget pseudoscience; its methods can't be formalized or routinized and its conclusions are uncertain.*

As one eminent rhetorician, a college dropout named Kenneth Burke, once said of his practice, "The main ideal . . . is to use all that is there to use" (PLF 21). Which on the face of it is about as helpful as Henry James's characteristically obscure advice to a young writer about how to become a novelist: "Be one on whom nothing is lost." Just how does one go about following such advice? What are the steps and procedures? What axioms, principles, and laws regulate these procedures? How might one falsify conclusions produced by these means? Does one really need to go to school or even read a book to discover how to be "one on whom nothing is lost" or one who uses "all that is there to use"?

Who can respect a field of knowledge that looks less like a "real discipline" than it does a bag of tricks, a collection of proverbs and aphorisms available to anyone regardless of education, character, intelligence, or intentions? Real disciplines like medicine, accounting, or chemical engineering are above all autonomous, which means they hold the power to exclude the weak minded through testing and educational requirements and root out those of weak character with ethical standards and conduct boards. Real disciplines possess intellectual rigor in the form of stringent tests routinely applied to claims and conclusions in order to prove them true or false. Real disciplines adamantly withhold their assent to any claim pending strong proof in support of that claim. The practice of rhetoric, on the other hand, lacks gatekeepers and overseers, has no code of conduct, and is an equal-opportunity supporter (nay, puffer) of any claim, no matter how shoddy. Because it proclaims its right to comment on every imaginable subject, it has no borders and hence no autonomy. Anyone may use it to any end.

Little wonder that rhetoric has become the refuge of last resort for those seeking to justify the unjustifiable or to render the impossible plausible. Just look at some of the most prominent practitioners of rhetoric in contemporary American culture. Those quacks and mountebanks on late-night TV who flog fat-burning elastic belts practice rhetoric; those "Sabbath gasbags" who pontificate endlessly on Sunday news shows practice rhetoric; those shameless mopes who phone during dinner and plead with us to buy a time-share in Orlando practice rhetoric; that ingratiating little weasel who sat next to you in French and got a C on the midterm but managed to wheedle a B- out of the teacher practiced rhetoric.

Even rhetoric's Greek origin myth, the story of its birth, underscores its utter lack of cachet. According to Protagoras, one of the first professional rhetoricians, the basic tools for practicing rhetoric were distributed by Hermes, acting on orders from Zeus, equally to everyone regardless of intelligence or status. In fact, so rudimentary were these gifts—the capacity to discern the just from the unjust, to revere justice, and to be shamed by injustice—that those who lacked them were to be put to death. So every warm body, as it turns out, is entitled—indeed obligated—to practice rhetoric. No wonder Socrates, to whom Protagoras tells this story, makes short work of his pretensions to real knowledge and foresees—correctly, it would appear—the sorry state the world would fall into if ever rhetoric were to triumph over more rigorous and principled modes of thinking.

Indeed, today one can put paid to contemporary rhetoric's claims for itself simply by rehearsing the anti-rhetorical arguments of Socrates and his student Plato, who records those arguments in his dialogues. Whenever Socrates invites rhetoricians, then known as Sophists, from whence the term "sophistry" is descended, to defend their practices, they offer up a flowery speech. And each time, Socrates responds by slicing and dicing their effusions, reducing their vague generalities to a series of stark contradictions that reveal finally the emptiness of their claims. In the end, Socrates arrives at certainty by following a rigorous logic, by reducing the Sophists' boldest propositions to two opposing choices, two possible meanings, and then inviting the rhetorician to select one; once the rhetorician chooses (sometimes with a nudge from Socrates pointing up the absurdity of his first choice), Socrates breaks that proposition down into two further choices. And so on, until at last there is one and only one possible conclusion to the exchange. We have arrived at The Truth. And it rarely looks anything like the claim that launched the hapless Sophist's oration; in fact, as often as not the poor fellow must reluctantly agree (sometimes he storms offstage or disappears into the crowd to avoid having to acknowledge the sorry pass to which the dialogue has brought him) that the conclusion Socrates has helped them reach is the very opposite of his opening claim.

The contrast could not be starker. The rhetorician *speaks at* people; Socrates *talks with* them. The rhetorician promotes causes that suit his interests; Socrates promotes The Truth whoever it suits or doesn't suit.

The rhetorician uses emotional appeals and anecdotes to aggrandize his cause; Socrates uses mainly logic to deflate that cause. The rhetorician's claims are appealing; Socrates' conclusions are necessary or inevitable. And from the vantage point of the present, it appears that little has changed. But while latter-day rhetoricians appear to be winning with their tricks and flattery, we know enough to trust that appearances that deceive are vulnerable to arguments that prove and to have faith that some day new champions of truth will emerge and bring us to our collective senses with irresistible and pious arguments.

2. Rhetoric panders to the masses.

Even rhetoric's most ardent supporters, including the aforementioned Burke, acknowledge that it could not survive in a more perfect world. By Burke's own admission, rhetoric is a subject "concerned with Babel after the fall," one whose contributions to knowledge "often carry us far into the lugubrious regions of malice and the lie." In a perfect world where all humans possessed the same language and values, where no one was motivated to fool other people or to win their assent to ideas that ill-served their interests, where all were united by universal truths, there would be no place for rhetoric because there would be nothing to persuade anyone of. We would all know and believe the same things. Rhetoric can only hold sway in an imperfect world where words can have more than one meaning, where truth is not universally acknowledged, and where people are vulnerable to unprincipled, persuasive gambits.

The question that rhetoric begs in its suspiciously eager embrace of an imperfect world is whether it merely accepts those imperfections or whether it is in fact responsible for creating new ones. And if it is only arguably complicit in the deplorable conditions that it claims necessitate its practice, rhetoric is most certainly derelict in meeting the most fundamental obligations any discipline owes to those who come seeking enlightenment from it—the duty to teach the truth as it knows it, and to make clear how such truth is to be acquired. Virtually every major Western philosopher over the past 2,000-plus years has consequently criticized rhetoric for scanting these obligations in favor of helping people win over audiences. Instead of dispelling false notions, rhetoricians teach their students how to exploit them. If an audience believes the world to be flat, rhetoric does not compel us to persuade them that it's actually round. Instead, it urges us to use that audience's fallacious belief in the service of our own ends. Perhaps, for example, we could convince some of them to replace those outmoded world "globes" in their dens with our new line of "lighted earth boxes, ($49.95, bulbs not included)"; or, if some of them were contemplating transoceanic voyages, we might persuade them to buy our travelers insurance covering them in the event they "sail over the earth's edge." Like judo masters who win their matches by accelerating opponents' motion in whatever direction they are already inclined to go, rhetoricians win over audiences by embracing their most fallacious beliefs and most irrational fears and making them the premises of their arguments. Rhetoric gets its way not by resisting or challenging people's ideas, no matter how cockamamie, but by flattering their prejudices.

For rhetoric, the clearly defective claim that "Fifty million Frenchmen can't be wrong" could well serve as its motto. What matters is not the truth of a statement but its effect on an audience. By believing a statement, an audience renders it true; by disbelieving it, an audience renders it false. If a speaker can persuade the right people—those with the power to make the speaker's interests prevail—to hold the right opinion, that opinion is equal to truth in rhetoric. When Benjamin Franklin suggested that getting people to believe you are virtuous is just as good as actually being virtuous, he spoke as a true rhetorician.

3. Rhetoric is at best amoral, at worst immoral.

Speaking of virtue, there is in the field of rhetoric no equivalent of anything like business or medical ethics, military justice, or a professional creed of conduct. There is no Golden Rule of rhetoric, no "Do unto Others," and no categorical imperative directing you always to act as you would have all others act. The closest rhetoric might come to a universal moral imperative is something along the lines of "Just win, Baby!", the mantra of the Oakland Raiders football team, whose mascot is a pirate, whose players annually lead their league in penalties, and whose owner leads it in lawsuits. The victors will write history, so by winning at all costs you assure yourself of being right for posterity no matter how scurrilous the means used to attain victory.

The failure of rhetoric to impose an austere moral code on itself can be traced back to its murky approach to reasoning. According to Aristotle, the godfather of rhetoric, one of the distinguishing characteristics of the practice is its capacity to "prove opposites," thereby violating the Law of Contradiction, upon which all rigorous forms of reasoning and coherent ethics must rest. According to the Law of Contradiction ("X cannot both exist and not exist"), a single act cannot be simultaneously just and unjust or good and evil any more than water can be simultaneously hot and cold or a dog can be simultaneously large and small. Given opposing claims A and not-A, one must be false and the other true and it is the job of reason to discover which is which. It is most surely not the job of reason to prove that both are true and to create arguments that make the case for whichever one works to the advantage of the person making the case. Rhetoric has, in sum, no scruple against "proving" any claim no matter how logically indefensible or morally repugnant. And as the German philosopher Hegel reminds us, "He must be a poor creature who cannot advance a good reason for everything, even for what is worst and depraved."

To say that rhetoric has no coherent ethic is not to say that its adherents don't lay claim to an ethic or occasionally assume ethical postures. And the field of ethics is sufficiently capacious to accommodate rhetoric along with some other dubious inhabitants—hedonists, subjectivists, objectivists, and their ilk. Indeed there is at least one established ethical school that would happily claim rhetoric as one of its own. That would be the once highly touted "situational ethic" espoused a half century ago by French existential philosophers—and that today flies under various banners such as "multiculturalism" or "cultural relativism" or "social constructivism." According to the existentialists, one does not look to any moral law or code when determining the right thing to do in a given situation. Every individual is free to pursue their own course according to the particulars of the situation. What was right for one person yesterday, in a different locale, is not necessarily what is right for this person today in this particular locale. Which makes it pretty much impossible to determine if one choice—or one culture or one value system—is ever better than another. Everyone finds their own way in their own situation, which in turn sounds a good deal like Aristotle's legendary definition of rhetoric as "the capacity to find the available means of persuasion in a given circumstance." Rhetoric and situational ethics appear in fact to be two sides of the same ethical coin. Situational ethics invites us to act by our own lights according to the particulars of the situation while rhetoric promises to help us find the means for justifying our acts by our own lights, citing only those particulars. Rhetoric, the means for justifying anything, turns out to be the perfect handmaiden for a situational ethic that permits everything.

4. Rhetoric encourages agonistic behavior and possesses all the gravitas of a professional wrestling match.

Apologies for the outburst of Latin here. A bit of explanation is in order. "Agonistic" derives from the Greek word "agon," meaning "contest." Today it possesses negative connotations associated with extreme gamesmanship, the capacity of some people to turn the most routine interactions with others into opportunities for displaying their superiority of intellect, athleticism, wit, or whatever other quality they think is being contested. Agonism is associated with adolescent boys whose capacity to convert everything into a competition is immortalized in that most agonistic of tropes, the "peeing contest." At the more serious level, the American justice system is often criticized for turning justice into a game between combatants who are required by their own standards of professional behavior to exercise "zeal in advocacy" on behalf of their client, even if they might strongly suspect that said client is as guilty as Tony Soprano. The search for a just outcome, many critics of American jurisprudence have argued, takes a backseat to lawyers' agonistic displays of legal virtuosity. And in ancient days, when education followed the Greek model and rhetoric was at its core, boys (girls were not educated at the time) were taught to write and think by having to defend propositions and debate one another. The schoolroom was a continuously noisy agon and the search for truth fell perpetual victim to the quest for victory. If we wish to submit our youth to such corruption and reduce learning to sport, all we need do is allow the nose of rhetoric once again in the tent of education.

Gravitas meanwhile refers to the seriousness, the heft, of something, typically an individual's character. When we say that someone possesses *gravitas*, we mean that they are people to be taken seriously. Conversely, when we say someone is a "lightweight," we mean they lack this very *gravitas*; they fail to manifest the solidity of character, depth of commitment, and thoughtfulness of manner that command our respect and attention. To say someone has *gravitas* is to suggest that they are authentic, not given to game playing, deceit, or insincerity, that they are steadfast in their beliefs to the point of suffering or even dying for them. In what's been said so far about rhetoric, one may well presume that *gravitas* does not loom large among the traits valued by those who practice the craft. One would be right in that presumption. In distinguishing those with *gravitas* from those without it, we will hereafter designate the former as "Serious People" and the latter as "Rhetorical People." Serious People reach noble heights through self-reliance; Rhetorical People reach compromises by talking among themselves.

Rhetorical People, as we have seen, trim their principles to fit their circumstances. In this regard, as in so many other regards, their kinship with politicians is evident. If the voters want lower taxes, by golly, they do too; and if voters want better schools, they, by crackee, are the "education candidate." Stronger defense? "Just call me 'Hawk.' " As comedian Groucho Marx once put it, "Those are my principles. If you don't like them, I have others." And when out on the campaign trail, every audience at every whistle-stop is assured that the pol is deliriously happy to be in Brokenspoke, or Hackysack, a place "near and dear" to them for some transparently manufactured reason. In observing politicians and other members of the rhetorical tribe use language in this way, one can't help but feel that one is watching a performance rather than a straightforward act of communication. They are like actors reading from scripts. Some read their lines more persuasively than others, but all of them manifest a public self, a persona, whose resemblance to the private person is never totally clear.

This uncertain relationship between the mask and the face of Rhetorical People results in an uncertain relationship between audiences and actors, between words and meaning. Such uncertainty does not confound the communication of Serious People, who wear no masks and speak from the heart rather than from some script. Whereas Serious People aim for clarity and simplicity of language—preferring action to mere words whenever possible—and strive always to be understood literally as having only one meaning, Rhetorical People use a range of linguistic devices, everything from lies and equivocations to ironic statements and metaphors, to render their words ambiguous and open to multiple interpretations. Like Shakespeare's Hamlet, a murderous and impulsive youth who views all the world as a stage and likes to use "indirection to find direction out," Rhetorical People revel in role-playing, double meanings, and indirection, in tricking and beguiling people with words.

Rhetorical People are, in sum, sad parodies of their more serious counterparts, forever reducing the earnest business of life to a contest played by shameless self-seekers, oblivious to the fact that their ruses are readily apparent to ever vigilant Serious People. Serious People, guided by the beacon light of their ideals, follow a straight and narrow path toward an end that lies beyond this fallen world. Rhetorical People, meanwhile, go through life adopting this mask or that cause depending on which pays the most or best serves their interest. Light as gossamer, blown hither and yon by every new wind of change and fashion, never looking beyond whatever advantage is to be gained from each exchange, they hopscotch their way through life.

The Rhetorical Retort

So much for our critic. In truth, our Anti-Rhetoric Spokesperson has scored more than a few valid points against Rhetorical People. Then again, also in truth, our Anti-Rhetoric Spokesperson is actually Anti-Rhetoric *Spokespersona*, a mask we donned, a rhetorical device we employed to set up our arguments in support of rhetoric as a legitimate way of understanding the world. He is, thus, himself implicated in a rhetorical exercise of the very sort he's been railing against for the past several thousand words. In setting him up like this, we were simply following the example of his hero, Plato, himself a master rhetorician not above using his Sophist foes like ventriloquist dummies to mouth his self-serving script. And that's the first point to be made in the case for rhetoric's significance—its ubiquity. Every symbolic act, including some that appear not to be symbolic, has a rhetorical dimension. Even the most rabid of our critics has to use rhetoric to criticize us, or anything else for that matter, from artificial turf to monotheism. Thus while our Anti-Rhetoric Poseur may wish to place himself above the fray in some realm that is "objective," where truth is self-evident and no one else's approval is needed for his truth to stand, that's clearly not where his audience resides. Why, if we are all in (or up) there with him, would he feel compelled to seek our assent? And why does he use persuasion rather than a series of declarations to gain that assent?

But even if we invented our critic to do a job of rhetorical work for us, we can't make him disappear simply by revealing his embarrassing lack of existence. Even if he's totally invented, we—that is to say, Rhetorical People—have to deal with what he has to say about rhetoric. That's one of the rules of rhetoric. Or more precisely one of the nonrules of rhetoric. Anyone—even made-up, supercilious twits—can offer any argument they wish, and so long as it makes it into the conversation of rhetoric, our "endless talk" that he finds so cheap, it requires an answer. No rule will automatically disqualify it, only another, better argument can trump it, with "better" determined by the parties to the conversation.

This model of the conversation is central to understanding rhetoric in contrast to more "methodical" approaches to understanding the world put forth by our excessively earnest critic. It suggests a voluntary association of people on a more or less equal footing engaging in symbolic activity both for pleasure and enlightenment. There's little formality to conversation and nothing equivalent to Robert's Rules of Order, let alone the Scientific Method, to dictate procedures. Conversations are oral and are seldom recorded. Conversations never attain the sort of closure and certainty yielded by methods; indeed at times it may be difficult to discern the prevailing topic let alone the prevailing view of conversants toward their topic. It may be lighthearted, or serious or heated, it may be a wildly subjective airing of opinions, or a solemn rehearsal of pieties. But for all its deceptively haphazard trappings, conversation is central to our existence. It's how most of us learn best, it's how most civilized societies conduct their public business, it's how colleagues and coworkers typically puzzle out solutions to problems, how families maintain connectedness, and how friends and lovers establish intimacy.

All of which is not to say that conversation is true and method is false and thus that we can, with Platonic aplomb, toss method aside and claim conversation as the sole province of truth. That would be a most unrhetorical thing to do. Rhetoric rejects the idea that the world consists entirely of true things that are real and untrue things that are illusory and that reason is the process by which we sort them out and rid the world of error and illusion. For rhetoric, the world is full of overlapping partial truths and the task of reason is to figure out which is truest—most meaningful, most effective—in a given situation, setting the others aside for the time being, possibly holding them in reserve for a different occasion when one of them may be the more appropriate choice. Conversation does not, thus, "cancel out" method. Indeed, to the extent that conversation and method are overlapping categories, employing one entails the employment of both. As it turns out, they have a good deal in common. And the name we will give to their common ground is "the way."

Before There Was Method, There Was Hodos

The word from which "method" derives, the Greek "hodos," in fact means "way." "Method" evolved from hodos when "met" or "after" was tacked onto the front of "hodos" to yield "met-hodos"—"the way after." "After what?" remains to be determined, but the important shift here is to the past tense. "The way" as conversation, we contend, is a present-tense version of "the way" as method. After conversations produce insights, solutions, agreements, and empathy among the conversants, methods simplify and edit the results and make it possible for others to replicate those results in different settings by following some sort of procedure or routine produced by "boiling down" conversations to their essentials. As we shall see, especially in Chapters 4, 5, and 6, the conversation that is rhetoric does result in some procedures that are methodical, if not exactly methodological in the scientific or social scientific understanding of that term. However, in its emphasis on individual cases, particularly its stress on intersubjective consideration of those cases by observers with multiple points of view as opposed to objective consideration by unbiased observers and instruments, and in its unwillingness to privilege explanations with the fewest steps, contemporary rhetoric remains closer in spirit to the original "hodos" than to the latter-day "method." But the more important point for our present purposes is that method and conversation share a common ground in "way" and as such they can be said to complement each other as surely as they oppose each other.

Before we go any further, we need to clarify this somewhat-mysterious notion of "a way." As noted earlier, the Chinese "Tao" and the Navajo "Dine" both mean "way," as does the Indian word "Dharma." All of these versions of "way" turn out to be distressingly open ended, particularly to those who are not part of the culture or historical period from whence the terms arose. Indeed there was a vogue twenty years or so ago of books with titles declaring their subject to be "The Tao of This (or That)," including everything from leadership to money to physics and, most recently, to Elvis. And in many cases it was hard to say what exactly it was that rendered the approach to the subject a "tao" approach or what one book had to do with another. At the risk of further exploiting an already overexploited idea, however, the following generalizations will be offered about "tao" as a representative way.

The "way" that *tao* refers to is comprehensive; it is the way of the world, the laws and regularities that govern the physical universe and its human inhabitants. The secret to achieving happiness according to the followers of *tao* was to yield to these laws and regularities and forgo the futile quest to rise above or master them. Eventually a formal religion arose out of this loose set of beliefs. The lowercase "tao" became the uppercase ism "Taoism," and the way was written down and translated into a set of laws and institutions. The way gradually became less an activity, a verb one did, and more a doctrine, a noun one subscribed to. All of which is more or less the story of all the world's "ways." The way of justice turns into an institution of laws, the way of civility turns into codified rights and obligations, the path of enlightenment turns into the possession of truth. And the way of "hodos" turns into the "way after" of method as over time conversations get written down, then read, then turned into textbooks for classes that turn into curricula that turn into degrees. By the same token, amateurs sitting around marketplaces, coffee houses, and wine shops talking and arguing eventually become certified professionals, with titles and salaries, who ride airplanes great distances to talk and argue and quibble with each other at conferences, and then fly home to classrooms where they teach others how to talk and argue and quibble like they do. Or maybe they stay home and write books like this one.

But in every case, some of that looser, more imaginative, and open-ended truth of the way remains part of the methods that evolve out of it. For all their apparent differences, the original way and the doctrines that formalize and institutionalize it are intertwined. The nature of their relationship is captured neatly in the Chinese symbol for the *tao*, which consists of a circle containing the yin (dark) and the yang (light) separated by a serpentine line. Yin is associated with the feminine and the nonrational, yang with the masculine and the rational, which in terms of our present analysis would align the yin with conversation and the yang with method. Out of yin and yang's fundamental tension are generated the "ten thousand things" comprising the totality of the universe. Always, in all those things, both principles are to varying degrees present. And so it is with rhetoric, which is remarkable among the various Western modes of knowing for maintaining a balance between the two principles and for keeping faith with those original, imaginative ways that so scandalize Serious People.

One can see this balance perhaps most clearly in rhetoric's employment of proverbial wisdom—aphorisms, parables, maxims, adages, and the like—to do the work of axioms, laws, and principles of formal method. In the earliest days of rhetoric, these bits of popular belief and folk psychology distilled out of ordinary people's collective experiences and preserved in stories and lore were referred to as "commonplaces." They have remained an important element of rhetoric ever since, which is why so many of them will show up in this book. And for all their apparent differences from the more methodical tools beloved of Serious People, they do share some important similarities. Most importantly, rhetoric's proverbial wisdom consists of general statements applicable across a range of situations and times. And while these dictums may not have passed the sort of formal truth tests favored by Serious People, their soundness is attested to by their having survived the tests of time and experience and having proved useful to countless people in a variety of situations. That said, no one will confuse these pieces of folk wisdom with the formal methods of Serious People because they collectively violate the Law of Contradiction—virtually every pithy piece of folk wisdom is contradicted by another equally pithy piece of folk wisdom—and they regularly fail to compel only one conclusion.

Just how rhetoric's proverbial wisdom can manage to enlighten us without necessarily eliminating uncertainty is best seen by turning to an example, in this case, a line of poetry from Theodore Roethke's "The Waking." While this line of poetry might not fit a folklorist's official definition of "folk wisdom," it does represent a solid piece of advice that sounds a good deal like the advice one finds in traditional folklore. Indeed poetry and fiction are full of such nuggets, pithy quotes of the sort Renaissance schoolboys once collected in "commonplace books." Because literature serves as a storehouse of proverbial wisdom that offers "glimpses and inklings" of larger truths useful in all those eternally recurring situations, Kenneth Burke refers to it as "equipment for living" (PLF 293). Here is Roethke's line.

"I find my way by going where I have to go."

Where exactly the narrator of Roethke's poem may be off to is unclear. It doesn't seem to matter much, though, because the narrator's going is clearly meant to stand in for all our going. (The line ends the poem and the last lines of poems often serve a function like that of the morals that end fables, universalizing the message and converting it to a rule.) And whatever destination we might conjure up—love, truth, success, adventure, or a livable city with good schools—we are assured that we are to find it in the act of going. Which may sound, at first blush, like a pretty backward way to conduct one's life. But then there is that second notion, the imperative one, that we only go where we *have* to go. The idea of simultaneously "finding" our way and going where we "have" to go is confounding. How does one go freely where one is driven to go?

As it turns out, we do it all the time. How we do it requires another digression—we may have to concede that our most solemn critics are right about our propensity for hopscotch—in this case a consideration of a couple of terms from Burke, "Act" and "Motion," which represent two fundamental types of movement. (We capitalize them so as not to confuse them with ordinary, everyday act and motion, which is easy to do since Act and Motion are produced by exaggerating differences between acts and motions.) One of the major distinctions between Act and Motion is that while both inanimate and animate objects may experience Motion, only animate objects may Act. No rock, thus, can ever Act, though if dislodged from a mountainside it can certainly evidence Motion. To qualify as an Act, a movement must be voluntary and purposive and must result in something new happening or existing. In the strict sense, only humans can Act. If we were to line up all the "ten thousand things" of creation along an Act-Motion continuum, thus, human beings would line up along the Act end of the continuum. (Before we congratulate ourselves too heartily about that fact, it should be pointed out that both good *and* evil are Acts and what is worst about our species, as well as what is best, derives from our capacity to Act. Thus while ballistic missiles require Motion to reach their targets, what's required to set the missile in Motion is a series of human Acts: imagining the possibility of missiles, justifying their expense, building them, arming them, justifying their use, aiming them, pushing a button to launch them, assessing their accuracy, rationalizing the "collateral damage" they cause, and so forth.)

At the farthest reaches of the continuum as we approach the pure Act, the differences between Act and Motion are most clearly visible. But there is no such thing as pure Act. Every Act retains elements of Motion. No act is totally free, no purpose is entirely my own, no product of an Act is entirely new. Indeed, some of what passes for human Action is clearly little more than human Motion. When I reflexively perform work that is routine and repetitive, my movements are mostly Motions. Or when I do more challenging work inattentively, I literally "go through the Motions." And when I lie on the floor scratching my dog's ears while watching baseball games on TV (more on this later), I have more in common with a falling rock than a doctor of philosophy.

Which brings us back to Roethke's puzzling advice to find our way by going where we have to go, his seemingly casual confusion of freedom and necessity. Where does one leave off and the other begin? Even at the outset of our journey, even before we've taken our first step along the way, we have inclinations, beliefs, and mental equipment that incline us to follow one path over another. We inherit language and DNA, not to mention biases and doctrines, from those who precede us, and we are certainly creatures of our time and place, our culture and history. But that said, I am still not *determined* by all these factors; they are not my destiny and no one could predict precisely where my way might take me simply by examining them. With each Act, I change myself and/or my world however slightly; I realize one potential and foreclose another. At every step, I freely choose among options, though I am not free to create all the options from which I choose.

One way to think about this curious mixture of Acts and Motions that we are calling the way is to compare it to the Act of writing a book, the very model of free and creative activity. Even here, in this purest of Acts, I encounter restrictions. When I sit down to write a book, I have many options open to me, but not an infinite number. For one thing, I have a limited number of models before me of what it means to write a book. Someone sitting down to write a book in 1400 has different options to choose among than someone sitting down in

2000; the fifteenth-century writer is unlikely to write a piece of New Journalism (or old journalism for that matter), and the twenty-first century writer is unlikely to write an epic in rhyming heroic couplets. Every conceivable genre of book is governed by conventions, and those conventions reside in the minds of readers in the form of expectations, which if violated may cause readers to put the book down in frustration or disappointment. (Even the most avant-garde writing of any age must appeal to avant-garde audiences with notions of "avant-gardeness" that govern their expectations.) Among choices of genre theoretically available to me are some that I am temperamentally unsuited to write and others whose audiences and subject I don't know well enough to undertake. And since I probably know only one or a handful of languages, I am limited by the resources of that language in what I might say.

And once I actually begin writing, filling the blank pages with my thoughts, I find that each creative Act begets a train of restrictions. Once I commit to a theme, an argument, a voice, or to a certain kind of character, I am not free to change them at my will without violating an implied contract with my readers and with my subject. Indeed, many authors report that by the time they finish writing a novel, their characters have minds of their own and seemingly write their own dialogue. So it is with the "way" that Roethke is talking about. Every one of my freely made choices in life—choice of school, major, profession, job, significant other, and so forth—brings in its wake limitations, commitments, and responsibilities that bear heavily on future options. But the environment that limits my choices is also a place I've had a hand in creating. Am I "finding" my way or am I going where I "have" to go? Am I Acting or am I being acted upon? Only the most ardent Serious Person would insist on a definitive and certain answer to that question. And only the most zealous advocates of the Law of Contradiction would insist that in characterizing such a life we must choose between free will and determinism and dismiss the rejected alternative as an illusion.

Which brings us back to the way of rhetoric. Like Roethke's narrator, those who follow rhetoric's way freely choose and are compelled to choose. The term we use to describe this mixed bag of free will and determinism is "motivation." While Motions are "caused" and pure Acts "express inner purposes," the symbolic acts comprising rhetoric are "motivated." To say that one is motivated to do something is not to say that one *must* perform the act in question or that one performs the act solely to fulfill one's purpose. One is inclined to do it, and there are reasons for that inclination though the actor may not be consciously aware of all those reasons. We experience our motives sometimes pushing us from behind like causes and sometimes pulling us forward like purposes, but always both forces are at work. We have conscious motives ("You evidence a strong need to be successful . . . ") and unconscious ones (". . . perhaps because your father never valued you?"). To the extent that motives are conscious and purposeful, they are Act-like, while the extent to which they are unconscious and lie beyond our control, they are Motion-like. Some people spend many years talking to trained professionals, trying to sort out this perplexing combination of motivations that push and pull them along their way and to reassure themselves that they are something more than a loose bundle of impulses, urges, and compulsions.

This belief in limited human freedom and motivation is an item of faith essential to rhetoric. On the one hand, if rhetoric were to hold that people had no capacity to change their minds or attitudes and no capacity to cooperate with others to alter the world in accordance with those changes, it has no function. But on the other hand, if everything were possible, rhetoric would be nearly as useless as it would be in a world where nothing was possible. Making the determination of what is possible in "any given circumstance"—in this particular time and place, for this particular audience in response to this particular sort of symbolic act—is what constitutes method in rhetoric.

Serious People have great difficulty recognizing this sort of thing as methodical in part because their models for method are derived from the sciences. In science, one deals mostly with Motions and causes rather than Acts and motivations. Because things in Motion have no minds of their own, they tend to observe the laws of science much more sedulously than we observe the general principles of human behavior. We have a tendency to "swerve" in unaccountable ways and to be less uniform in our responses to a given set of causes. And while rocks are not influenced by the law stating that all objects, including rocks, fall at thirty-two feet per second squared, human beings, when told that children who don't read by third grade are likely to drop out of school, may well act to counter the effects of that principle, a phenomenon known as the "feedback effect." These differing assumptions between rhetoric and other disciplines about the nature of their subject account for most of their differing assumptions about the nature of method. Serious People assume a more or less stable and uniform world in which events conform more or less predictably to laws derived from long observation of the world's regularities. Variability and singularity are the enemies of prediction and control, the primary ends sought by Serious People from knowledge. Rhetoric, while acknowledging the existence of such regularities and sometimes employing them in constructing arguments and interpretations, is more often concerned with anomalous or singular events requiring some measure of original thought. Which is why rhetoric is sometimes counted among the so-called "sciences of single instances." Rhetorical People assume that while each situation resembles previous situations of a similar type, the distinguishing characteristics of each particular case must be understood before one can select the principle or rule that best fits the situation or choose the best course of action.

To borrow another metaphor from our central metaphor of the way, Serious People will consult a map—a precise visual representation produced by experts—prior to embarking on their journey and will follow the most efficient route to their destination. What happens along the way will not influence their route or manner of travel and one can predict their end point and time of arrival with great precision. Rhetorical People, meanwhile, know the way generally from talking with others who have preceded them; but at every fork in the way they will consult with each other to determine if the past way best suits their present situation, which is likely to have changed since they set out and will almost certainly have changed since those who initially advised them made their journey. And if the changes in their route are sufficiently significant, Rhetorical People may even decide to seek an altogether new destination.

The significant difference in the modes of travel favored by Serious and Rhetorical types has to do with the role of experience. Serious People do not totally ignore experience: If for some reason the route dictated by their map fails repeatedly to get them where they're going in a timely fashion, they will, however reluctantly, alter their maps eventually. And by the same token, Rhetorical People do not rely wholly on experience. They too have a representation of their journey, available to them at the start in the form of wisdom accumulated from prior travelers; and the choice to ignore or amend that wisdom requires persuasion with the burden of proof resting on those calling for change. But in the end, Serious People are less likely to pay attention to experience, the particulars of the journey, and the voices of other travelers, than are Rhetorical People. And that makes all the difference.

> You never step in the same river twice.
> —*Heraclitus*

> You step in one river, you've stepped in 'em all.
> —*Parmenides*

Actually, the Greek philosopher Parmenides, an ancient Serious Person, didn't really say that. But he may as well have. What he really said was this: "Nothing cannot exist." What he meant by this was that change is impossible because for change to occur, something must come into existence that previously did not exist. And if there is no such thing as "nothing," then everything that could possibly exist already exists. Existence is like a landlocked city that can't grow because there's no more open space, no "no-thingness," for it to annex. While the equally ancient Greek Heraclitus imagines that the river we took the first step into is sufficiently changed by the time we take the second step into it to qualify as a different river, Parmenides would say that the river we stepped into is exactly the same as the old river and for that matter every other river we might step into, and we can take as many steps as we like into any river and it remains the same; a river is a river is a river and no new ones will ever exist because there is no place for them to hang out not existing until they actually exist.

All of which is by way of initiating a return visit to the ancient battle between philosophy and rhetoric that our anti-rhetorical friend declared—prematurely as it turns out—a blowout for philosophy. If either of these two philosophical views were to prevail, rhetoric would indeed be in trouble. If Parmenides is right, Motions, let alone Acts, are impossible because the world is a frozen block of sameness. A famous story attributed to his student Zeno makes this point emphatically. If the fleet-footed Achilles were to race a turtle, and the turtle were given even the slightest head start, Achilles would never catch the turtle, claims Zeno, because to get even with the turtle he'd first have to go halfway, and to go halfway he'd have to go halfway to halfway, and so on, forever. We end up not with a race but a picture, a snapshot of Achilles and the turtle forever hunched over in the starting blocks staring blankly ahead. In Parmenides' world there can be no rhetorical way and no journeys, just a giant map of how things are. For Heraclitus, meanwhile, it's all Motion all the time. Locked into an eternal present, one would be unable to find one's way because there would be no past to consult. In either case, experience is useless. It's useless for Heraclitus because whatever one knows from the past is irrelevant to a world that changes totally moment to moment. For Parmenides, meanwhile, experience in all forms, including footraces, is useless because it is an illusion; everything we need to know is already on the map.

As it turns out, Parmenides and Heraclitus are typical of philosophers of their day in their hostility to experience. Much of the struggle between philosophy and rhetoric in the early days centered on this issue of experience. Remember, philosophy was a new enterprise at the time. In order for it to catch on among the people, most of whom put a great deal of stock in experience as the best teacher, philosophers had to persuade them that real truth was only attained through reflection, preferably by removing oneself from the hurly-burly of experience and entering one of their tranquil, reasonably priced academies. Prior to people like Parmenides and Heraclitus, knowledge got passed down through myths and stories and fables of the sort favored by Rhetorical People. The emphasis traditionally had not been on the search for *truth*, but on the accumulation of *wisdom*, insights and understanding earned through past experience and applicable to future experience. Truth for its own sake was a foreign concept among people who valued knowledge and understanding mostly because it helped them act effectively in the world. Backsliders who continued to think that experience was the best teacher were anathema to philosophers who stressed how untrustworthy experience really was. Rhetorical People of the day, along with their confederates—the poets, the storytellers, and assorted other lovers of experience—consequently got short shrift from the philosophers.

In refusing to concede to the ancient philosophers that experience necessarily led people astray, the rhetoricians and their allies took a more or less commonsense position. Footraces, they duly noted, did actually take place and while such races did not always, as the Old Testament reminds us, "go to the swift," prudent people did not bet on turtles. And they also believed that while rivers surely did change constantly, such changes were not of sufficient magnitude to justify renaming them every time you took a step. But however powerful their bias toward experience, Rhetorical People have never subscribed to a strictly commonsense view of the world. (Indeed, some of the early Sophists took perversely uncommonsensical positions, standing philosophers' views upside down just to show that it could be done.) While they recognize that any proposition must make sense to people for it to have any force in the world, they also recognize the worrisome tendency of common sense to promote reactionary views. What is often touted as common sense, according to Rhetorical People, is in fact not commonly or even widely viewed as sensible; it is instead an article of faith among a small group of like-minded people blind to the limits of their beliefs. And it certainly lacks the force claimed for it by some of its more zealous adherents who would have us believe that common sense is as irresistible a force in the realm of human affairs as axioms are in the realm of geometry. All too often, Rhetorical People have noted over the years, calling something "common sense" was done to paper over a lack of evidence or weak arguments in support of some generalization. That women were too irrational to vote was for centuries a claim supported, with devastating effectiveness, by nothing but common sense. And in countless other cases, large and small, change has been successfully resisted on the grounds that it violated common sense. There is a "whatever is is right" bias in common sense, a latent strain of Parmenidean thinking that reacts to novelty by contending in knee-jerk fashion that if the proposed change were good it would already exist.

The source of common sense's failures, and the trait that sets it apart from rhetoric, is its inability to question or to amend itself in any organized way. And this failing may in turn be traced back to limitations in the language of common sense. The language of common sense is a literalist language, a doggedly unimaginative vocabulary that blinds itself to contradiction and ignores ambiguity. Whatever a word has always meant is what it is supposed to mean; whatever traits are shared by members of a terminological class are essential traits unaffected by time and circumstance. If some people come up with different meanings for a term or if other people challenge the traits associated with a term, the commonsense response is simply to point to existing conventions and dismiss the challenge. (In Chapter 5, such people will be discussed in their role as "PC-proponents.") In its attitudes toward language, common sense is an anti-rhetorical practice. The way of rhetoric can be understood as an organized attempt to discover ambiguity and to use those discoveries to leverage new possibilities for meaning. For rhetoric, the greatest danger we face is to become victims of our "terministic screens," our vocabularies that direct our attention to some things and divert it from others. Burke's God, thus, may have the language of common sense in mind when he tells Satan in a dialogue that ends *The Rhetoric of Religion* that "where Earth-People are concerned any terminology is suspect to the extent that it does not allow for the progressive criticism of itself" (ROR 303). To understand how rhetoric encourages self-questioning we return to our metaphor of the way and its dynamic of the Act.

> Circumstances alter cases.
> —*Kenneth Burke*

The way of rhetoric, as it turns out, is a dynamic of "recurrence," a middle way between constant flux and permanent stasis. While

Heraclitus depicts experience as a succession of unprecedented events and Parmenides depicts it as a frieze of one eternally repeated event, rhetoric depicts experience as a series of related but not identical *acts* (which we'll cease capitalizing now). In rhetoric an act must result in something new. Which means that the relation of one act to another can't be one of identity. Motions may repeat each other exactly, but each act is different from those preceding it, which is why prediction is an art, not a science, in the realm of human affairs. But no act, as will be recalled, is ever pure. The novelty any act brings into existence is incremental. Only magic or divine fiat can create something absolutely new out of nothing, and rhetoricians claim for themselves neither magical nor divine powers.

In rhetoric, thus, experience is simultaneously old and new, a series of acts similar to and different from one another. Much of what we need to know in ordinary existence is a product of past experience, providing that the differences among acts are small. Common sense, habit, and reflexive motions get most of us through most of our day. Rhetoric comes into play only when acts and their consequences are sufficiently different from what experience has led us to expect that those affected by the act must reach a new consensus about the meaning and value of such acts. The commonsense agreement about the meaning of experience must now be consciously reconstructed through rhetoric.

Recurrence and the Law

In the abstract, this may seem a bit obscure. Down on the ground, it's much easier to understand. In this case, the "ground" we'll examine is the law, specifically the American judicial system. The law, which is also often named as a "science of single instances," is a particularly good place to examine the rhetorical dynamic because legal and rhetorical principles are so intertwined and because the law as an institution has formalized and made visible and explicit many rhetorical principles that are otherwise usually tacit. In particular, the law, like rhetoric, relies heavily on past acts, in the form of legal precedents, common law, constitutional principles, and so forth, to shape its view of new acts. The basic unit of the law's way is "the case," a complex act that meets a set of conditions proper to the law—e.g., it has been adjudicated in a formal legal setting and has been officially recorded following conventions of legal discourse. When the case in question is sufficiently different from those that precede it, and/or does not "fit" precisely with an accepted legal principle, the law cannot simply be followed, it must be made, consciously reconstructed through rhetoric in much the same way that ordinary experience requires the occasional intervention of rhetoric to reevaluate and redefine the meaning of everyday acts.

All of which is not to suggest that rhetoric and the law are identical. The law is considerably more "methodical" than rhetoric and has in place procedures that operate almost like algorithms to resolve routine legal issues with little or no intervention by human agents. For example, in uncontested divorces occurring in states that have "no-fault" divorce laws (no fault need be found with one or both parties to justify the divorce), parties may choose to feed all relevant information into a computer and let it spit out a decision. Many cases, even criminal cases, constitute the legal equivalent of motion: The act in question involves a violation of an unambiguous statute based on well-established legal principle; the legal precedents for such a violation leave little doubt about the appropriate punishment for the violation; there is no doubt about the guilt of the accused. Such cases seldom require courtroom proceedings of the sort we see on television, replete with rhetorical thrusts and parries.

Those legal cases that are most significant, on the other hand, all call upon the rhetorical skills of lawyers and judges. Important legal cases in fact comprise "hard cases" of the sort that many Serious People believe necessarily make for bad law. Any time the law is not simply "followed," like a cow path, Serious People will be distressed. They will grow especially agitated if the need to make new law is attributed to forces outside the law. For Serious People the law is supposed to be as methodical and as autonomous as science. It is supposed to be objective, unaffected by anything outside itself. But as it turns out, major changes in the law are almost always motivated by changes outside the law, changes in community attitudes, social values, economics, technology, and so forth.

In this regard, consider the Supreme Court's 2003 ruling that executing the mentally retarded constituted "cruel and unusual punishment," despite having come down on the opposite side of the issue only thirteen years earlier. According to the majority opinion, what had changed in the intervening years were community standards as reflected in the fact that a number of states had moved to forbid the execution of the mentally retarded and that increasing numbers of Americans and Western Europeans expressed opposition to the practice in opinion polls. The majority felt that the court must be responsive to " 'the evolving standards of decency that mark the progress of a maturing society.' " Some decidedly Serious justices dissented on the grounds that the decision found "no support in the text or the history of the Eighth Amendment" and relied on "irrelevant" polling data to establish that people opposed executing the mentally retarded. According to the dissenters, the majority was playing that old rhetorical game of pandering to the masses.

At the heart of this debate lie different views about the nature of meaning. For the dissenting justices, the meaning of a phrase like "cruel and unusual punishment" is immanent in the text of the Eighth Amendment. One need never look beyond the words on the page to know what they mean. Whatever was meant by those who wrote the words originally is exactly what they should mean today. For the majority meanwhile, "cruel and unusual punishment" means whatever those who use the words mean by them in a given time and place. In deciding whether a given punishment is cruel and unusual, they do not limit themselves to what people in the eighteenth century may or may not have had in mind, but what it means today to those who must live by the standard and bear the responsibility for enacting it. In agreeing with the majority that meanings cannot be fixed, Rhetorical People would point to the mountains of evidence, including authoritative sources such as the *Oxford English Dictionary*, which record countless changes—often dramatic—in the way virtually every English word has been used over the centuries. The more significant the word, in fact, the more likely it is to undergo important shifts in meaning.

Because the Constitution is such a difficult document to amend, one must either interpret its words flexibly in light of changes in circumstances, or spend one's days reconstructing the founders' original intent and laboring mightily to deny all attempts to take new circumstances or unintended consequences into account. While there are Serious People within the field of law, sometimes called "originalists" or "strict constructionists," who claim to follow the latter path, one would be hard pressed to find any who actually pull it off in practice given the tendency of this ideology very quickly to run afoul of broadly held American values—for example racial and gender equality—not explicitly championed in the Constitution. Like those who appeal to "common sense," those who appeal to "original meaning" and the "founders' intent" often as not start off with a set of values and beliefs that they then claim to find inscribed in a source held in high regard by their audience. If they were completely right about the self-evident truth of the Constitution, there would be little need for a Supreme Court in the first place.

In the language of the law, "originalist" judges prefer to offer "narrow" rulings tightly tied to the particulars of a case, in the process denying connections between the case in question and any larger context outside the law. In one particularly infamous Supreme Court decision, *Plessy v. Ferguson* (1896), which upheld the legality of a Louisiana law requiring railroad companies to maintain separate seating for black and white passengers, the prevailing justices argued that maintaining such facilities did not necessarily imply that blacks were racially inferior. And of course, in and of itself, divorced from two centuries of history and any knowledge of slavery, the KKK, mob lynchings, employment discrimination, inferior school facilities, and so forth, one could say with a straight face that the Louisiana law did not "require" one to draw any pernicious conclusions about its racist implications. However, Rhetorical People would argue, as later courts rejecting the ruling did in fact argue, that because "circumstances alter cases" one must look beyond the words on the page to the circumstances that gave rise to them and to the consequences that flow from them to determine how to understand and judge them. There is, to be sure, no hard-and-fast rhetorical rule to follow about how far afield one should pursue the circumstances of a case, no sure way of fixing what Burke calls the "circumference" of a case. As we will see later in discussing persuasion, making that judgment is one of the most crucial, least visible, and most contestable acts performed in rhetoric. But whatever circumference one might choose, no Rhetorical Person would ever hold that the words on a page are in and of themselves sufficient.

What the above discussion should make clear is that every act of legal judgment, like any other rhetorical act, entails an element of creativity. The movement from legal principle to legal decision, from legal precedent to the case in question is never automatic in significant cases. In such cases, connections between old and new, the same and the different, the particulars of the case and the circumstances surrounding the case, must be *made*, must be argued for. What is new, thus, is not the decision per se, but the written opinion that justifies and elucidates the decision and constitutes a new addition to the ongoing conversation of the law. If Supreme Court justices were allowed simply to pronounce a decision without a written opinion, they would in effect be doing nothing more than what an umpire does in calling balls and strikes. The rules of baseball are not clarified or modified with each call; one rule is repeatedly applied to a uniform set of circumstances and nothing new is ever added. The role of the umpire in calling balls and strikes could probably be filled nicely by a machine, something like the earlier mentioned divorce computer, because it is little more than a motion.

If each pitch in baseball is independent of the subsequent pitch in the eyes of an umpire, the same cannot be said of cases in the law in the eyes of those who judge them. The relationship of one case to the next in law is one of "recurrence." Recurrence implies that each case is related to previous cases, but how that relationship is to be understood and which cases are included in that relationship must be adjudicated. In turn, recurrence implies neither a "causal" relationship nor a "categorical" one. When we say that one case provides a good precedent for a subsequent case, we are not saying that the previous case is the *cause* of the subsequent case; neither are we saying that the latter belongs to the category of the previous case—*is* the previous case. The cases share some common ground, they fall under a given principle such as "Eighth Amendment cases" or "cases involving conflict between changing community standards and definitions of criminal acts (e.g., pornography cases)." But this common ground, unlike less ambiguous categories such as, say, subcompact cars or migratory birds, is much looser in membership. Those cases sharing the common ground often lack the numerous, readily discernible traits marking less controversial classes. Differences among the members of the class are much more readily discerned and membership is thus more readily contested.

By the same token, the relationship between a given case and its precedents does not appear to be anything in the nature of a causal relationship. The influence of previous cases on the pending case is not direct and decisive in the way that the effect on water of a 212-degree temperature is direct and decisive. The relationship is not even as clear as the relationship between a diet heavy in saturated fats and obesity. Previous cases may be said to "lead to" the still-pending case, but "leading to" in this case is analogous to the way events in a historical narrative, or a good novel for that matter, lead to one another. They point to an evolving, unresolved legal issue, but seldom allow one to predict how that issue will be resolved. The cases resemble each other in interesting ways and the relationship among them is worked out by means of exploring those resemblances. The relationship between one case and another is thus more tentative, more in the nature of an analogy or a metaphor in which one term allows us to see another term in a particular way. Instead of seeing the case before us as something totally new or singular, we are allowed to see it *as*, or *under the sign of*, or *in terms of* a better understood case.

Rhetoric Is the Art of Proving Opposites

Which brings us, then, to the matters of sincerity, gravitas, and ethics that so vexed our friend the Anti-Rhetoric zealot. The law requires that advocates for two sides of any given legal issue plead their cases vigorously in front of a jury and/or judge. So long as one assumes that the truth is already known or clearly knowable through methodical means, such a system of advocacy seems artificial, an invitation to chicanery and various forms of theater hostile to the ends of justice. Serious People would prefer that "experts" study the evidence and reach a decision in the calm of their offices or studies, unaffected by emotional testimony, flowery speeches, and legal technicalities. Only if one believes that the outcome of the issues under adjudication is unknown does our judicial system make sense. It only makes sense if justice is seen not as a given end that is waiting to be "found," but as—at least in part—a product of the proceedings themselves, a complex dialectical process in which two different ways of seeing the issue are tested against one another.

In this regard, consider the reported behavior of one of America's best-known legal figures, Supreme Court Justice Oliver Wendell Holmes. According to the testimony of his law clerks, Holmes would enter the office each day and demand of them that they "State any proposition and I'll deny it!" Clearly such behavior constitutes a major breach of Serious Person etiquette. It is gamelike behavior, playful and arbitrary and distinctly un-gravitas. In some cases, he must have inevitably argued against propositions he held dear. Indeed, given the nature of the game he was playing, one would assume that his clerks outvied each other to identify those propositions that he would find most difficult to deny. Is this how we wish judges on the highest court in our land to act?

In a word, yes. Think for a moment about the ideal of justice, a concept so intimately associated with the origins of rhetoric. Consider the icon of justice itself, a blindfolded female figure with the scales of justice in one hand and a sword in the other. The figure of justice is blindfolded, as we all know, to indicate her objectivity, her lack of prejudice on either side of any case that comes before her. But mere disinterest is not enough; judges cannot stop at being unbiased (an impossible, if admirable, ideal that we'll return to later); they have to be actively open to both sides of the issue, willing and able to entertain the rightness of either side no matter how improbable a task that might seem at the outset of a trial. In the end, judges act by offering an opinion that is different from the arguments presented by the lawyers. The quality of a judge's opinion rests on her ability to imaginatively identify with and actively listen to all the arguments and produce an argument that goes beyond them. A first-rate legal decision handed down in a hard case, thus, could well strike an observer of the entire process like the ending to a good piece of fiction, at once surprising and inevitable. Clearly Holmes was exercising these imaginative capacities in his daily sparring matches with his law clerks. And just as clearly, these capacities, which are related to the rhetorical capacity to "prove opposites," will result in much more substantive, weightier arguments than those produced by people unable to entertain, let alone "prove," multiple points of view in an argument.

Is such a capacity "ethical"? Not in the sense that most Serious People understand the word. If one equates ethics with obeying unambiguous rules and keeping faith with bulletproof principles, exercising one's imaginative capacities in the above manner is a dangerous business. It might well tempt one to commit various impieties. But then again, pieties that depend for their existence on avoiding or squashing challenges from impieties will not long remain in force. Unchallenged pieties have a tendency—and history provides numerous examples—to harden and rigidify and to result in negative consequences unforeseen by those who originally promulgated them. Even the most conservative of religions, thus, allow for the possibility that canonical truths may be overturned by revelation.

That said, "proving opposites" is not to be construed as an ethical activity in and of itself. If Justice Holmes were to treat those who came before his bench in the same way he treated the clerks in his office, if he were to write every opinion with an eye to coming up with the most surprising resolution to the case, taking the position most at odds with the arguments and evidence presented by the two sides, his behavior could hardly be considered admirable or ethical. Only if proving opposites is understood as a "capacity," a proficiency that contributes to the best possible outcome, can it be seen as ethical. In this regard, proving opposites may serve a couple of purposes, one of which only *looks* ethical because it is in the service of an already-accepted ethical view, the other of which only looks *unethical* because it serves no particular doctrine.

On the one hand, the capacity to prove opposites may be a mere technique used in the service of a propagandistic end, a tool used to promote a doctrine considered beyond question by those promoting it. In an earlier age, thus, Jesuit priests were extensively trained in rhetoric to propagate (a word with the same root as "propaganda") the word of the church. For them, "proving of opposites" was simply a technique for anticipating opposing arguments that they were then in a better position to refute. Only to the extent that we already agree with whatever doctrine is being promoted would we consider such behavior ethical.

On the other hand, rhetoric may play a more ambitious, less coercive role. Rather than simply serving as a marketing tool for an already-established ethical good, rhetoric can serve as a means for generating ethical goods. This productive facility is a critical, often-overlooked dimension of ethics. It is overlooked because the prevailing Serious People view of ethics frames ethical choice as a straightforward matter of selecting between what we know to be The One Right Thing To Do and various seductive alternatives that tempt us, thanks to our weak moral character. But while the thoroughgoing, always-already-in-the-know ethical Serious Person is faced with a choice between one luminous "ought" and a legion of shoddy "ought nots," the rest of us face a more complex task. Before we can figure out what "ought" to be done in a given situation, we must first determine what "can" be done in that situation. The "best choice" among these possible options, meanwhile, is a matter to be decided by those responsible for the consequences of that choice; they must determine which one best comports with prevailing values and beliefs. Rhetorical conversation is the best mechanism both for generating such choices and for reaching a consensus on the most appropriate choice. While this version of rhetoric's ethical role does not prescribe a particular ethical stance or rule, it does serve those who subscribe to given stances and rules to ensure that they will be in a position to make the best—most appropriate, most defensible—choices by their own lights, whatever those lights may be.

We will return to this complex relationship of ethics and rhetoric in later chapters. For now we return to the way of rhetoric and some final comments on the manner and pace in which it is traveled.

I Wake to Sleep and Take My Waking Slow

This is the first half of the sentence that concludes Roethke's "The Waking," the line before "I find my way by going where I have to go." Under the guise of offering a description of a singular event, it also offers general advice useful to pilgrims along the rhetorical way. And like the line that follows it, this line comes in the form of a paradox, the sort of mysterious statement one is forced to linger over, not unlike a Zen koan such as "What is the sound of one hand clapping?" that those who follow various Asian "ways" favor. In what sense does one "wake to sleep"? For most of us, waking is the opposite of sleeping. Certainly for Serious People, one must be either awake or asleep or else be in violation of the Law of Contradiction.

But however much our language may fool us into thinking that we must choose between the two states, we all know better. Who has not described themselves as being "half awake" or "half asleep," drowsy or wakeful? In our lives we experience the two states as lying on a continuum that we forever move along, experiencing more of one and less of the other but never fully "outside" either state. Indeed, our most active mental states, those moments described by some psychologists as moments of "flow" when we are lost in our thoughts, totally immersed in solving a puzzle or imagining a solution, are often experienced as moments of effortlessness and relaxation more akin to sleep than to work. And in our deepest slumber, we frequently find ourselves actively, sometimes frantically, working through the psychic dilemmas of our waking hours by staging little mental dramas we call dreams.

What the poet is doing with waking and sleeping is not unlike what we earlier saw judges and rhetoricians doing with arguments. But instead of "proving opposites," Roethke is showing us that opposition itself may be an illusion. The two states no more cancel each other out than opposing arguments disprove or "debunk" each other. In fact, the two words "wake" and "sleep" very much need each other to make any sense. If either word/concept disappeared from the language the other would disappear with it because it would cease to name a useful distinction. Together, they name a series of states marked by various degrees of waking and sleeping. And we take our waking slow because in doing so we retain access to both states, the dreamlike, imaginative world of sleep and the crisp clarity of being fully awake, the capacity to engage in prolonged reflection and the resolution to take decisive action. While Serious People are concerned mostly to keep the world ordered neatly in categories and to render thought more efficient through method, Rhetorical People, like the poets, are forever smudging the boundaries and mixing and matching incongruous pairings just to see what one thing looks like *in terms of* another.

The tendency of rhetoric to slow things down, to force people to contemplate all sorts of variables that Serious People carefully exclude from their methods, has always been seen as one of its greatest weaknesses. It was one of the reasons why Plato saw it as an inferior form of thought—more like "cosmetics and cookery" than science or philosophy. In refusing to ignore mere appearances provided by experience, it was forever getting bogged down in superficial matters. It might be a useful tool for tarting up an explanation or for spicing up a weak argument, but it was no fit instrument for ridding the world of error. And maybe Plato was, in a way, right. Maybe rhetoric is like cookery. For a rhetorician, after all, such a comparison does not have to be an insult. It can be a challenge. What happens if we think of rhetoric "in terms of" cooking?

Rhetoric and the Slow-Food Movement

In all likelihood, Plato himself was not much of a cook, which is why he could be so dismissive of the culinary arts. Being something of Puritan, he probably ate plain, bland food, skipping meals to dream up dialogues and fasting for long periods of time to keep himself sharp (though he did apparently like wine). For people like Plato who are indifferent to cooking, it's all of a piece. But for those who care about food, its preparation, presentation, and consumption, not all meals are created equal. It can be as trivial a business as Plato makes it out to be, or it can be a way of transforming the ordinary and everyday into the luminous. Moreover, cookery, like rhetoric, is not something we can choose to do without; we can only choose to do it ill or well. And so, if we are to understand rhetoric in terms of cookery in some fashion, let us understand it in this second way. In keeping with the recommended pace of rhetoric, let us understand it as analogous not just to any sort of cooking, but to the sort of cooking championed by the so-called "slow-food movement."

The slow-food movement took hold in Europe in the last decade of the previous century in response to the invasion of European cuisine by American fast-food restaurants. The fast-food restaurant involves the extension of industrial management and production techniques to the restaurant business. It is methodical in ways sure to gladden the heart of any Serious diner. Its devotion to method is a function of its original purpose. Fast-food restaurants came about in order to rival and eventually replace the countless American diners and family restaurants, places with names like "Elmer's" or "Hank's Playmore Park," offering a hodgepodge of local favorite foods of highly uneven quality. Travelers and newcomers unfamiliar with the area and its cuisine—and such people comprised an increasing proportion of those eating out in the ever more mobile 1950s and 1960s—placed an increasing premium on predictability, which was above all else what fast-food restaurants provided, along with foods high in fat and sodium and low in nutrients. They offered a narrow, uniform menu of entrees that were methodically prepared in precisely the same way at every franchise. One major fast-food franchiser went so far as to create a "Hamburger University" to train employees exactly how long to cook each patty, at what temperature, and with how much oil. This uniformity in quality and type of food allowed them to franchise their product, "brand" their food, and advertise it intensely at the national level. Thanks to the volume generated by advertising, the de-skilling of minimum-wage workers needed to prepare and serve the food, and their ability to buy massive quantities of food from distributors on the cheap, fast-food chains were able to severely undercut prices charged by local establishments and thus to drive many of them out of business.

The production of fast food is, in short, the culinary version of motion. The production of slow food, meanwhile, is quintessentially an act. And the dynamic of slow-food production is very much like the dynamic of rhetoric. Just as each rhetorical act will be incrementally different from the rhetorical acts that precede it, each slow-food meal will be incrementally different from meals of the same name that precede it. The meatloaf served on Thursday night will be subtly different from the meatloaf served by the same slow-food restaurant on Wednesday night. And it will certainly be different from the meatloaf served by the slow-food restaurant down the street, which insists on using rosemary instead of cumin and is excessively timid in its use of garlic.

Over the course of the year, slow-food restaurant menus change as different ingredients come into season. Because slow-food restaurants are committed to locally grown foods, they resist buying frozen or otherwise preserved foods from outside the area. Because local soil and climate conditions are different, different varieties of different ingredients will be used in different areas. And flavors will be changed by the growing conditions, which in turn calls for different spices to complement the different flavors of the ingredients. Each meal, or "case" as it were, is an expression of the local conditions, "the circumstances" as it were, as well as being like all meals of the same name. Slow-food preparation is "inefficient" in comparison to fast-food preparation. One cannot reduce slow-food preparation to a sequence of tiny steps readily mastered by high school students indifferent to the culinary arts. One cannot control the market through which one buys one's ingredients any more than one can control the local climate and soil conditions that limit one's choice of foods. The slow-food cook must adapt to local conditions, learning from those before him who've worked within constraints posed by the same conditions how to prepare those foods most appropriate for the conditions. There is no recipe that can guide the slow-food cook in adapting to the ever changing circumstances he must work within any more than there is a map sufficient to guide the rhetorical wayfarer.

The slow waking celebrated by Roethke is the same slow pace celebrated by slow-food cooks and rhetoricians alike. In all three cases what slows people down is attention to the particulars of experience. In the end, if one is to make fine food, poetry, or persuasive cases, one must adjust to the ineluctable limits of one's environment and the singular needs of those who will eat, read, and hear what one produces. In a world where ever greater efficiencies deliver "just in time," ever less substantive food, for thought or for sustenance, telling people to slow down and pay attention to all those variables that fast thinkers, fast-food vendors, and fast capitalists have eliminated from consideration is perhaps a quixotic act. But if one produces poetry and food and persuasive cases not just to please, but to change and educate those one serves, one has no choice but to make one's way and take one's waking slow.

2

❦

Rhetoric and Identity

Of the three major relationships discussed in this and the next two chapters, the relationship between rhetoric and identity is perhaps the least widely acknowledged and least well understood. While nearly everyone associates rhetoric with persuasion, and many associate it with interpretation, few would associate rhetoric with identity without being prompted. And yet arguably the most important function served by rhetoric is the work it does in service of identity formation. Who we are, who we wish to be, and the amount of control we have over either of those two matters depends significantly on our rhetorical skill. In the rest of the chapter, we'll examine why so many matters of identity formation fall into the province of rhetoric and just how rhetorical skills may help us in that process. Our starting point for that examination is the common denominator of rhetoric and identity—language.

You would never think of rushing up to a stranger at a party, and with little or no preamble demanding of them, "What do you *mean*? What's your *definition*?" as if they were some exotic noun you were encountering for the first time. Well, maybe you would, but if you did you would be committing a social blunder. It's simply too flat-footed, too impertinent, too invasive a way to begin a conversation. Some, though certainly not all of you, might, however, start things off by asking, "So, what's your story?" That's a bit abrupt, but possibly acceptable, depending on the nature of the gathering. At least you've elevated the other person from a noun to a full-fledged narrative.

But having said that, many of the clearly acceptable questions we do put to people on first meeting them are designed to elicit some of the same information sought by the above questions, information about their meaning. Take, for example, that old standby, "And what do you do?", which is immediately taken to mean, "What do you do for a living? What's your job?" Or, if you're a college student, "What's your major?", meaning, "What do you plan on doing for a living?" Certainly in American society, anyone interested in discovering our meaning, our story, would be able to infer a great deal about us from our answer to questions about our vocation. If one person were to answer, "I'm a bounty hunter," while another answered, "I'm a heart surgeon," we would begin making all sorts of assumptions and drawing any number of inferences about differences in their respective levels of education, intelligence, socioeconomic status, physical condition, and even their character. We would, of course, be guilty of stereotyping; but so long as our assumptions took the form of hypotheses that we were willing to discard as the conversation progressed and confounding evidence emerged—the surgeon may prove to be a blockhead whose sole interest is offshore tax dodges while the bounty hunter may prove to be an engaging, morally complex student of constitutional law—we remain within the normal bounds of identity interpretation as that art is universally practiced.

If People Are Words, Why Don't They Live in Dictionaries?

Later in the chapter we will return to this crucial relationship between identity and vocation. For now, however, we are mainly interested in the relationship between identity and language, between our selves and the words and stories we use to represent those selves that lie behind questions about vocation. It is this interdependence between identity and language—our capacity to use language as a means of representing our identity to others and in turn to interpret others' representations of themselves—that makes rhetoric such a powerful tool for understanding, forming, and preserving identity. That is not to say, however, that identity is *nothing but* language; each of us is, to be sure, more than a collection of words. But whatever we may be beyond language is largely inaccessible, even to ourselves. The extraverbal dimension of our selves is like the tree that falls in the forest when no one is around to see or hear it fall. We assume of course that unwatched trees do in fact fall down, not to mention grow up, burn to the ground, drop their leaves or cones, suffer from bark beetle infestations, and everything else they might do with someone watching, just as we assume that we persist pretty much intact even while we sleep. To believe otherwise, to believe that nothing exists unless we are conscious of it, is to be delusional. But few of us give much thought to the offstage existence of things, including our selves, when they are beyond the reach of perception or language, and that indifference seems not unreasonable. (And did you ever stop to wonder how, if no one was around to hear that tree fall, the person posing that question knows that it has in fact fallen?)

Essence v. Substance

In making this rough equation between identity on the one hand and consciousness and language on the other, we depart from traditional notions of identity based on "essence," here understood to be some part of us—perhaps physical, perhaps spiritual—that makes us who we are, that which if removed from our identity would change our identity. While philosophers don't spend much time these days pondering essence, the assumptions underlying essentialism sprout like hardy perennials in everyday conversations about identity. Thus, for example, some among us spend inordinate amounts of time and sometimes money "finding themselves," or "getting in touch with their inner [fill in the blank]," thereby suggesting that a "real," as-yet-undiscovered self, not to be confused with the bumbler who is doing the searching, abides and awaits their discovery. Once found, presumably, their authentic existence will begin.

Once upon a time, this sort of search was not the province of amateurs. For centuries, philosophers were so bent on naming *the* human essence—everything from souls to angels to playfulness to pineal glands has been nominated—that they devoted a major branch of inquiry, known as ontology, to the effort. Over time the search for essence branched off in two basic directions: While some set out in pursuit of a property or set of properties that make us uniquely who we are in all our glorious particularity, others set out in pursuit of a property or set of properties that make us members of a larger class—"God's creature" or "human being" or "rational being" are often cited—that constitutes the most venerated class in which we may claim membership. Paradoxically, thus, my essence may name that which makes me identical to other members of my species, or it may name that which makes me unlike any other member of my species. In the first case, the most important aspect of my identity is understood to lie outside myself: Thanks to my possession of a certain set of properties I can be equated with all other creatures possessing those same properties. In the second case, my identity is understood to lie wholly within myself: Thanks to my possession of a unique set of properties—a sort of ontological version of DNA—I am distinguishable from every other creature.

Eventually a schism developed among essentialists, who, as is the habit of serious, logical sorts of people, resolved the contradiction by choosing up sides and rejecting the alternative notion of essence. One side, which held sway for two millennia, claims that the significance of any single identity pales in comparison to the glories of our common identity. The other side, which started regaining traction just a few centuries ago, retorts that the glory of our identity lies in our absolute uniqueness and our freedom to make of ourselves what we will. Today, the divide between these two essentialist camps mostly follows the fault line separating religious and secular thought, with the "collectivists" being strongly identified with religious thinking and the "individualists" with secular thinking. In practice, of course, the two get confused all the time. Unable to square the two senses of "essence," and unhappy living without the alternative sense of the term, some essentialists simply bifurcate the two senses of the term and define themselves alternately by whichever one suits their circumstances. In the workplace and the marketplace, they assure us, they are essentialists of the secular sort ("I'm a self-made man!"), while at home they are essentialists of the religious sort ("I'm God's creature!"). The contradiction they resolutely ignore is not unlike the one finessed in the credit card commercial whose honey-toned voice-over reminds us that "There are some things money can't buy," all the while showing us money buying all manner of things apparently *necessary* for the state of being that money can't buy, and then concludes with the reassurance that "for everything else there's MasterCard." Faced with the same contradiction, others unwittingly confuse the religious and secular senses of essence. The old textbook depictions of evolution as a pyramid with human beings at the apex represents a secular version of categorical essentialism, while the peculiarly American belief that "God wishes me in particular to get rich because I'm a uniquely worthy member of His creation" is a religious version of secular essentialism.

Why "I" Is a Metaphor

Meanwhile, rhetoricians, who it will be recalled revel in the practice of "proving opposites," knowingly embrace the paradox of identity that bedevils the essentialists. They can do this because they don't view identity as being reducible to a "set of traits" or a single quality that permanently identifies us like a dictionary definition; rather they view it as a succession of acts, a project like a manuscript, a work in progress. At the heart of that project is the ongoing struggle between our need to identify and affiliate with people and ideas outside ourselves and our need to preserve as much control as possible over the nature of our affiliations and identifications and their influence on us. We wish to act as self-determining agents in charge of our own destinies while at the same time serving as responsible citizens in our communities and stewards of our environment. And the only language supple enough to embody that struggle is the language of metaphor, the only language—other than nonsense—that ignores the Law of Contradiction's insistence that "A cannot both exist and not exist." The language of metaphor is the playful language of "both-and," not the more serious, logical language of "either-or"; it is the language of transformation that allows categorically different entities to merge.

By way of illustrating the dynamics of metaphor, consider Shakespeare's metaphorical equation of an old man and a deciduous tree, a figure with some obvious implications for a discussion of identity.

Sonnet

That time of year thou mayst in me behold
When yellow leaves, or none, or few, do hang
Upon those boughs which shake against the cold,
Bare ruin'd choirs, where late the sweet birds sang.

In me thou see'st the twilight of such day
As after sunset fadeth in the west,
Which by-and-by black night doth take away,
Death's second self, that seals up all in rest.

In me thou see'st the glowing of such fire
That on the ashes of his youth doth lie
As the death-bed whereon it must expire,
Consumed by that which it was nourish'd by.

—this thou perceivest, which makes thy love more strong,
To love that well which thou must leave ere long.

If we look up "old" and "man" and "yellow" and "leaves" in a dictionary, we will find nothing to link the terms. The connections between them are not denotative or direct, they are connotative. Connotations are emotional connections and colorations that words take on because of the way in which they are actually used in specific environments. Old men, beyond the categorical traits of being human males beyond a certain age, are identified with any number of qualities. Which ones come most immediately to our minds is a function of our personal experiences with members of the class and with cultural values and attitudes that shape those experiences. We may think of old men as pathetic, noble, wise, diminished, tyrannical, charitable, rigid, prudent, garrulous, mute, or any number of things in between. The point is, the terms always do more than simply name members of a class; they conjure up associations and feelings that are not entirely random or idiosyncratic. And hard as we sometimes work to eliminate these associations from the language, they endure. Technical languages and jargon are from time to time invented by specialists to rid words of their shady pasts and unfortunate connotations; but after awhile those near-invisible tints of meaning (what will be later discussed as "unearned increments" of meaning) inevitably sneak back in as divisions develop within the community that coined the terms and they come to be associated with dangerously radical or hopelessly outmoded ways of thinking. Hence the very term "essence," once the starting point of any serious discussion about human identity, is today rarely invoked—though many people continue to talk about identity as if it were an essence without using the term—except by the occasional theologian and the marketers of fragrance and wine. In the seventeenth century, meanwhile, the enemies of connotation were so exercised about the mischief wrought by these sneaky, uncodified word associations that a bill was brought before the British Parliament to outlaw metaphors from the language. (That the bill's sponsor was a fellow with the unfortunate—connotatively speaking—name of Sprat, has always struck me as more than mere happenstance.)

Back to Shakespeare's sonnet and his equation of an old man and the leaves from a deciduous tree. For the metaphor to work, Shakespeare has to limit the equation to a narrow subset of traits shared by the two categorically distinct entities, traits clustered around the image of winter as a season and as a time of life. Consider the opening stanza:

> That time of year thou mayst in me behold
> When yellow leaves, or none, or few, do hang
> Upon those boughs which shake against the cold,
> Bare ruin'd choirs, where late the sweet birds sang.

Shakespeare, following the "both is and is not" logic of metaphor, defines the old man by telling us what he is not as well as what he is. Again, according to Burke, all acts of definition follow a similar logic: In designating what a thing *is* we must designate what it's *not*. He calls this phenomenon the paradox of substance. In the case of Shakespeare's old man, he is and is not a tree; more to the point, he is and is not a tree full of golden leaves and singing birds. He *was* that, and a few yellowed leaves perhaps remain to remind us of his glory before it fled. He *is now* denuded of leaves, silent and cold. The tree's currently bleak condition resonates with us because of the contrast with its previously robust condition. If we only see the tree and the speaker as old, if we see decrepitude as their defining "essence," they are simple, flat figures. But if we see them as at once young and old, warm and cold, beautiful and ruined, singing and silent, they become compellingly complex figures. And like most profound metaphors, Shakespeare's is built on a simple truth: We do in fact tend to perceive longtime acquaintances (most especially ourselves) cumulatively. That is, we tend to perceive them like a series of stop-action pictures, with afterimages of the person they were perpetually superimposed over the person they are. So it is with couples who've been married for 50 and 60 years reporting that they continue to see in the 70- or 80-year-old next to them, the person of 18 or 20 that they first married. Language that restricts itself to logically consistent statements about the world is ill-equipped to capture this complexity.

A Brief Mind Experiment

Only by looking at what the old man is not can Shakespeare begin to give a fully rounded picture of his subject. To describe him as he is inevitably misses the point. To test this for yourself, I invite you to undertake a task that a former teacher of mine, Ann Berthoff, used to help a seminar of college English teachers better appreciate the intricacies of language. She had us select an object at random—the only qualification was that it had to fit in our hand—and write an extended description of the object without naming what the object was. Since I was living with my family at a beach during the seminar, I used our evening walks along the shore to collect interesting objects. After discarding a number of items, I settled on a small crab claw, detached from its owner, entangled in a mass of seaweed. After about a half page of trying to describe it, I had run through all its apparent traits—weight, color, shape, size, texture, etc.—of the sort taxonomists would use to classify the object. Continuing to stare at it was not producing any new information. Out of desperation as much as anything, I began comparing it to things it wasn't: a starfish, a clam shell, and all the other beach flotsam that I'd discarded before selecting the claw. From these comparisons, its "story"—what it *meant* as opposed to what it *was*—began to emerge.

Thanks to an extended meditation contrasting the crab claw to a starfish, I eventually landed on the notion of "crabbiness." Whereas the starfish was absolutely flat, self-effacing, rigidly indifferent, the crab claw was at once menacing and amusing, in the same way that crabby people are often irritatingly aggressive and laughably ineffectual. This smallish, pink and white, brittle, bumpy-shelled object with its fearsome little pincers was the perfect embodiment of irascibility and small-scale hostility. It was the Danny DeVito of crustaceans. Setting out to describe something, I circled back and discovered the roots of a metaphor that through long familiarity had lost its bite, so to speak. Having started out trying to present an exhaustive catalog of its traits, assuming vaguely that they would somehow "add up" to the crab claw, I ended up offering a decidedly partial, but much more satisfying, account of my subject.

The Gist—A Provisional Essence

Defining anything in any sort of depth, including ourselves, requires that we direct people's attention toward some aspects of our subject and away from others, to see what X is "in terms of" Y and for the moment to ignore what it might mean "in terms of" Z, A, B, or C. In effect, each of the terms we choose to understand our subject "in terms of" serves as a provisional essence. Out of numberless acts of understanding X in terms of other things grows a sense of what X means. Out of numberless acts of understanding ourselves in terms of other people, ideas, beliefs, etc., comes a sense of who we are and who we are not— our sense of identity. To cite a simple example, if a stranger were to ask, "Who are you?" you'd probably tell them your name. But unless you were formidably famous your response wouldn't be overly helpful; and there's no dictionary of proper names for them to look you up in. Your most enlightening response would entail an account of those relationships—attractions and associations, animosities and aversions— that were most important to you. Such an account would tell them both about your "place" in the world and what mattered to you, your self as defined by your circumstances and your self as defined by your acts and attitudes. Our fullest possible account would attempt to chronicle the sum of all our entanglements, voluntary and involuntary, and our attitude toward them. But such an account would be endless, and so we content ourselves with offering partial accounts of our most meaningful entanglements.

The term we will use to describe these selective accounts of meaning is "gist." Confronted with any complex text, like Shakespeare's poem, or multilayered event, or upon first meeting a fascinating person, our first response—certainly a rhetorician's first response—is to offer an initial take on its/his/her meaning, to come up with a gist. A gist is not to be confused with an essence, a definition, or a summary. Whereas an essence attempts to name that which *makes* something what it is, a gist attempts to name what we *make of* something. A gist, moreover, refers to a linguistic construct, a phrase or brief statement, while an essence, presumably, refers to a thing. And whereas definitions attempt to fix the meaning of a term, a gist is simply a single "take" on the meaning of something. To arrive at a gist, someone must perform an act of interpretation; to arrive at a definition, one may do nothing more than open up a dictionary. So perhaps a gist is more like a summary? Here again, there are important differences. When summarizing something one does not, ostensibly, intrude on whatever is summarized. In theory, a summary merely "miniaturizes" or reduces the scale of the original. In fact, no summary can do this because summarizing requires that certain features of the original be highlighted and others be ignored. But summary connotes "impartiality" and objectivity as surely as gist connotes partiality and the subjective presence of an interpreter. And a summary is supposed to be "definitive" in the sense that for any given phenomenon there is one correct way to summarize it. But gists, we know, may change as circumstances and interpreters change.

Perhaps the most appropriate way to sum up this discussion of summing up is to offer an analogy, one that returns us to our original example and to the relationship between language and identity. If in response to the question "What do you do?" the stranger encountered at a social gathering were to silently hand us their résumé or curriculum vitae, they would be handing us the equivalent of a summary of their worklife. If on the other hand they launched into a narrative account of their job, full of anecdotes and asides and flashbacks and flash forwards, telling us how they got interested in their work, their hopes for the future, how the work has changed over the years, the hardships and joys of their job, and so forth, they would be offering us a gist of their worklife in the context of their full life. And later on, if that same person, in a job interview, were to offer a different gist, highlighting different features of their worklife and emphasizing different attitudes and beliefs about their work, they would not necessarily be lying, or even exaggerating. They would simply be editing that perpetual work-in-progress that is their identity, selecting a different ensemble of relationships to see it "in terms of," in acknowledgment of, a new purpose and a different audience for their performance. In the rest of the chapter, we will consider some terms and some ways of thinking about identity that will

hopefully equip us to construct gists that will do us and those we interpret justice.

Know Thyselves: Three Dimensions of Identity

The idea of a multidimensional identity is hardly new. That it might
consist of three parts goes back at least to Plato, who divided the human soul up into passions or appetites, reason, and spirit. Similarly,
Freud claimed more than two thousand years later that the human psy-
che (a modern version of soul) consisted of the id, ego, and superego.
So our own tripartite division of identity into the given, the readymade,
and the constructed (or homemade) has some rough precedent, though
our own division is less neat than its predecessors. These three divisions
of identity are overlapping as well as complementary and sometimes it
is difficult to say exactly where one leaves off and the other begins. Or,
as Kenneth Burke has suggested, "The individual is composed of many
'corporate identities.' Sometimes they are concentric, sometimes in
conflict" (PLF 307). To complicate matters further, one of our three
identities, the readymade, turns out to contain three further subdivisions (workplace readymades, consumer readymades, and cultural
readymades). But they are all three sufficiently distinct and important
to receive separate consideration, and to the extent that we are able to
form and defend our own identities, it's crucial to understand the inter-
action among the three.

So what is the "gist" of each of our identity types? The given identity includes all aspects of our identity that are inherited or acquired
willy-nilly rather than by choice and/or by creative act. And while our
given identity is not necessarily unchangeable, it constrains our
choices, sometimes decisively so. The most obvious aspects of our given
identity include our genetic and family structure; the time, place, and
circumstances of our birth; and our pasts. The readymade, meanwhile,
includes those identities that we have not ourselves constructed, that
have been prefabricated by others and are on offer through the workplace, the marketplace, and the cultural space we occupy. To varying
degrees, these readymade identities may serve our interests, but not before they serve the interests of those who construct or exploit them—
those who employ us, those who sell us goods and services, or those who
have an interest in influencing and shaping the priorities of our larger
culture. Our constructed identity, meanwhile, is as much a negative capacity as it is a positive one, insofar as none of us constructs an identity
all on our own out of nothing. We construct our selves based on avail-

able models and within the limits of that which we've been given. But each of us has the capacity to reject some models and accept others and to modify what we've been given.

In many ways, the given is the least interesting of the three dimensions of identity insofar as it is the one over which we have least control. However much I may desire to be an NBA center, no matter how hard I work, if extraordinary height is not in my DNA, my dream is doomed. To be sure, through plastic surgery I can change my body's appearance; through regimens of diet and exercise I can resist time and the various biological "set points" that govern weight and muscle tone; through radical surgery, I can change my sex. I can take pills or drugs to alter my personality. But I can't do much about the time and place in which I'm born or the people who conceive and rear me, and I have little control over many of the early formative experiences that shape my identity: growing up rich or poor, a student in a public school or an exclusive boarding school, a farm kid or city dweller, an only child or the youngest of five. Indeed my motivation to modify or accept various of my given traits is largely determined by my time and place. No nineteenth-century British citizens longed to be NBA centers and probably few aspired to be seven feet tall. And my desire to change my sex would be strongly influenced by the prevailing readymade models of gender in my time and place, not to mention the availability of surgical procedures to effect my transformation.

One of the major reasons why equations of identity and essence lost favor had to do with the large proportion of one's identity essentialism assigned to the given. Depending on the particular type of essentialism one espoused, one could do little or virtually nothing about one's identity. One might occasionally become something improbable, rising up, say, from humble origins to play a major role on history's stage; but such transformations were matters of destiny (or, in Puritan terms, "election"), prefigured by one's essence, and the vast proportion of the world's population was not so blessed. If wealth was what one was born to, wealthy was what one was meant to be. And if one was born the son of a peasant, one was unlikely to die anything but a peasant. Women's roles were clearly and narrowly defined with little help from actual women. Social or geographical mobility was severely limited and one's "place" in the social hierarchy was determined by one's place in the Great Chain of Being, which had been set up by God and wasn't open to gerrymandering. Looking back, from the perspective of the twenty-first century, the system that conferred identity on the Western world's population looks far too deterministic, leaving the individual little room for growth or change. And in a world where one's identity was an essence conferred by a divine creator, the idea of acquiring or constructing an identity wasn't just incoherent, it was heretical.

There's no one particular moment in the history of Western thought one might point to that signaled the broadening of identity to allow for readymade and constructed identities. The emergence of Protestantism, with its emphasis on the direct relationship between individuals and their deity, out of Catholicism, with its emphasis on hierarchy, marked an important turning point. The corresponding shift away from monarchies and the divine right of kings toward democracies and individual rights furthered the impetus toward self-determination. But that impetus accelerated most dramatically during the eighteenth and nineteenth centuries due largely to fundamental changes in the nature of work and of the economy in the wake of the Industrial Revolution. During this period, the share of our identity we attributed to the given shrank considerably. And as it did, the notion of "the self-made man" and the appeal of the readymade identity grew apace for reasons we'll now explore.

While most work had for centuries been done in the home, the fields surrounding the home, or in a small shop attached to the home, increasing numbers of nineteenth-century workers spent their days in factories, mines, and large retail establishments. And the tasks they performed on the job were considerably different from the ones they'd performed at home or on the farm. Countless intermediary positions and entirely new professions emerged throughout the nineteenth century as agricultural economy gave way to an industrial economy. When people left home to go to work, they no longer produced their own food and basic necessities and seldom built their own homes; now they had salaries to buy the goods produced elsewhere. People were needed to build and run a greatly expanded transportation infrastructure—roads, railways, canals—required to get the goods to market. People were needed to keep track of what was shipped and accounts of what was sold. People were needed to manage those who made the goods while others were needed to sell and market the goods. And a much greater proportion of people needed banks and bankers to look after their surplus cash, which was transformed into the capital needed to finance further economic expansion. By the end of the nineteenth century, countless displaced farm families found themselves living among large numbers of strangers in a new urban environment, doing the sorts of jobs that previous generations of their family had never heard of; in offices, stores, and factories of the sort their parents had never seen; and earning sums of money that were unthinkable in their parents' genera-tion. People were certainly freer than their place- and identity-bound ancestors, but they were also less secure about just who they were sup-posed to be both at home and on the job.

The stage was thus set in America for a new science—the fabrica-tion of readymade identities for domestic and vocational purposes. The primary creators of readymade *consumer* identities in America were ad-vertisers, who plied their trade mainly in the weekly magazines that peo-ple started subscribing to en masse in the early twentieth century. The job of creating readymade *workplace* identities, meanwhile, fell to a vari-ety of people, including those who wrote the fiction and essays featured in those same magazines, those who wrote books about how to achieve success, and most especially those members of the emerging science of management. Because advertising is arguably the most important rhetor-ical art to emerge in the twentieth century, it will be discussed later on in this chapter and subsequently in Chapters 4 and 6. But now we'll turn to the process of constructing readymade identities for the American workforce.

Selecting a Suitable Workplace Self

In the wake of arguably the bloodiest, most strike-torn period in American labor history, extending from the last decade of the nine-teenth century through the first decade of the twentieth century, large companies and corporations began to pursue "kinder, gentler" ways of persuading their employees to be more productive and less belligerent. Exploiting the anxieties felt by many workers and middle managers of the day who were unsure of their role in the workplace and lacked mod-els of workplace identity from previous generations of workers, people like Frederick Taylor, father of the "Taylorist workplace," and others began to prescribe models of workplace behavior emphasizing docility, cooperativeness, and strong identification with the company.

Large corporations, using many of the same persuasive tools em-ployed by advertisers, began touting themselves to workers as benevo-lent, familial institutions, an alternative to civic community. Subsequently, self-help books, often written by upper management and corporate publicists, were among the first best-sellers in the twentieth-century book trade. Stressing various strategies of "appearance manage-ment," these books appealed particularly to those in sales and manager-ial positions and bureaucrats of various sort. Such people seldom produced tangible goods, which made it difficult for them or anyone else to assess their performance. Moreover, the measures of their performance were often affected by matters over which they had little control. By becoming a certain *sort* of person, by conforming to the pattern of a readymade workplace identity thoughtfully provided by their employer, they could achieve at least some measure of security. They could *fit in*. But the price for fitting in was high. The prevailing models of workplace identity were considerably more congenial to company interests than to the psychological health of the worker. In today's argot, what the worst of these books commended was tantamount to "identity theft." Books like *How to Win Friends and Influence People* basically showed us how to efface ourselves and become whatever our customer or manager needed us to be. Success, in the form of the sale or promotion, would be ours at the price of our autonomy. More sophisticated versions of these books continue to sell in huge numbers today as more and more members of the American workforce find themselves taking up positions in a new economy that is if anything more opaque to those who work within it than were the industrial, consumer, and service economies of old.

The Trickle-Down Effect of Workplace Readymades

While all this may seem remote from the immediate concerns of those who don't work in corporate America, these works, because they are valued and invoked by so many powerful individuals and companies, have a significant "trickle-down" effect on all sectors of American life. (The effects are global, to be sure, but the immediate impacts are most visible in this country.) The language of these works, featuring terms such as "excellence," "champions," "accountability," "brand," "reengineering," "stakeholders," "leadership," and . . . "trickle down" to name a few, creeps into the vernacular of politicians, educators, and government bureaucrats. And with this language come the values and belief systems that inform it, because, as we have seen, language is never innocent and never neutral. To redescribe the world using these new terms is to reevaluate and reprioritize the world.

The way in which this phenomenon occurs, the circulation of terms from one realm to another, varies considerably. But in general, terms that move into a new realm are initially experienced in that realm as metaphors, as substitutions of an unfamiliar term for a familiar one. We can see this most obviously in the case of poetry, which is a sort of engine of linguistic change, forever substituting unfamiliar for familiar terms. In the case of Shakespeare's poem, for example, a tree in winter is "substituted for" an elderly man. Poetic metaphors such as this are not categorically different from metaphors of the everyday sort, they simply retain their strangeness over time. In the normal scheme of things, metaphors lose their "both-and" tension and just name things in the way that "crabby" now names a particular human disposition without calling to mind a crustacean. Rhetoric teaches us that this process is inevitable and not necessarily sinister; but it also teaches that we must pay attention to these inflections of meaning and "discount" terms as they pass from one realm to another, much as we discount currencies as they pass from one economy to another, in order to minimize misunderstanding and misuse. Otherwise, as numerous critics have pointed out in recent years, language may use us as readily as we use it. Or, to borrow Kenneth Burke's analogy: "Sometimes we drive in traffic and sometimes traffic drives us" (LSA 49). To the extent we borrow language from another realm without remaining mindful of *both* its original sense *and* the sense in which it's now used, we are particularly vulnerable to being used by language.

Seldom, it appears, are terms imported from the literature of workplace identity, a genre I've elsewhere termed "success rhetoric," seriously contested or thoughtfully discounted. In this regard, consider one of the most sacred and mystified notions in all of this literature: "leadership." Leadership is to success rhetoric what heroism once was to ancient myth: the personification and exemplification of the dominant values and beliefs of the domain within which the hero/leader performs. Unfortunately, it is far more difficult to discern precisely what values and beliefs a contemporary leader might represent than it is to determine those an ancient hero stood for. Too often leaders are identified in much the way that—contrary to their own doctrine—Puritans once identified the elect: according to their worldly success. Because they have been successful, as measured by an extremely narrow metric that itself remains largely unquestioned, they must be leaders. To the extent that the leaders featured in success rhetoric can be said to exemplify an established *ethos*, the details of their lives are tortured to fit the model in much the way that the particulars of saints' lives once were tweaked to fit a different model. But most of the time leaders' values and beliefs don't receive any sort of extended attention. Bromides and slogans, which are unlikely to offend or challenge a mass readership, do the work of values and beliefs while a bulk of the attention is reserved for the tactics, the 5, 7, 9, or 12 steps/stages/traits that comprise the leader's secrets for success. In converting a single life into a formula that readers can imitate, most books on leadership reduce human action to a form of motion. And in failing to question the ends of those actions, in failing to ask, as Burke requires us to ask, just what "tests for the tests of success" (P&C 101) have been applied, they represent severely impoverished models for human identity.

Terms like "leadership" enter our vocabularies innocently enough. But all too often they end up redefining our realities and remolding our identities by "naturalizing" some acts and virtues and rendering others deviant. Burke's notion of a "terministic screen" nicely captures the sense of this process. Like so many of his terms, it is a pun of sorts that exploits the basic ambiguity of "terministic," which can be taken simultaneously as a reference to linguistic terminology and to the state of being terminal or finished. So understood, it nicely illustrates a proverb from the French artist Georges Braque, who once declared that "*Le conformisme commence à la définition.*" ("Conformity begins in definition.") Once something is defined, assigned a term, it is indistinguishable from that which "terminates" it. Only metaphors, puns, and the like, which wear their ambiguity on their sleeves and exploit that ambiguity to open up new possibilities of meaning, can readily escape the "*conformisme*" that follows definition.

To illustrate the process by which the unconsidered choice of terms can lead to dangerous conformity, consider a couple of different examples from the worlds of education and business. When schools are supposed to be "accountable" instead of, say, "effective," the debate over "tests for the tests of [educational] success" is short-circuited. We assume that the "objective" measures of accountancy provided by standardized tests are valid while broader, more complex measures requiring interpretation are "too subjective" to fit neatly in our accounting ledger. Hence we end up arguing over what to do about "underperforming" schools and whom to blame for their failure while setting aside discussions about what success and failure might actually mean. And students likewise are invited to internalize the judgment of a multiple-choice test that defines them as smart, dumb, or average.

Or, to cite another example, when corporate "families" give way to corporate "stakeholders," the pecking order of the various constituencies subtly changes. By itself, of course, use of the term "stakeholder" causes nothing to happen. But a stake is "literally" a financial term and only "figuratively" a reference to nonpecuniary interest, which means that the interests of those who own shares in a company are likely to be privileged over the interests of those who work for the company. The term "family," meanwhile, was a popular term for describing corporate culture when that culture emphasized the reciprocal obligations of the company (long-term security) and its employees (loyalty) to each other. In an age that prefers to talk about stakeholders, family is deemed a deviant or "paternalistic" term. But picture for a moment the rhetorically delicate task facing the corporate spokesperson sent out to announce the latest exercise in "rightsizing" the workforce if that workforce is conceived of as part of a family: "In order that our cousins the shareholders may see their meager returns boosted by at least 13 percent, we are letting go 50,000 of our brothers and sisters in the employee family and cutting health benefits to 100,000 of our grammies and gramps in the retiree family. On behalf of all surviving members of the Bogusheart family, we thank all our former kin for their selflessness and wish them all the best in their search for new families."

Consumer Readymades: How to Be a Harley Guy

The effectiveness of success rhetoric in constructing readymade workplace identities and shaping larger social values represents one of many challenges to our rhetorical capacity. It is notable primarily for being so little remarked, meaning that before one can critique the practice, one must first persuade people that it is real. On the other hand, the challenges posed by advertising, and the sometimes toxic models of readymade identity that it has created over the years are visible to just about everyone. Thus, to cite one particularly notorious example, advertisers' reliance on extremely thin female models creates an ideal of female identity that is unrealizable for most and unhealthy for almost all young women. That the increasingly skeletal appearance of the models parallels increasing instances of eating disorders in adolescent and postadolescent women—and increasingly in young men—is hardly news.

Because we are so wary of advertisers' claims and savvy about their ploys, most of us have become adept at using rhetoric—the very means they use to gull us after all—to protect ourselves against their wiles. But advertisers have responded in kind by becoming themselves ever more sophisticated at flying beneath our radar and circumventing our critical responses. They are particularly good at the art of ingratiation, of not appearing to have designs on us, of wanting nothing more than simply being our chums, our confidants, a source of earthy amusement in a world full of sham and pretense. It's hard to offer a sober condemnation of a medium so adroit at appearing not to take itself seriously. Which is why advertising critics often end up sounding like those excessively earnest people who analyze humor and tell us why we really should not be amused by jokes that make us laugh uproariously.

Take the case of beer ads. No one would argue that beer does much for the health or character, not to mention the appearance, of the American consumer. But millions of Americans, particularly young American men, drink enormous quantities of the stuff. Which is why beer ads are often humorous and focus on beer as part of the male-bonding experience, or as an important adjunct in the pursuit of young women, or as the catalyst for "bad boy" or chauvinist behaviors that leave other young American beer drinkers helpless with laughter. Criticizing beer ads by citing statistics showing the extent to which beer is implicated in drunk driving accidents and deaths, liver disease, obesity, fetal alcohol syndrome, chronic absenteeism, battery and sexual abuse, and so forth, is unlikely to get one very far. In the eyes of beer drinkers, any bluenose who trots out those numbers is simply missing the point since those pictured in the ads and those responding positively to the ads don't see themselves affected by whatever grim statistics one may produce. Beer is associated with good times and "time-out" ("It's Miller time") from the pressures and rules of the workaday world in which many beer drinkers have a particularly precarious foothold. Beer ads accept, make that *embrace*, the associations between alcohol and delinquent behaviors. Part of the genius of advertising lies in its ability to co-opt critics by including ideas hostile to the advertisers' interests—"People who drink beer are sometimes boorish and chauvinistic? Absolutely!"—into their ad so as to naturalize the connection and neutralize potential criticism. Instead of countering objections to their products, they celebrate what's objected to in a tongue-in-cheek manner—think Joe Isuzu, think Miller man—thereby disarming potential critics.

In our final chapter, "Rhetoric and Everyday Life," we'll return to some of the strategies employed by advertisers to sidestep or blunt rhetorical critique. For now we want to focus on one example of consumer marketing, less to expose the underhanded ways of advertisers than to illustrate how those targeted by marketing are sometimes complicit in the consumption and modification of readymade identities, and how those identities may be adapted to serve consumers' interests as well as those of the advertiser. Our emphasis here is intended to underscore the agency of consumers—which is to say, all of us—in the dynamic of identity formation and the role played in that process by consumer readymades. The product we have in mind is the Harley-Davidson motorcycle. And rather than closely reading one of its ads—the sort of thing we'll do in our final chapter—we'll focus on the basis of its appeal, an appeal underscored by its overall marketing plan as much as by any particular ads or ad campaigns, and the implications of that appeal for identity consumers.

To understand the relationship between a particular brand of motorcycles and identity, one must understand the place of motorcycles within the larger culture. First of all, motorcycles are a mode of transportation. And in America, the symbolic import of the means we use to transport ourselves about is far greater than the practical import. The vehicle we choose for transportation—be it a car, truck, van, SUV, scooter, or motorcycle—goes a long way toward defining our consumer readymade identity.

Not everyone would accept that there is a strong connection between our identity and our means of getting from place to place. Indeed, some people reject any linkage whatsoever between consumption and identity. Some people in fact take great pride in buying cars that they are sure will tell us little about their identity. They select utilitarian vehicles: inexpensive, reliable, boxy-looking cars that take them where they need to go at unremarkable speeds using minimal gas. And automobile manufacturers produce just such products for just such consumers, who as it turns out aren't really opting out of the car-identity game by buying purely functional vehicles; they are simply marking themselves as part of a particular "psychographic" (a way of sorting consumers based on their psychological makeup and tastes, as opposed to a "demographic" that sorts them by location, age, income, and so forth) that is extremely practical and value conscious. Knowing someone's choice of car, assuming the choice is not driven strictly by financial limitations, marketers can place them in one of sixty-two "psychodemographic" categories and predict with chilling accuracy where that person is likely to shop for clothes and what brand of cereal they will select for breakfast.

But however asymmetrical the competition between consumers who wish not to have their identities determined by the products they consume and marketers who spend billions of dollars a year studying the relationship between people's beliefs about their identities and the sorts of products they buy, consumers always have the final say, not just in their choice of products, but in *how they consume* those products. Which brings us back to Harley-Davidson motorcycles. The first thing that sets the Harley apart from other modes of transportation is its singular lack of utility. Few who ride motorcycles—for motorcycles are "ridden," like horses, not "driven," like milk trucks—use them to commute. They tend to ride them in their leisure hours. After all, unless one lives in a place with mild winters and little rain or snowfall, motorcycles can't be relied upon to get one where one needs to go much of the time. They are not the safest vehicles in the world, as anyone who has ever tried to buy insurance for one soon realizes; they are not the quietest and most comfortable vehicle around; they are not, relatively speaking, the least-expensive vehicle one might choose, particularly if one chooses a high-end bike like a Harley; and they are not very useful for hauling around groceries, pets, kids, elderly people, or more than one passenger of any age. All of which means that most people who choose to ride motorcycles are doing so to satisfy other needs: the need for speed or immediate contact with the environment, the nostalgic desire to relive childhood bicycle trips, . . . or the wish to be perceived as the sort of person who rides a Harley.

In sum, Harley-Davidson bikes, because of their minimal utilitarian function, clearly serve a symbolic function that is less obviously served by all other forms of transport. While they may also satisfy a need for speed, a lust for wind blowing in our face, or a secret longing to do "wheelies," it is their capacity to confer an identity on those who ride them that best explains their appeal. And the identity they confer is in turn a product of Harley-Davidson's marketing, their artfully cultivated association between the Harley "brand" (here understood to be a company's self-proclaimed gist, or, for those of a metaphysical bent, its soul), and a highly desirable prefab identity. But before we can understand the nature of this dynamic, we need to better understand the raw material of the "consumer readymade," the "cultural readymade." Cultural readymades are derived from cultural myths that are transmitted in the form of narratives, icons, characters, jokes, props, scenes, and so forth. Advertising makes extensive use of such cultural readymades for obvious reasons. In appealing to a reader/viewer whose attention they have purchased for a very short time at a very high cost, they need a store of readily recognizable images and themes. Stock characters, typical scenes and situations, recognizable "status details" that signal the characters' age, tastes, beliefs, income, etc., all are manipulated by marketers to create messages that can be read in the time it takes to fly past a billboard or to watch a TV ad. The basic dynamic of this process is as-sociational rather than logical. No advertiser needs to claim that their product will make you more masculine, more sexually desirable, more hip, more secure, or more anything else. They only need to present their product in close proximity to easily recognized representations of these qualities.

In the case of the Harley-Davidson motorcycle, the cultural ready-mades from which its consumer readymade identity is compounded are among the most ubiquitous and easily recognized in our culture. Big motorcycles like Harleys instantly evoke associations with actual outlaw gangs like Hell's Angels and actual devil-may-care risk takers like Evel Knievel. These associations also owe much to classic films like *The Wild One* (1953) with Marlon Brando and *Easy Rider* (1969) with Peter Fonda and Jack Nicholson, and songs like "Born to Be Wild." Riding motorcycles has long been associated with antisocial, though not unsympathetic, characters living life on their own terms out on the edge. And what Harley-Davidson did was to draw upon those cinematic and cultural associations, those cultural readymades, and identify them with their product, thereby turning a potential turnoff to consumers—it's not safe to ride motorcycles—into an appeal—you're just the sort of go-to-hell person who loves risking life and limb. It is sold as the authentic motorcycle, the Real One, still recognizably the same product that most of us grew up watching rumble by on the streets and on the screen. This last emphasis developed in response to heightened competition during the 1980s from Japanese bikes, which were less expensive, sleeker, and capable of performing all the nonsymbolic functions of motorcycles at least as well as Harleys. By selling symbolic, cultural associations versus mere performance, Harley took advantage of its unique position as a cultural icon, a ground on which Japanese manufacturers could not compete. And in recent years, in a classic case of "brand extension," Harley-Davidson further exploited their symbolic advantage by creating a line of clothing and accessories that allow Harley riders to "dress the part" created by actors like Marlon Brando and James Dean in their studded black leather jackets and chaps.

Hence the local phenomenon known as "The Harley Guys," small bands of middle-aged, often bearded men, fully togged in Harley accessories, down to the orange and black "do-rags" they wrap around their heads in lieu of helmets, roaring up and down the not-so-mean streets of Scottsdale, Arizona, on Harley Hogs, stopping off along the way not at biker bars, but at coffee shops where they order expensive espresso drinks and discuss their portfolios, the college choices of their children, . . . and their latest plans to accessorize their bikes. In the world of work, these are largely professional men—lawyers, bankers, and brokers. (And according to Harley-Davidson's marketing department, the local Harley Guys represent a fairly typical cross section of Harley owners, who in 2000 averaged forty-four years of age and had a median income of $70,000.)

Are they deluded Hell's Angels wannabes taken in by Harley-Davidson's slick marketing campaign? Escapees from a midlife crisis out looking for Peter Pan's Land of Lost Boys on high-priced pieces of chrome powered by 1200 cc engines that sound like they're calling out "potato potato" as they pass? Well, surely some are. But for many, being a Harley Guy is clearly something of a theatrical role that they enjoy playing rather than an "alternative lifestyle" that they adopt without any sense of irony or aesthetic distance. Harley-Davidson, drawing on a rich store of cultural readymades, created a brand image with, as their CEO put it, "a little bit of naughty" in it. Harley Guys use that image to ensure that people read their dress and behavior appropriately, so as to distinguish them from people who ride bikes mainly for more pedestrian reasons on the one hand, and from biker outlaws who are way beyond "naughty" on the other. Middle-class professionals who don elaborate biker costumes and ride around on expensive motorcycles are asking to be "read" like metaphors, not mistaken for criminals. Their everyday identity is so far removed from the one that they are asking to be understood "in terms of" that the merger of the two is unlikely ever to lose its strangeness. And by the same token, when a group of local lesbians form a team called "Dykes on Bikes" to perform on Harleys in Gay Pride parades, they stretch the metaphoric connection even further. They "appropriate" (a term used to describe the process of taking a readymade symbol and turning it to unforeseen uses) a venerable icon of American machismo, playfully reclaiming the icon from its exclusive association with heterosexual male identity. Through their performances, Dykes on Bikes call attention to the artificiality of a readymade identity, "denaturalizing" the connection between bikes and macho and establishing a new connection between two seemingly remote terms—"Harley Hogs" and "lesbian theater."

The Higher Purpose of Cultural Readymades

In our example of the Harley Guys and Dykes on Bikes, we get a glimpse of the way that workplace, consumer, and cultural readymades interact, alternately using and being used by human agents in the process of identity construction. But in this process we have slighted somewhat the complex role played by cultural readymades. In the above case, advertisers and individuals alike appropriate a cultural readymade to forge communal identities that on the one hand increase loyalty to a given brand and on the other hand alter perceptions of a community's members. But cultural readymades are more than just raw material for consumer readymades. Those who wrote the films and the songs that contributed to the cultural status of motorcycles clearly had more in mind than the creation of an icon useful in the representation of an identity. In the case of *Easy Rider*, for example, the protagonists use motorcycles and drugs to similar ends: to escape middle-class respectability and the violence of the Vietnam War. In the end, they die violently and randomly at the hands of poor whites who are themselves marginalized members of the very society the bikers are fleeing. In the end, the film serves as a critique of American culture in the late 1960s, and while some of the characters achieve martyrdom, none are truly heroic. The film does not simply try to "sell" a particular identity, it offers up an account of the sometimes treacherous process of identity formation in a given time and place, thereby rendering us more reflective of our own processes, more tolerant of alternative identities, less likely to adopt uncritically an identity fabricated by others.

Cultural readymades are closest in spirit to constructed identities by virtue of their emphasis on the negative. Powerful films and literary works—which may or may not be "classics"—often serve to remind us how important it is to maintain a critical attitude toward the identities we are proffered on all sides by parents, educators, communities, companies, advertisers, peers, and so forth. They teach us not just who we might be (for inevitably they privilege and publicize some models of identity and ignore or vilify others), but also how to critically evaluate our options. Thus early on in life we may absorb models of identity offered up in children's books, comic books, or fairy tales read or told to us by parents, grandparents, or siblings and on TV shows watched raptly with little sense of critical distance, almost the way a plant absorbs nutrients. But over time we encounter more complex works that play with the patterns and characters familiar to us from our earliest stories. Perhaps, as in the old *Bullwinkle* cartoons, they offer up "fractured" versions of our beloved fairy tales, poking fun at their heroes and heroines, rendering the wise-cracking villains more sympathetic, twisting the ending to suggest a different, less-than-expected conclusion—perhaps the "wrong people" live happily ever after. We begin to develop an appreciation and an eye for novelty, for departures from the tales we once loved for their familiarity—as children we love to have the same story read to us over and over—and fidelity to patterns as much as anything else. By the time we are adults we may well possess dual allegiances to movies and books, valuing them both for their comfortable repetition of familiar patterns, patterns whose rightness we view as an article of faith, and for their constant ability to surprise us, to force us to question our comfortable assumptions about life. Which is to say, we may value a book because it is a real "page-turner" and/or because it makes us "really think."

Cultural readymades that fall into the second category are particularly important to the process of identity formation. What they offer are complex models of identity in the form of multiple characters with conflicting and even antithetical beliefs and attitudes, each in their own way capable of engaging our sympathies. Much is left to us in terms of sorting them out. From these texts we learn how to think about who we are and what we value. They are, to once again use Burke's term for literature, "equipment for living," a storehouse of proverbial wisdom and scenarios that illustrate the process of determining which proverbs ought to guide us in given circumstances.

Death of a Salesman: The Cultural Readymade as Equipment for Living

We can see this process at work in a play like Arthur Miller's *Death of a Salesman*, a work that comments both on the vagaries of workplace identity in midcentury (1949) America and on the stifling conformism of domestic life that might make escapist adventures on motorcycles an appealing alternative. Willy Loman, the hero of Miller's play, is a traveling salesman who in late middle age loses his job. An ardent believer in "appearance management" of the sort preached by self-help books of the day, he is suddenly faced with the fact that being "well liked" and making a "fine appearance" aren't enough to keep a job once you grow old and quit making your sales quota. Willy spent his life conforming to other people's expectations—or not conforming and lying to himself and others about his deviations—and in the end is penniless, jobless, and baffled, unable to discern reality from fantasy. According to one of his sons, there is more of Willy in a front stoop he built onto his home than in all the sales he made. But as Willy's brother Charley reminds us in the play's final scene, when he begs us not to "blame this man" after Willy has committed suicide, making a living as a salesman and retaining some degree of personal autonomy are not easily reconciled ends. Salesmanship, at least as Willy understands the notion—and countless self-help books of the era affirmed his understanding—is primarily a matter of self-effacement, even self-abnegation, of mirroring others' expectations and keeping all conversations focused on them. Which is why, Charley declares, it was an "earthquake" when customers quit returning Willy's smiles.

In the end, Willy reminds us about the dangers of dreaming *other people's* dreams, of blindly consuming identities readymade for us by forces that do not have our best interests at heart; he reminds us too how important it is that we actively participate in the process of determining which readymade identities suit our circumstances and the givens of our existence and that we adapt these identities to our needs. And he reminds us finally just how difficult that task is.

The Rugged Individualist: Cultural Readymade as a Tool of Manipulation

If Willy errs on the side of failing to take responsibility for the identity he adopts, the second cultural readymade we will discuss errs on the side of taking complete responsibility—and credit—for his identity. He is the anti-Willy whose very existence serves as a rebuke to Willy's. So successfully has this figure dominated our collective imagination that many Americans don't think of it as a prefabricated identity; in many people's minds, it is synonymous with pure authenticity. The figure we have in mind here is the so-called Rugged Individualist. He (and Rugged Individualists are almost always masculine) is the archetype behind the self-made man of business, the code hero of Western films and hard-boiled detective fiction, the political "outsider," the organizational maverick, not to mention that latter-day knight of the road, the biker. He's a simpler figure than Willy, a larger-than-life character straight out of the American myth. And indeed his simplicity is what we find most attractive about the Rugged Individualist. Beholden to no one, he promises complete self-determination without the slippery compromises and tedious negotiations entailed by our rhetorical model of identity. Faced with a difficult choice, the Rugged Individualist rejects conversation and consultation in favor of immediate, intuitive action; and thanks to the fact that his intuitions are uncorrupted by a civilization from which he's always maintained a wary distance, they are always right. In some ways, the Rugged Individualist can be seen as a sort of action/adventure figure version of Serious People from the previous chapter. He is a literalist for whom there are no grays or ambiguities, and for whom ethics is a matter of instant obedience to an unquestioned code. He is often depicted as a man of few words, a stoic who keeps to himself until it's time to act, which he always does decisively, sometimes violently. But the violence is never arbitrary because the Rugged Individualist unerringly recognizes evil and hence is justified in skirting social conventions and institutions such as the law.

In American culture, the Rugged Individualist is an extraordinarily influential cultural readymade. The reasons for its influence are numerous. Partly, it's a matter of our history. One might expect that in a country founded on revolution, rebels would be accorded special status. And in an age far removed from those revolutionary roots, an age that affords us few opportunities for decisive, consequential action, we may well be especially anxious for the spirit of Rugged Individualism to be resurrected. In fact we appear to be so eager for its reappearance that we happily attribute the status to virtually any public figure, real or fictional, with the temerity to claim it—no matter how flimsy his claim, no matter how badly the seams of his costume show, no matter how scripted his speech, and no matter how visible the strings that animate his motions may be. Actors who play Rugged Individualists are thus automatically accorded that status in their daily lives. (My favorite example here is John "Duke" Wayne, who years ago appeared in a movie entitled *Hondo*, the previews for which announced that "John Wayne *is* Hondo," a doubly ironic claim in light of the fact that John Wayne wasn't even "John Wayne," let alone an intrepid gunfighter named Hondo; his real name, Marion Morrison, was in fact changed after being adjudged a tad too effeminate for such an icon of masculinity.) Politicians who claim they are "outsiders," immune to the corruption tainting those "inside the beltway," are often gratefully believed no matter how long they've been in politics or how clearly beholden they are to special interests.

The powerful appeal of the Rugged Individualist, our urgent need for it to be real, can be understood in part as an expression of a related psychological tendency termed "False Attribution Error" (FAE). According to the social psychologists who coined the term, FAE refers to our tendency when viewing scenarios involving human agents to attribute a much greater share of responsibility for the scenario's outcome to the actions of the agent(s) rather than to the circumstances even when the circumstances would, by any rational reckoning, seem to deserve more credit. Thus when a team suffers a losing record in an injury-riddled season, we call for the firing of the coach. When a company is swept along in the wake of an accelerating economy to a year of record profits, we insist on giving the CEO a huge bonus. And any time a celebrity or public figure is profiled, the theme of overcoming hardships, doing things their own way, eschewing the popular and "easy" path will be foregrounded if at all possible, no matter how badly that scenario fits the subject's actual life. The children of wealth and privilege, the offspring who find themselves running family businesses at an early age, the sons and daughters of entertainment figures who follow in the footsteps of their illustrious parents will inevitably dismiss the influence of circumstances and credit hard work and an iron will for their success; and apparently, given the popularity of the genre and the ubiquity of the myth, we are eager to believe them.

All of which is not to dismiss the good that may sometimes come from the presence of people aspiring to be Rugged Individualists. Any community needs a certain number of people capable of manifesting the virtues of Rugged Individualism at key moments. When collective action degenerates into mass conformism, when, in Yeats's words, "the best lack all conviction / the worst are full of passionate intensity," we welcome the Rugged Individualist willing to step forward in the name of values we may have temporarily lost faith with. Martyrs, whistleblowers, gadflies, and war heroes often possess the "real stuff" of the Rugged Individualist. The problem with the identity type lies in our tendency to forget that like all readymades, its appeal serves some interests better than others and it can't serve as a universal model of identity. For example, poor and vulnerable populations, when measured by the standards of the Rugged Individualist, may appear weak and contemptible, not deserving of help from Rugged Individualists and Rugged Individualist wannabes who are less poor and vulnerable.

And like so many heroic figures that serve as models for readymade identity, a basic contradiction lies at the heart of the Rugged Individualist. Those who qualify for the class are, by definition, exceptional people who have beaten some long odds; the longer the odds in fact the more esteemed their status. It is a statistical certainty then that most who model themselves on these exemplary figures will fall short, probably far short, of their exemplar's standards. And unlike other identity models, the responsibility for falling short rests totally on the shoulders of the aspirant. The dark side of the "self-made man," of whom there are few, is the "self-made failure," of whom there are many more. And in the process of striving to be Rugged Individualists, those who fail may manifest some of the less happy traits of the breed. Rugged Individualists, after all, hardly ever play well with others. And when Rugged Individualists are wrong, their capacity for mischief is as disconcerting as their capacity for good is commendable. Their willingness to uphold, sometimes belligerently, unpopular views is far less attractive when those views also happen to be pathological. History is littered with examples of Rugged Individualists who did not wear well when the times did not favor them. Britain adored the strong leadership of

Winston Churchill in wartime, and resented his high-handed ways in peacetime; Charles Lindbergh was seen as a symbol of the intrepid American spirit when he flew across the Atlantic, but fell from grace like Icarus when his anti-Semitic, Nazi sympathies were revealed.

To the extent that we believe in the model of the Rugged Individualist identity, we are, ironically, rendered particularly vulnerable to the appeals of those who invoke the figure in getting us to do their bidding. The tougher the sell, the more that's asked of people in the way of credulity, conformity, and self-betrayal, the more likely it is that the Rugged Individualist will be the vehicle for the appeal. In selling products that are particularly unhealthful for ourselves and/or our environment, thus, advertisers are especially likely to link their product to Rugged Individualism and that "go to hell" spirit of people who won't be pushed around by health officials, scientists, environmentalists, and other timid souls. Which is why smoking cigarettes is associated with Marlboro Men and movie tough guys; by implication those who smoke are gutsy, independent types not about to be dissuaded from their addiction by the mere prospect of lung cancer.

Moreover, the appearance of Rugged Individualism is used frequently to paper over actual dependencies. In the Western United States where I've spent most of my life, for example, the two most revered tokens of Rugged Individualism are the pioneer and the cowboy. Having "a pioneer spirit" and being "a real cowboy" are words of high praise, albeit in very different ways, in many quarters of the West. Pioneers are "can-do" people, stoic and ready to take on any risk in the name of progress. Cowboys are tough, ornery types who refuse to be tamed. They represent the opposite of risk-averse urban dwellers and effete "dudes," roles that today are often assigned to "government bureaucrats." But this much-touted, often-invoked opposition between the West's Rugged Individualists and the Washington bureaucrats belies the powerful, long-established dependency of the West on federal help necessary to build the massive infrastructure to support a large population on fragile lands. Without military protection and government land giveaways at the American West's inception, followed by the building of dams, canals, land grant universities, and roads, and the granting of federal grazing rights, and so forth, considerably fewer Rugged Individualists would be privileged to roam the West's often-inhospitable landscape.

And even Harley-Davidson, the ride of choice for fiercely independent souls, was rescued from bankruptcy by the federal government in the early 1980s at the very moment it was developing a market campaign associating its product with the spirit of self-determination. A staunch free-trade administration, headed by a president well known for portraying Rugged Individualists in films, was persuaded by Harley-Davidson to impose tariffs on Japanese motorcycles that rendered them less competitive with Harley Hogs. So long as anything is done in the name of Rugged Individualism, it appears, we will happily surrender our own agency and blithely disregard the limitations of others. The lesson we should take from this is that when products and people are being touted to us based on their association with Rugged Individualism, we should be especially vigilant that our own interests and agency are not at risk. In this regard, we do well to follow the advice of Mark Twain when he cautioned about dinner guests who proclaim their piety too loudly and offer up a mealtime grace that goes on too long: Be sure to count the silverware the moment they leave. We owe it to ourselves to be no less suspicious of those who profess their allegiance to the cult of Rugged Individualism and enlist us to their cause.

Unconstructed Identity: The Case of P-Dog

If you were to direct the question, "Who are you?" to my dog, Penny, a.k.a. P-Dog, her stub of a tail would start rotating manically and she would inch closer to you until she was sitting on your feet, all the while staring expectantly up at you through her one chocolate-brown good eye and her one milky, opaque bad eye. You could even say to P-Dog, as I sometimes do, such things as, "I just don't even know you anymore P," or, "P, how could you be so naive as to believe that essence precedes existence?" and she would react in pretty much the same way. What she will not do is respond to anything you say with a verbal rejoinder. Which does not stop me from asking her questions or holding extended one-sided conversations with her. I simply fill in what I imagine she would say in return based on my reading of her demeanor and her habits. That she enjoys these confabs is evidenced by her affable smile and her quivering body. Any time sound is being directed toward her by her master that's a very good thing.

So based on everything we've said about identity so far, P-Dog's identity seems to be in question. Without language, what sort of identity can she have? She has a given identity, to be sure. She has a proper name supplied by someone else, she's a member of a particular breed (Australian shepherd, mostly, we think), she's got a past that influences her. Her inveterate sniffing of the ground and her need always to keep us behind and to the right of her when out walking are the marks of a dog bred to herd. And to some extent, she seems to have a readymade identity in that she has accepted a certain role imposed upon her by others and has been trained to do and not to do certain things. She seems in fact eager—perhaps to a fault—to fulfill that role and please the two humans she lives with. It's only when it comes to a constructed identity that P-Dog seems clearly deficient.

What P-Dog lacks is the ability to say no, to conjure up some alternative to the givens of her existence, to select from among multiple readymade possibilities, or to critically analyze her choices. For all these acts, one needs language. She can of course be trained—up to a point—not to do some things that she would otherwise do without human intervention. But it takes a great deal of effort and basically her training takes the form of substituting one compulsion for another. Put another way, what P-Dog is not capable of is Acting as that term was defined in the previous chapter. She cannot initiate a significant change in her life or adopt a novel identity. The impetus for change in her life must come from without. Then again, she is not simply pure Motion. She has a certain minimal level of volition. Specifically, P-Dog is capable, by our lights anyway, of disobedience, which is not something one can say of minerals or plants. So what might one call this mode of being somewhere between Action and Motion?

The term we'll use to name this Action/Motion hybrid is "Behavior." P-Dog Behaves, meaning that most of the time she will do what she has been trained and bred to do. When she does not do what she has been trained or bred to do, we may choose to call what she has done misbehavior, though P-Dog would never apply such a label to anything she's done. In P-Dog's world there is no such thing as evil or good, behavior or misbehavior. P-Dog's life resembles the lives of Adam and Eve before the nasty incident with the apple—she just does what she does in total innocence. The term "behavior" is, of course, broadly used to refer not simply to the behavior of P-Dog or dogs in general, but humans as well. In normal usage it refers to human acts that conform to codes of conduct ("You kids either behave yourselves or I'm stopping the car!"), or etiquette ("She behaved rather badly in yesterday's meeting"), or psychological/physical training ("The subject's behavior was inconsistent with his conditioning"). All of which explains why you can "misbehave" but you can't "misact." In the context of human identity, people who conform to others' expectations and the readymade identities foisted off on them may well be "behaving" in pretty much the way P-Dog behaves. When one is young, this is how one learns to inhabit an identity; but at some point, one must learn to Act, to take some responsibility for the construction of one's identity or one may well end up leading a very hollow life.

Because P-Dog is incapable of Acting, she is incapable of constructing her own identity, and hence will experience neither remorse nor regret. To feel remorse or regret, as opposed to simple unhappiness, suggests that we've acted in a manner that we feel is inconsistent with our self-understanding—our sense of who we are. What we "make of" ourselves, our "gist," does not include the sort of actions or attitudes we've just exhibited. Either we must condemn ourselves for falling short of our model for what good people say, do, and believe, or we must rethink our model. P-Dog, meanwhile, has no model of behavior apart from how she in fact behaves in each moment. She is, as my wife must often remind me, "the best Penny she can be." Lacking language, she can't "make of" herself anything apart from what she is. Consequently, she cannot "make" a self, construct an identity, in any meaningful sense either. She cannot reflect on her past actions or contemplate her future ones. She does not foresee her death or worry that she performs no work to earn her keep and no tricks to entertain the two humans from whom she demands inordinate amounts of attention and daily walks, all the while running up some not inconsiderable kibble and vet bills. P-Dog cannot think about one thing "in terms of" another or imagine how anything, including herself, might be different than it is.

Which means, more or less, that we've come full circle and have now returned to our point of departure, which was the equation of identity and language. As we've seen in the case of P-Dog, any creature may possess a rudimentary sense of identity, that which is given and that which is ascribed to it. But in order to possess an identity in the fullest sense of the term, one must possess the capacity to say no to some of the given and ascribed elements. And before one can imagine saying no, one must possess a capacity for language, the only tool we have for entertaining multiple possibilities and inventing new ones. And to use language astutely in the construction and defense of an identity requires at least a nodding familiarity with the way of rhetoric.

Subverting the Negative Identity: Saying "No in Thunder!"

Much of the time most of us are no more conscious of our identities than is P-Dog. Few of us are struck like Saul on the road to Damascus and transformed on the spot into Paul. And perhaps given some of Paul's not-altogether-charitable notions about gender and identity, that's not all bad. Most of us muddle along, making incremental changes, gradually working our way through stages, adapting to new roles, sometimes modifying those roles in the name of a better fit, finding a way to make our identities work for us in our ever changing circumstances. The great exception to this generalization occurs when we find others casting us in a role or ascribing an identity to us that ill-suits, offends, or even outrages us. All of us suffer such moments. If we're lucky, they are brief and the humiliations they bring in their wake are not too severe. Adolescence is a particularly difficult passage for many people and a time when some may suffer their most memorable identity crises. The tendency in high school to sort people into a finite number of carefully circumscribed categories arranged in a scrupulously graded hierarchy is one expression of adolescents' massive insecurity about identity. High school cliques are developed with the same scrupulous attention to detail that once marked the construction of the Great Chain of Being: Mobility between the cliques is proscribed, and one is supposed to know and keep one's place in the order—wear the right clothes, eat lunch in the appropriate places, take the right people to the right social gatherings, participate in the right activities—the whole catastrophe. Social hierarchies being what they are, only a few can attain the uppermost reaches. While these elite may be no more secure in their position than the lowliest of the low—and given the hierarchy's lack of any meaningful principle of gradation, how can anyone feel that their place has been properly earned?—the lowliest of the low are doubtless more acutely aware of their dismal lot on a daily basis. Many people who have gone on to have remarkably happy and productive lives still shudder at the memory of time spent consigned to their high school's untouchable caste.

For other people, the experience of being cast into the lower reaches of a rigid and irrational hierarchy is a more permanent and more serious business. Within any society, some people will be offered a considerably narrower range of readymade identity options than the dominant members of that society, and those options will be far more difficult to modify or evade. And unlike adolescents, they may find themselves in these straits for an entire lifetime. In such cases, the power of the negative, the human capacity to imagine alternatives and to critique the status quo may be severely strained. The result is often violence, of the literal sort, the linguistic sort, or both. Before looking at a specific instance in which a writer performs linguistic violence in an attempt to free herself from a dysfunctional identity ascribed to her

by her society, let's take a closer look at the characteristics of a defective readymade identity.

The common term used to refer to such an identity is "stereotype."
Literally, a stereotype refers to a rigid print mold from which numberless, identical copies are produced. If one thinks of the mold as the category and all the copies as the members of the category, you have a
stereotypical category. There is no variability within the class. Every
member of the class will have more in common with every other member of the class than they would with anyone outside that class.
Moreover, like the countless identical paper copies produced by a
stereotype, the members of a stereotypical class are passive recipients of
their identity. One may stereotype others and one may find oneself "being stereotyped," but we don't normally set out to construct a stereotype
for ourselves. In effect, the members of a stereotypical class are denied
the basic human right of saying no to a readymade identity, an act that
the dominant majority views as their birthright. And within any society, the dominant majority works very hard to ensure that members of
the underclass do not deviate from their ascribed role. Thus stereotypes
are tirelessly represented in an extremely narrow range of ways in jokes,
ads, films, TV shows, and so forth. And when those identified as members of a stereotypical class deviate from the expectations created by
those representations, the response to their deviations will be excessive
by any reasonable standard. When members of a stereotypical class act
out of character, after all, they threaten the very structure—and the
very arbitrariness of that structure makes it extremely vulnerable to
even the mildest threats—that gives meaning to those who ascribe
their defective identities to them and who derive no small measure of
their self-worth from looking down on the members of the stereotype.
Not so many years ago, African-Americans who showed signs of "not
knowing their place" were labeled "uppity," an epithet never applied to
even the most boorish graspers and strivers of the dominant class. On
the other hand, the more members of the class "stay in their place" and
behave in conformity with the expectations of their type, the more
fondly and patronizingly their "betters" view them.

Clearly a number of traditional stereotypical identities and defective readymades have been dramatically challenged over the past century. Women and African-Americans have through a variety of
means—civil protest, political action, athletic and artistic expression,
individual accomplishment—challenged and even shattered prevailing
stereotypes. In both cases, the negative power of language has been

strongly in evidence as a tool of identity construction; and in both cases the powerful resistance to identity construction and redefinition has meant that this power has sometimes been experienced as a form of violence.

Clearing a Space for a Self: Sylvia Plath

One of the most influential, certainly one of the most famous, expressions of this phenomenon occurs in the poetry of Sylvia Plath, an important figure in the feminist movement of the mid-twentieth century. As in the work of any serious writer, Plath's poems are not easily summarized. In particular, it's not always clear to what extent she is in control of her language or her language is in control of her, an ambiguity she appears intentionally to exploit and thematize in her work. As many feminist thinkers in recent years have suggested, the very logic and dynamic of language itself (especially its tendency to function as a series of binaries) may work against those trying to transcend the boundaries imposed by ascribed definition. To challenge that definition, thus, she must use language in unconventional ways that may pose unsettling difficulties for her readers. But however painful her work may sometimes be to read, it makes clear the oppressive effects of stereotyping on the stereotyped and the importance of the negative in clearing a space for identity construction.

Perhaps the most famous of Plath's poems, and surely one of her darkest, is "Daddy." The poem was, she once claimed, autobiographical, and concerned her troubled relationship with her father, Otto Plath, a German-born scientist who died when she was ten. While one can certainly read the poem as a psychological account of a deeply disturbed father-daughter relationship, the wider implications of the poem for female identity are unmistakable. Casting her father in the role of a Nazi, a villainous figure of global and even mythic proportions, and herself as a Jew or perhaps a gypsy—both groups were victims of Nazi genocide—she uses the poem as a vehicle of escape from his oppressive presence in her life. But however clearly she announces her liberation in the poem's conclusion, she leaves unresolved many of the problems with her identity and with her self-acceptance that are revealed throughout the poem.

The poem has clear affinities with perhaps the oldest of poetic genres, the curse poem, which in ancient times Irish bards directed against their enemies prior to battle. Such verses were supposed to have magical powers; vanquishing your enemies in rhyme assured you of vanquishing them in fact. Thus, in the poem's last stanza, Plath assures the Daddy figure in the poem

> There's a stake in your fat black heart
> And the villagers never liked you.
> They are dancing and stamping on you.
> They always knew it was you.
> Daddy, daddy, you bastard, I'm through.

For all that bravado, it would appear that Plath's poem may be no more effective at exorcizing her father's presence from her life than Irish curse poems were at vanquishing alien armies, or running stakes through people's hearts were at ridding villages of vampires. This magical use of language is characteristic, after all, of children, children of an age to refer to their fathers as "daddy." Children often use language to dramatize and resolve conflicts in their lives (e.g., staging mock battles between action figures or dolls to represent sibling or peer rivalries that threaten them), or to practice inhabiting adult roles. The imagery invoked by the narrator of "Daddy" to represent the father figure underscores her infantile perspective. In attempting to impart her own sense of his immensity, she conjures a figure "with one gray toe / Big as a Frisco seal /. . . . And a head in the freakish Atlantic / Where it pours green bean over blue / In the beautiful waters off Nauset." It's an image at once terrifying and lush, a fairy-tale monster presented in the manner of an illustration in a children's book. Clearly the narrator is at once attracted to and repulsed by the image and by the satanic Daddy figure whom she alternately curses and deifies. "Every woman adores a fascist," she claims, prior to revealing that she'd "made a model" of her father, "A man in black with a meinkampf look" and promptly married him.

In the end, "Daddy" is a tale of enchantment and victimization, and the language of the poem embodies the difficulties faced by someone who has had an identity imposed upon her like a fairy-tale spell and has no language, no magic words, to modify or reject that identity and no fairy godmother to serve as a guide. She "lived like a foot" in the black shoe that was her father and when she tries to talk to him, "The tongue stuck in my jaw / It stuck in a barbed wire snare. / Ich, ich, ich, / I could hardly speak." The poem is an eloquent tribute to one who lacks a critical vocabulary adequate to the task of imagining an alternative existence. As the perpetually ten-year-old child of her father she is absorbed and wholly defined by the relationship as surely as a member of a stereotypical category is defined by that membership. She cannot define herself metaphorically "in terms of" her father, in terms of the similarities and differences that might ultimately yield a "third thing," an independent figure that is both and neither the father and the child. She can't begin to imagine such a thing until after she has destroyed or debunked her father and created a space for herself to work out a new language, her own language, and not the foreign language of her father, a language supple enough to manage the dialectic of merger and division and thereby transcend the arid dualism that ensnares her. While Plath's narrator may not manage this feat, Plath herself offers a poem, a most useful piece of "equipment for living," that redefines the problem for others who may share the narrator's fate and who may benefit from an admonitory tale like "Daddy."

3

~꽃~

Rhetoric and Persuasion I

AN INTRODUCTION TO ARGUMENT AND THE RHETORICAL SITUATION

I n Chapter 1, we considered how rhetoric is situated in relationship to other ways of understanding the world. At a general level, we discussed rhetorical practices insofar as they differ from other methods of knowing. In Chapter 2, we considered rhetoric in relationship to identity. Again, our concern was to show in *general terms* the important function rhetoric serves in the process of identity formation. Henceforth we'll be taking a more fine-grained look at the range of tools available to the tribes of rhetoric and the range of uses to which rhetoric may be put. In this chapter and the one to follow, we'll consider rhetoric's most prominent use, sometimes taken to be its only use, as a tool of persuasion. In Chapter 5, we'll consider a less prominently featured use of rhetoric, as a tool of interpretation. Along the way, we will argue that these two uses of rhetoric are mutually interdependent and difficult to disentangle insofar as what we persuade others about and what others persuade us about are for the most part different interpretations of the world and alternative vocabularies for describing the world.

We've already seen this process at work in the previous chapter. The process of identity formation is largely about the struggle to control our meaning, to construct an identity consonant with our values, and to defend that identity against the misinterpretations and misappropriations of others. We are assaulted on a daily basis by various pitches for readymade identities proffered by advertisers, employers, writers, and propagandists. While these appeals often come disguised as information, entertainment, advice, or recommendations to purchase a good or service, they all promise to transform us. In this regard, the process of identity formation exemplifies all rhetorical processes. How I go about defining and defending my sense of self is not significantly different from how I go about defining and defending my sense of "justice" or "the good." In fact how I define justice and the good is a remarkably good indicator of my self-definition. And my capacity to resist, oppose, and entertain divergent beliefs—to understand my ways of talking about the world "in terms of" alternative ways of talking about the world—is a fundamental expression of my humanity.

Why Persuasion Matters Today

As we saw in the previous chapter, our identity has not always been such a problematic matter. While our incorrigible tendency to go astray, a condition known to our Puritan ancestors as "innate depravity," has always meant that we might lose our souls, our essences, our citizenship, our membership in a family or community, or whatever other status fixed our identities, we were assured a reasonably unproblematic existence so long as we "behaved" by observing the laws and conventions appropriate to our place in a fixed order. Absent a fixed order that assigns everything a value, meanwhile, we are free to construct and choose our identities; but with that freedom comes the necessity of evaluating and negotiating our options. Which means in turn that our beliefs, values, relationships, status, and all the things that matter most deeply to us are also subject to negotiation and evaluation.

Obviously, not everyone would agree with this conclusion. Many people subscribe to systems of belief that, for them at least, fulfill the role of the old fixed orders in laying out their priorities and defining their choices. None of these systems is, however, universally subscribed to and there are few if any places left on earth where the inhabitants may freely ignore the alternatives. No matter how secure people may be in their faith that their particular system is absolute and universal, no matter how strongly they may believe that everyone *ought* to join them in subscribing to their particular doctrine, getting others who do not share their beliefs to cooperate with them—and some form of cooperation is always required—or to adopt their beliefs means they must either use force or persuasion. And as recent history amply illustrates, when dominant belief systems attempt either to ignore alternative belief systems or to coerce them into compliance with their own, they pay a very high price for their intolerance. As media, modern transport, and the globalization of commerce combine to shrink the world, we have little choice but to acknowledge alternative belief systems and to take them into account in making decisions. Increasingly, matters that were once determined by authority now must be submitted to discussion and negotiation.

Rhetoric as a Pluralistic, versus Relativistic, Activity

For some people, the above description of the world might be dismissed as "relativism," a doctrine with which, as we've seen, rhetoric has long been associated. But relativism involves more than the disavowal of one absolute value system and a tolerance for multiple belief systems. Relativism also holds that it is impossible to "converse" across belief systems, that the denizens of different belief systems cannot modify each other's views, and that it's futile to try. Moreover, relativism also leaves open the possibility that each individual may constitute an independent, autonomous belief system, leaving each one of us free to pursue our own interests, under no obligation to accommodate others' interests or to reconcile our ends with anyone else's. (Ironically, the proponents of rugged individualism, a form of relativism on stilts that might with equal justice be termed "brawny subjectivism," are among those most exercised by the specter of relativism–or at least by everyone else's relativism but their own.) If rhetoric really were reducible to relativism, it would be a tawdry business indeed. But it's not. First of all, rhetoric can't be reduced to any sort of radical subjectivism (formerly known as solipsism) because of its inherently social nature. A rhetorician espousing radical subjectivism makes as little sense as a pope espousing atheism. To the extent that either were successful, they would soon be out of jobs; in the first instance, people would no longer have a motive to communicate with others whose reality was, after all, chimerical, while in the second instance, people would no longer have a need for an institution to intercede on their behalf with a deity who didn't exist. Moreover, even less radical forms of subjectivism are incompatible with the inner dynamic of rhetoric. As we've seen, truth for rhetoric can't be reduced to an agreement between a word in my head and a thing in the world. Truth for rhetoric is a public matter requiring agreement among people. Indeed, the most fundamental motive for practicing rhetoric is to achieve identification across differences of class, race, gender, nationality, ideology, age, or any of the other numberless ways we have devised to divide ourselves up categorically. Which is why Kenneth Burke sometimes characterizes persuasion as courtship, whereby we use all manner of guile in the amorous pursuit of the Other, an endeavor at once morbidly self-interested and gloriously selfless. Burke's metaphor transforms difference from a disability into a virtue–"Vive la difference!"—and a goad to identification.

Given its thoroughly social basis, rhetoric can more accurately be described as pluralistic rather than relativistic. Because of their mutual opposition to absolutism, pluralism and relativism are sometimes confused, but while relativism emphasizes the differences among individuals and classes of peoples, pluralism emphasizes the commonalities. Because of this emphasis, pluralism holds out the possibility that different "sorts" of people may achieve identification with one another and thereby tolerate each others' differences in the name of cooperation. But in saying that categorical differences among people may be bridged in a pluralist world, we are not suggesting that people will be less passionate in their commitment to their faiths and beliefs, or less ardent about proselytizing on behalf of those beliefs. In a pluralist world, people simply accept that there is no universal court of appeal in which they can prove the rightness of their position, no master vocabulary that will assign *their* meanings to the world. Unless we are willing to impose our views on others by force, we have to work out among ourselves views that are mutually acceptable and represent us as fully as possible in a given circumstance. Truths arrived at through such a process, while they may not be absolute or universal, are not capricious or subjective in the way that relativist truths may be.

In the best of all possible worlds, rhetoric would be unnecessary because human beings would recognize their fundamental kinship and arrive automatically at conclusions that best harmonized their superficial differences. In the worst of all possible worlds—and here we have considerably more experience to draw on—rhetoric would be useless because right would be determined by might. Any given system of belief would be as absolute and universal as the power possessed by those subscribing to the system. Those critical of rhetoric tend to contrast its ways to those that would prevail in the best of all possible worlds; those supportive of rhetoric tend to contrast its ways to the ways that would prevail in the worst of all possible worlds. Rhetoric viewed as an alternative to force and coercion is considerably more attractive than rhetoric viewed as an alternative to sweet reasonableness. To borrow an epigram from Kenneth Burke's *A Rhetoric of Motives*, rhetoric understood in the first way is dedicated *ad bellum purificandum*, "to the purification of war." Recognizing the inevitability of difference, competition, even enmity among people who live "in the state of Babel after the Fall"(ROM, 23) Burke uses rhetoric to transcend strife and transform it into dialectic. Wars are won by transforming enemies into casualties; wars are "purified" by transforming those same enemies into interlocutors.

The Conceptual Range of Persuasion:
From Coercion to Pure Persuasion

So let us start from the perspective of rhetoric as an alternative to coercion and an old joke. The late comedian Jack Benny was famous for his skinflint ways. Much of his humor centered on his unwillingness to spend or loan money. In one particular comedy sketch on his weekly TV show, Jack is locked out of his house, peering in through a window to see if he can get his wife, Mary, to let him in. Suddenly a masked man appears and sticks a gun in Benny's back: "Your money or your life!" he barks. A lengthy silence ensues. Benny looks thoughtfully upward. More time passes.

> "I said, 'Your money or your *life!*'" the robber demands, this time more loudly.
> "I'm *thinking!* I'm *thinking!*" Benny sputters at last.

The crux of the joke lies in the fact that Benny hears a proposition where virtually any rational person would hear a command. For Benny, the gunman is offering up for his consideration a claim of the sort Aristotle called "deliberative" involving a decision about some future—and the future is now in this case—action. Clearly the speaker/gunman favors the course of action in which Benny gives up his money, hence his prominent use of a persuasive tool touted by Chinese leader Mao Tsetung, who once opined that truth is most reliably found "at the end of a gun." From a rhetorical standpoint, the weakness of the gunman's argument lies in his failure to account for the unorthodox views about life and money of his immediate audience. For the miserly Benny, the two possess roughly equal value, thereby neutralizing the gunman's most forceful persuasive appeal. Presumably, as he stands there with his hands raised, a gun in his ribs, Benny is busily "proving opposites" in his head, working out the costs and benefits for each of his two choices for future action.

What this joke illustrates is the sometimes blurry line separating persuasion from coercion. What distinguishes the above case from most cases where the line between the two is blurred has to do with the direction of the confusion. It's not typically the audience who transforms overt acts of coercion into persuasive appeals; it's typically the speaker/author who sets about masking coercion as persuasion. Coercion, when it takes the form of a symbolic act, relies primarily on the suppression of alternatives. In its strongest form it presents as fait accompli, necessary, or inevitable what is in reality contingent and subject to human agency. It turns "could" into "must" or "should" or "did" without acknowledging its sleight of hand. In more diluted forms it simply loads the dice strongly in favor of a conclusion by distorting or withholding reasonable alternative conclusions. One of the distinguishing marks of our age is the increasingly sophisticated and subtle way in which coercion may be disguised as persuasion.

In saying that coercion must be distinguished from persuasion, we don't mean to suggest that one can construct a simple binary—persuasion (good) versus coercion (bad)—that does justice to their subtle interactions. Rather, we would argue that coercion lies at one end of a continuum marking the range of persuasive practices. In its pure form, it would lie off the end of that continuum just as pure persuasion would lie just beyond the opposite end of that continuum. But in their pure form, coercion and persuasion are rare indeed. Torture—which Aristotle, not normally known for his sense of humor, refers to, deadpan, as an "inartistic proof"—is about as purely coercive as it gets. But coercion can take far less obvious forms. Take for example one of my favorite philosophical oddities, Pascal's Wager, a sort of pseudological proposition aimed at persuading people to declare their faith in God. According to the wager, there are two possibilities regarding God's existence: God does or does not exist. In turn there are two possible attitudes to adopt toward God's existence: I can believe or disbelieve. That gives rise to four possible combinations, four possible outcomes: I believe, God exists, and I exult in heaven after having lived a happy life full of faith; I believe, God does not exist, but I've spent a lifetime being happily deceived and in the end there's no heaven or hell anyway; I don't believe, God exists, and after a hopeless existence I go to hell; I don't believe, God doesn't exist, who cares? The absence of wiggle room here, the insistence on four and only four alternatives when more seem possible (e.g., who's to say an agnostic can't have a cheerful mortal existence?), inclines me to place it toward the coercive end of the continuum, though clearly no one is torturing me or sticking a gun in my ribs to gain my assent. It's the sort of fear-based argument that entices some of us to buy elaborate home security systems or to move to gated communities. It's hard to imagine anyone sustaining a profound faith based on the motives assumed by Pascal's Wager.

At the other end of the continuum, a complex play like *Death of a Salesman* persuades in a way that is probably about as noncoercive as possible, as evidenced by the long and continuing debate over its meaning and the values it promotes. But what about a teacher in a classroom using a series of questions similar to Pascal's to lead students to predetermined understanding? How does one avoid using coercion to move students reliably from a position of ignorance about a subject to an understanding already possessed by the teacher? This example may seem somewhat of a stretch if our model of education is, say, an intro to biology course in a contemporary American university. But what if our model were a nineteenth-century biology course promoting "eugenics," the pseudoscience of human breeding, or a German biology classroom during the time of the Third Reich when "Nazi biology" was being taught? The line between coercion and persuasion may not always be bright, and in an attempt to better understand when we cross it we'll consider a range of persuasive acts along the continuum from pure coercion to pure persuasion and note some of the traits that distinguish them from one another.

The Continuum of Persuasive Practices: From Propaganda to Literature

In imagining such a continuum we immediately need to give up the notion that it might be exhaustive. Persuasion takes countless forms. Moreover, any form of persuasion we may think to place along our continuum will itself constitute a "minicontinuum" of practices distinguished by similar means. Advertising, thus, may be deceptive to the point that its claims are legally actionable, or it may be a relatively straightforward presentation of comparable data from independent sources about price and performance reflecting favorably on the advertiser's product. And literary works may range from those that engage our critical faculties and require deep reflection about our values and choices to "novels of ideas" so heavily loaded toward a particular ideology that they are barely distinguishable from political tracts. Our neat continuum, thus, is perhaps more profitably pictured as a series of overlapping horizontal lines, each representative of one sort of practice.

By way of simplifying our task, we'll limit ourselves to three representative forms of persuasive practice. On the left end, where coercion predominates, we place propaganda; in the middle, where persuasion dominates but coercion lurks around the edges, we place legal reasoning, a practice already discussed in the first chapter; and on the far right, where persuasion approaches purity, we place literary texts. Clustered around the three points on our continuum one could place various allied practices. Near propaganda, thus, one might position marketing, advertising, salesmanship, talk radio call-in shows, political campaign speeches, and the like; near legal reasoning, one might place parliamentary debate, classroom lectures, and point-counterpoint TV and radio discussions among informed discussants; near literary texts, one might place various ceremonial speeches and sermons, extended essays, and small-group discussions aimed at achieving consensus.

What characteristics of propaganda cause us to place it on the left end of the continuum? How does legal reasoning end up to the right of propaganda and why would literary texts outflank legal reasoning? A number of different considerations play into these judgments. Most of the differences are of degree, not kind. Thus, for example, just to the right of coercion but on the same scale, many people, starting with the Greeks, have placed "advantage-seeking" or *pleonexia;* in theory, those who practice propagandistic persuasion are strongly motivated by a desire to seek advantage for themselves and their cause. Those who write literary texts, on the other hand, are sometimes depicted as having transcended advantage-seeking, in the name of truth and beauty for their own sake. While there's some justice in this division of rhetorical practices, it's far too neat. After all, even Gandhi sought "advantage" for his beliefs and to that end wrote an autobiography that is simultaneously a serious literary work and a passionate argument whose intriguing subtitle, *The Story of My Experiments with Truth,* underscores its rhetorical sophistication. (In determining what makes a text "literary," we do not require it to be fictional or purely imaginative work; any carefully crafted work, be it fiction, memoir, autobiography, essay, and so forth, that engages us and offers up "equipment for living"—even sometimes defective equipment—would be considered "literary.") It's not that literary texts never seek advantage for anything, it's just that the advantages sought are more likely to exceed the author's self-interests.

The seeming godlike aloofness of literary authors from worldly concerns stems less from their moral superiority than from the demands of their craft. When ideas are dramatized they are necessarily more elusive, less single-pointed. Our attitudes toward them will be complicated by our attitudes toward the characters who hold and express them and those who oppose them. If one experiences Willy Loman as pathetic and deluded, one will view the ideas he represents differently from another who sees him as nobly tragic. (And if our interpretation is based on a performance of the play, it will rest in turn on the interpretation of the character by the director and the actor who embodies the character.) To dramatize ideas is to submit them to dialectic encounter with other ideas, and if audience interest is to be held by these encounters, there must be some rough equality among them, some chance that the "losing" proposition may prevail, may be right. Burke refers to the requirements of craft depicted here as "self-interference" and sees it in turn as the dominant characteristic of pure persuasion. Whatever an individual's interests may be at the outset of creating a literary text, her devotion to her craft will force her to accommodate those interests to the needs of her text. Which, again, is why writing a literary text is an exemplary "Act" for Burke, who emphasizes how the act of writing can eventually render the agent a servant of her own act.

Propagandists, meanwhile, practice a form of self-interference that, ironically enough, improves their odds of realizing their self-interests. They make adjustments to texts almost exclusively on the basis of the effect of those changes on an audience. The propagandist relies on "cunning," to use Burke's terminology, to "address" an audience. The starting point of the propagandist's argument is always whatever an audience most strongly believes or most fervently wishes to be true; and the conclusion of that argument is always what the propagandist already knows to be true. Audience beliefs are rarely challenged, or complicated; rather, they become the means through which the propagandist realizes his ends. No matter how contrary the propagandist's ends may be to the audience's beliefs, the two will be made to appear consonant with each other such that subscribing to the propagandist's ends seems the surest way for the audience to act in the name of their beliefs. Which is why propagandists and advertisers study their audiences so acutely, reading and performing extensive research, forming "focus groups" to test appeals, conducting opinion polls, and so forth; as a general rule, the more to the left a persuasive activity is situated, the more thoroughly and scientifically do the practitioners study their audiences, not so as to learn *from* them but so as to find out how best to take advantage *of* them. (Among legal reasoners in the middle of our persuasion/coercion continuum, those at the left end of things would include the litigators who hire expensive jury consultants to help them select jurors most likely to sympathize with their client and arguments most likely to work on their client's behalf.)

While propagandists may sincerely believe that the doctrine or product they promote will best serve their audience—and one of the crucial differences between propagandists and advertisers is the former's sincere belief in their cause—their first commitment is to the doctrine or product rather than to the happiness of their audience. Thus when the first propagandists—or at least the first to self-identify as such—went forth on behalf of the Catholic Church to convert people to Catholicism, promoting the acceptance of church doctrine as a necessary condition for salvation was a higher priority for the propagandists than the salvation of souls. And when various Marxist economies of Eastern Europe began floundering in the mid-twentieth century, propagandists did whatever they could to save the doctrine responsible for misdirecting the Marxist countries' economic policies, however disastrous the consequences for the people to whom they promoted that doctrine.

Another important distinguishing characteristic among persuasive activities concerns their manner of presentation and what that manner reveals about their respect for audience autonomy. Propagandists' narrowly partisan visions often reflect a disdain for their audience's intelligence. Again to invoke terms from the first chapter, the goal of propaganda is to induce "Motion" in an audience, to bypass critical thought, and to cause an audience to respond *reflexively*, in the manner of an involuntary muscle movement, rather than *reflectively*, in the manner of an informed citizen. The more we move to the right, the more texts invite us to react critically and reflectively, and the less they are directed to us en masse as a member of a carefully researched cohort. Texts on the right end of our continuum address us as individuals free to respond differently to their message, and invite us to engage in conversation by way of negotiating those differences. Just as the way of rhetoric encourages us to slow the production of symbolic acts by taking into account the particulars of our circumstances, the products of pure persuasion force slower, "thicker" readings of themselves on us through self-referentiality and dialectic. To echo a familiar theme, the way in which texts are constructed determines their manner of construal.

Conversely, propagandists view the persuasive occasion not as a conversation but as a monologue, both in its manner of construction and in its manner of presentation. Propagandists start out knowing the truth, the right way of doing things, and see their function as "propagating" truth in much the way that people used to plant crops by propagating seeds. They don't see themselves as being responsible for testing and questioning the truths they propagate (modifying or hybridizing their "seeds"), any more than they see themselves as responsible for presenting their truths in a manner that invites others to test or question them. They don't consult various sources of information and different viewpoints to construct their arguments, and in fact they often make a point of ignoring "bad news" or any information that disrupts their settled view of things; "proving opposites" is not for them. Propagandists select data and viewpoints solely on the basis of their conformity to the orthodoxy in whose name they propagandize and then dress them up to look like the orthodoxies of their audience. By the same token, advertisers rarely question the social utility or relative worth of a product they've been hired to sell and seldom solicit the views of those who might be critical of the product. They target the audience most likely to buy the product; analyze their tastes, preferences, and beliefs; and do their best to associate the product with the audience's norms.

The law, meanwhile, exhibits a more complex relationship between audience and the construction of arguments. While lawyers are infamous for stretching arguments as far as they can in favor of their clients' interests, the structure of law makes it impossible for them to ignore contrary views in the process of constructing their own. They must anticipate opposing arguments, not to mention intervention from the bench if they fail to observe legal protocols for presentation of evidence, questioning of witnesses, and so forth. Witnesses, unlike unnamed sources in propaganda or paid spokespersons in ads, must give their testimony under oath. And whereas advertisers and propagandists are judged solely by popular reception of their "product," legal judgments are rendered by informed third parties, judges, and/or juries, who have been privy to arguments on both sides of the case. And those judgments, unlike the popular responses to advertising and propaganda, are unambiguous. While litigators may certainly tailor their arguments to the psychology of a given jury and the predilections of a given judge, they cannot construct arguments that ignore inconvenient points or the arguments of the opposition in the process. In effect, the law is an adversarial process constructed so as to *require* "interference" and to limit the legal reasoner's ability to seek advantage for their clients or to spin responses to their arguments.

While legal arguments are constrained by these external requirements, literary texts are constrained by the inherent requirements of literary craft, which force the author to "listen" to the divergent voices of her characters if her text is to be plausible and engaging. So, not only is there increasing "interference" with a writer/speaker's self-interest as we move from left to right across the continuum, the source of that interference is increasingly from within, increasingly the upshot of a creative act.

What the above analysis suggests is that "self-interference" is something of a misnomer. In the act of "interfering" with our established beliefs and assumptions, we generate new ideas and insights. By forcing ourselves to accommodate divergent views, even if doing so forces us to challenge the beliefs and assumptions of our audience, we are forced to engage our creative powers and enrich our arguments. While this process does not guarantee that the argument we produce will win the day with a given audience—propagandists' and marketers' more narrowly conceived arguments, which are often carefully and scientifically targeted at a given segment of the population, may be extremely persuasive—we are more likely to discover new ways of thinking about issues, new ways of representing and solving problems, new ways of identifying with our audience than we would have if we scrupulously accommodated our audience's existing beliefs, assumptions, and tastes.

It's this inventive power of argument that Aristotle calls attention to when he famously defines rhetoric as "the faculty of observing in any given case the available means of persuasion." Had he called rhetoric "the faculty of creating the winning argument every time," he would have been guilty of the crassest advantage-seeking of the sort that serious people charge against rhetoric. And in the process he would have slighted the distinctive power of rhetoric to discover new reasons, new solutions. To be sure, Aristotle goes on to emphasize the importance of effective argument and offers numerous techniques for winning over audiences by appealing to their beliefs and prejudices. But one's first responsibility is actively to seek out all the possible arguments that might be made, pro and con, in response to a given proposition, a practice that may well force one to change or modify one's argument. In effect, this first commandment of rhetoric represents the same sort of obligation to "self-interfere" that was previously identified with pure persuasion.

Make no mistake, rhetoric is always concerned with the effectiveness of arguments at persuading audiences, always operates under the assumption that people construct arguments in order to seek advantage of some sort and that ineffective arguments that fail to persuade audiences are more often deserving of judicious amendment than unswerving loyalty. But in discovering/observing all available means of persuasion, one not only discovers more arguments, one puts oneself in a position to discover "better" arguments that not only are more likely to win the day, but are more likely to serve the interests of all parties to a controversy. For whatever reason, one may not choose that better argument; rhetoric does not require one to choose it, and has no power to enforce such a requirement. But insofar as others are empowered by their understanding of rhetoric to oppose our arguments and do choose the better argument, our own argument may not fare well or last long in the marketplace of ideas.

How to Observe in Any Given Case the Available Means of Persuasion

Like most creative activities, finding the available means of persuasion is largely a matter of attending to those "given circumstances," the very contingencies that at first blush appear to be inhibiting one's creative capacity. Circumstances are like the rules of a game—the squares on a chessboard, the moves assigned to each of the pieces, the definition of winning—in combination with the progress of a particular game at a particular point in time—the position of the pieces on the board at various stages of play. One's strategy will flow from the limits imposed by these rules and by the prior moves made by each player. We calculate our possibilities, invent our moves and strategies, based on our close observation of all these seeming necessities. Each of the particulars comprising our given circumstances constitutes a "problem" that must be solved. But in the act of solving each of these problems, we define our task more clearly. Articulating the particulars of one's circumstances turns up multiple ways of representing those circumstances, many different "gists" that suggest many different strategies to pursue. In the case of our chess analogy, a player may consult various models of the game in progress selected from among previously played games that followed similar paths. This process of charting and naming one's situation turns out to be a very powerful discovery tool, and over the centuries numerous systems have been developed to help one work out, in a more or less systematic way, the potential means at one's disposal in a given situation. Like chess players who've studied their own games and the games of others in order to devise sets of strategies appropriate for various circumstances, rhetoricians too have devised their own stock of strategies useful in recurrent situations and roughly similar circumstances.

As noted in the first chapter, rhetoric is more or less a "science of single instances" such that no formula could be conceived that would be adequate for every possible instance. We likened the practice of rhetoric to the practice of the law insofar as each operates on a case-by-case basis even while each also recognizes many commonalities among cases that allow one to generalize about strategies and principles. In rhetoric, "cases" are typically referred to as "rhetorical situations." By studying a broad array of rhetorical situations, rhetoricians have devised many strategies and principles useful in discovering "the available means of persuasion" in a given situation. The various elements of a rhetorical situation constitute "places" we can look for new insights into the matter at hand. But before considering some of those strategies and principles, a word needs to be said about the vexatious nature of the rhetorical situation.

Those who are vexed by the nature of the rhetorical situation question the extent to which such situations are objective, independently existing entities, sitting there waiting for us in a more or less solid form, and the extent to which the rhetorical situation is constructed by a person free to define the situation as she wishes. Our response should be by now predictable: It's a bit of both. Like Wordsworth's view of reality, "half perceived and created," a given situation may be perceived as rhetorical, as calling for a persuasive response of some sort, or it may be perceived as simply the way things are and as such, not corrigible through rhetorical means. Two different people might look at the same state of affairs and legitimately reach opposite conclusions about it. But having deemed a given situation rhetorical, I must persuade others that my naming is appropriate. And insofar as both the situation I am characterizing and the people I am addressing are not mere creatures of my desires, I may have my work cut out for me. The things I name may not behave in a manner consistent with the names I give them; the people I address may be unwilling to entertain, let alone grant, my claims or share my vocabulary. There is, as we've noted, an indelible strain of "recalcitrance" in the world. Even in a socially constructed world, "saying doesn't make it so" unless one happens to be a magician or a denizen of Alice's Wonderland.

The nature of the rhetorical situation is perhaps best understood on the model of identity discussed in the previous chapter. There will certainly be an element of "given-ness" about the situation, elements already there, already formed, resistant as anvils to our importuning. And often as not the situation will arrive with a readymade label or labels already attached, courtesy of those privy to the situation, or similar situations, before us. But to the extent the situation in question involves human judgment we still are free to redefine it, reconstruct the problem, and persuade others that our reconstruction is better than the prevailing constructions. As we review the various elements of the rhetorical situation, we'll try to keep in mind this "tripartite" model of identity insofar as it characterizes the various elements.

Elements of the Rhetorical Situation

In what follows, we'll enumerate the elements of the rhetorical situation and exemplify each of those elements using a variety of examples, but always including one example taken from the 2003 State of the Union Address delivered by President George W. Bush. We'll be reading that address with the sort of close attention that's usually reserved for poems and other extremely complex and prestigious verbal artifacts of "high culture." We do so both to illustrate how consideration of the rhetorical situation deepens our understanding of an argument, allowing us to recognize its strengths and weaknesses, and also to show how any text, even an apparently simple one performing a job of work in the everyday world, can possess intricacies of construction and complexities of form not immediately detectable to the casual listener/reader. Drawing once again on the language of the law, these extended analyses of the president's address are labeled "sidebars" in honor of the conferences judges and lawyers sometimes hold out of earshot of the jury and courtroom audiences. They are asides to the main proceedings, but may play a crucial role in the determination of a case's outcome.

The Rhetorical Act

The first element of any rhetorical situation is the *rhetorical act* itself, which is usually, but not always, a verbal construct of some sort. The act can be further broken down into the act's *message* and its *medium* (sometimes referred to as *agency*). In "charting" the rhetorical situation, message is most fully treated under two rubrics discussed later: stases and Toulmin schema. Because it is the most obvious element of the rhetorical situation, it may seem as if all other elements are subservient to message, as if their importance is strictly a function of their influence on the message. In fact, all of the elements may play this role, serving simultaneously as the whole of the rhetorical situation and a part. It is, once again, a matter of perspective. No single part is understandable except insofar as it is understood "in terms of" another part. (Ideally all the parts will be understood in terms of each other, but the process can only occur one pair at a time.) The tendency of the parts of the rhetorical situation to appear at once independent and interdependent is illuminated by Burke's analogy of a hand, whereby the elements, like fingers, "in their extremities are distinct from one another, but merge in the palm of the hand" (GOM, xxii). For now, we'll be talking about the elements as if they existed independently of one another, though when it comes time to actually apply the terms to situations, it will be clear how interdependent they are.

Act as Message: Presence and Coherence

Since message will be discussed at length later on, we'll touch here on just two factors relevant to this element of the rhetorical situation: the language choices one makes in articulating one's message, in particular the degree to which one uses very specific, sensory language to embody one's message and lend it greater "presence," and the overall coherence of the message, the extent to which it all hangs together for an audience. (In ancient times, these matters would be discussed under the rubrics of *pathos* and *logos*.) Presence, as the term implies, has to do with the effects of a message on the sensibilities of its audience. In the broadest sense, presence results from the selection of what to discuss and what to ignore in one's argument. Anything that makes it into the argument can be said to have at least minimal presence. But in the stronger sense of the term, "presence" refers to examples, metaphors, illustrations, anecdotes, extended analogies, well-known allusions, and detailed descriptions—all the traditional storytellers' tools—that put the message immediately before the audience and invite their identification (*pathos*) with it. If one wishes to appeal to hearts as well as minds, if one wishes an audience not merely to assent to one's message but to act on it, one is well advised to imbue one's message with presence. In some circumstances, data, particularly when presented in a graphic form, can be said to possess presence. Or if data are presented in a particularly imaginative fashion, they can lend presence to an argument. Take, for example, the following: "If every SUV owner in America were to switch to a hybrid automobile, the subsequent reduction in our annual demand for oil would be equivalent to the amount we currently buy each year from Saudi Arabia." To the extent that arguments rely too heavily on presence—frequently the case in advertising—the effect may be to obscure the point of the argument by crossing the line from *pathos* to *bathos,* drowning the audience's sensibilities in sentiment and sensory detail rather than merely touching those sensibilities.

A coherent message is a logical message. But by itself logic, as we shall see, is an incomplete measure of coherence. In particular, logic treats coherence as a purely internal affair. So long as the parts of an argument do not contradict one another, logic calls it sound. But rhetorical coherence requires us to take external as well as internal relationships into account and demands more of internal relationships than mere noncontradiction. In addition to the consistency of a message's parts with one another, rhetoric considers the effectiveness of the parts' arrangement, and the relevance of the parts to the whole. A point that does not contradict an overall message may still be criticized as being irrelevant or barely relevant, or as being situated inappropriately given its importance to the whole argument.

Thus, while it may be perfectly logical for a church spokesperson to say, as a Phoenix spokesperson did, that the counseling and transfer of priests accused of child molestation was consistent with the Catholic Church's general policy stressing rehabilitation, few people found the statement persuasive in the context of an argument about the legal and moral culpability of the priests. The point made by the spokesperson is mostly irrelevant to the latter argument; it was as if a large energy company accused of defrauding ratepayers were to defend its actions by saying that company policies did not prohibit fraud. And had the spokesperson placed this claim at the conclusion of her defense of the church, she would have compounded her error by situating a weak claim in a place where audiences pay particularly close attention. According to the classic principle of Nestorian order, we expect to find the most important points in an argument in the conclusion, the part people are most likely to remember, just as we expect to find the most important information in a sentence at its end (sometimes referred to as the "emphatic" position in a proposition). By the same logic, one is advised to place one's weakest or least-important points in the middle of an argument or in the "second" position after one has completed the second-most carefully attended to portion of an argument, the opening, and well before the conclusion.

Coherence viewed as an external matter, meanwhile, may be thought of as a message's plausibility. If a message fails to conform to our overall sense of how the world works, it is unlikely to be persuasive. If an example is chosen to illustrate a principle and the choice strikes us as inappropriate or unrepresentative, we are likely to be skeptical about the principle being illustrated. Thus when opponents of federal estate tax on inheritances (which they dubbed "the death tax" to lend it a grim bit of presence) protested that the tax was bad because it prevented family farms from being passed on from one generation to the next, their protest was initially greeted sympathetically, thanks in part to the central place of family farms to the American *mythos*. But when no actual instances of the tax preventing a farm from being inherited could be found in the "heartland" state of Iowa, death tax opponents quickly moved on to other examples, none of which were drawn, it should be said, from the one class of people indubitably impacted by the tax—offspring of the nation's wealthiest 2 percent, who stood to inherit their family fortunes.

I cite this particular example because of my own experience growing up on a family farm. I found the example implausible on the face of it primarily because most of the family farms I grew up around were barely solvent, and none would ever have come close to the considerable dollars in assets that one must possess before estate taxes even begin to kick in. Some farmers are, to be sure, "land rich" to the point that they may appear to meet the inheritance tax thresholds, but in most cases they owe much of—sometimes more than—their land's worth to lenders they borrow from to get their crops in and harvested each year. Occasionally, farmland skyrockets in value when a city begins encroaching on it and developers bid to replace cornfields with subdivisions or shopping malls. But most states have provisions whereby such land continues to be taxed at its considerably lower value as farmland for as long as it is used for that purpose. The only way for it to be affected by "death taxes" is if its owners choose to get out of farming voluntarily. (In a recent Arizona case, a well-known family farm did precisely this; the owners claimed they were being "forced" out of farming not because they were losing money, but because they stood to make millions more selling to a developer than they could make from their agricultural operations.) To the extent that any argument relies on implausible examples—understanding that our sense of the plausible is influenced by our personal experiences and must eventually be tested against a wider sampling of experience—it will strike us as incoherent. The disconnect between the claim and the example is not a logical disconnect, it is a veridical one. The example doesn't "ring true," rendering us skeptical of the entire argument. If one's examples are implausible, they had best be obscure.

Act as Medium: The Physical Means of Transmission and Genre

Every rhetorical act must be expressed through a given *medium:* spoken, written, digital, electronic, visual, and so forth. Whatever form it takes, there will be an extraverbal dimension to that act—pitch, gestures, fonts, papers, sets and backdrops, lighting, costume, visual accompaniments, and so forth—and in some cases, the rhetorical act may be entirely extraverbal. In many realms, including diplomacy, finance, politics, and the law, persuasive messages are routinely sent via actions and decisions. Refusing to meet with a country's leaders face-to-face, demanding instead to meet with them through third parties, is a way of telling the country in question that they are less powerful than you and that you are not happy with them. Lowering interest rates is the Fed's way of signaling investors that they have little to fear from inflation. Awarding a huge settlement in a corporate fraud case allows a jury to "send a message" to potential perpetrators that they should rethink their business practices. Even criminals may indicate the nature of their displeasure with their victims by the manner in which they choose to "whack" them.

Every medium affects the messages it transmits. Every medium has its own set of protocols that must be observed, or else violated judiciously and mindfully by the author of a rhetorical act. Before participating in an Internet listserv, for example, one is well advised to lurk for a bit, observing how formally or informally people address each other, who is deferred to and who is ignored, how long people are allowed to go on about the matter at hand, how new threads are introduced, etc. Because of the nature of the medium and the circumstances in which messages are read, Internet communication generally encourages a more time-sensitive, terse style over more conversational or "chatty" styles. At the same time, the strong sense of community that develops among members of a listserv over time may render participants more tolerant of individuals "thinking out loud" about common problems without requiring them to reach some sort of closure. By the same token, a political speech given on TV and a live speech given over a handheld microphone on the quad of a university campus will require different deliveries. A speech that strikes one as inspirational when heard live in a large open space may strike one as strident and overly emotional when seen on a TV screen in the more intimate space of one's living room, particularly if crowd noises have been filtered out through the use of sensitive microphones and the camera remains "tight" on the speaker. While every message in some sense exceeds its medium, there is no question that one's message, verbal and extraverbal, will have to be adjusted to its medium for maximum effectiveness.

In addition to the physical medium of our persuasive messages, they all may be assigned to a readymade category of message known as a *genre*. Everything from office memos to State of the Union Addresses are read and responded to within the context of the history and conventions associated with that particular genre. A funeral oration full of invective against the deceased will probably not go over well with the assembled loved ones, even if the slurs are largely true and the loved ones might agree, "off the record," that the deceased was a most disagreeable fellow. When faced with an anomalous persuasive message that we can't immediately assign to a familiar genre, when we don't know what "sort" of message we're processing, we may well have great difficulty understanding, let alone assenting to, the piece's message. Some genres, particularly those aimed at narrow audiences of specialists or those associated with formal ceremonial occasions, are more rigid than others. One has, thus, considerably less latitude in constructing a National Institutes of Health proposal than in constructing an editorial calling for a change in tax policy.

SIDEBAR I   2003 State of the Union Address
(SOUA)—Its Message and Medium

The 2003 State of the Union Address, given by President George W. Bush, promises to go down in history as one of the most controversial State of the Union Addresses ever delivered. Not that there is a great deal of competition among such addresses for the title "most controversial." As a genre, State of the Union Addresses may occasion mild controversy, but seldom the sort of animus, long-term angst, and prolonged scrutiny this one occasioned. They usually serve as an opportunity for the president to celebrate legislative accomplishments, blunt criticism of failures or shortcomings, and announce new initiatives in the broadest and most agreeable of terms. But President Bush used this address to prepare the nation for a controversial war against Iraq and its leader, Saddam Hussein. This particular aspect of his address will be the primary focus of our analysis.

The State of the Union Address is delivered before a joint session of Congress and on live national television amidst a good deal of pomp and circumstance. The Joint Chiefs of Staff, the members of the Supreme Court, and a number of other worthies are in attendance, often in full regalia. In recent years, it has become pro forma for the members of the president's party to erupt in applause at key junctures of his speech, signaled by his rising intonation followed by a pause and a resolute gaze across the room. It is, in sum, a curious hybrid of state ceremony and stump speech. The address usually covers a lot of ground in a fairly brief period of time, which means that few extended arguments are developed. The speech mostly serves to announce the executive branch's agenda, its self-graded scorecard, and its spin on pending issues. More extended arguments are left to other venues and other occasions.

While ostensibly delivered directly to those in attendance, the more critical audience for the speech is the television audience. Winning over the millions of television viewers is seen as a necessary condition for getting Congress to act on the president's agenda. Hence the applause, however heartfelt by the members of the president's party, serves a function similar to that of a laugh track on a sitcom. Just as the laugh track signals us that the just-delivered line is funny and invites us to chuckle along, the applause signals us that something significant has just been said and invites us to nod along. Like the "call-and-response" of a church sermon, the "pronouncement-and-applause" of the address usually follows a predictable rhythm. Once that rhythm is established, a break or departure, like a break or departure from the pattern of a poem or song, typically signals a particularly important passage.

In the case of the 2003 State of the Union Address, the interjections of applause come very quickly in the beginning, every

40–50 words. They then lengthen out to 50–200-word intervals until, near the end of the speech, the president begins a long narrative, over 900 uninterrupted words, enumerating the evidence of Saddam Hussein's duplicity and evil intentions. In contrast to earlier "sound-bite" proclamations, this applause-free interval frames the passage in a lengthy, steepled silence that implies a rapt audience hanging on every word and lends great weight to the president's words. Appropriately situated near the speech's conclusion, it serves as the high point and climax. The remainder of the speech serves as a denouement or "sorting out" of the type one encounters in the fifth act of a play. A response is announced (we will not wait until danger is imminent), the future is foretold (yet-to-be-taken diplomatic steps are outlined, and allusion is made to American forces assembling in the region), and a stirring call to action is issued.

Given the president's desire to win popular support for the Iraq war, and given the urgency of that desire—troops were already gathering in Kuwait, budget estimates for conducting such a war had already been submitted, and "military consultants" to news organizations had been on talk shows stressing the importance of invading before the heat of Iraq's summer set in—it is not surprising to find him lending great "presence" to several key points through graphic presentation. Thus, in order to underscore the futility of the U.N. presence in Iraq, and to dismiss U.N. weapons inspectors' contentions that no weapons of mass destruction were to be found in Iraq, the president likens the inspections to a "scavenger hunt" conducted by 108 inspectors "across a country the size of California." And to underscore the threat posed by the weapons putatively being hidden by Saddam Hussein, he ticks them off by name, quantity, and killing potential. Thus he mentions "25,000 liters of anthrax; enough to kill several million people," and "38,000 liters of botulinum toxin; enough to subject millions of people to death by respiratory failure." He goes on to say that "intelligence officials estimate" that Hussein possesses raw materials adequate to produce up to "500 tons of sarin, mustard and VX nerve gas" capable of killing "untold thousands" more, and "nearly 30,000 munitions capable of delivering chemical agents." And finally, by way of linking the Iraqi threat to the disaster of 9/11, and bringing the litany of threats and dangers to an apocalyptic finish, he calls upon his audience to "Imagine those 19 hijackers with other weapons and other plans, this time armed by Saddam

Hussein. It would take one vial, one canister, one crate slipped into this country to bring a day of horror like none we have ever known." While he goes on to dismiss the idea that America should wait until a threat is "imminent" to act, he clearly establishes a strong sense of imminent peril in his lengthy, uninterrupted, graphic depiction of a threat, a threat posed not by a nation but by a single unstable and evil person, Saddam Hussein, who is named seventeen times in the passage cited above, and who allows us to put a face at last to a faceless enemy and "shadowy terrorist networks" that are everywhere and nowhere.

Just as he highlights his bill of particulars against Saddam Hussein by breaking the rhythm of his talk, by placing it toward the end of his address, and by lending it particularly strong presence through metaphors, numbers, examples, and a hypothetical scenario lifted from the script for a summer blockbuster, the president downplays some less happy information by slipping it seamlessly into the classic "second" position, by avoiding any of the devices that might lend it presence, and by, in some cases, avoiding any mention of it altogether. Given the remarkable brevity of the bad tidings and their position within the speech, one would be excused for overlooking them altogether. After a ceremonial opening statement and a portentous allusion to "the decisive days that lie ahead," the president gives an upbeat start to his address by citing four major accomplishments from his administration's two years in office. Refusing to deem these accomplishments "a good record," he concedes they constitute "a good start" but now calls for some "bold steps" vis à vis the economy, which was sputtering. The bad economic news is delivered in a fifty-word passage bracketed by applause lines that blends neatly into the happier passages that precede and follow it. The sentence that announces the shift goes like this: "After recession, terrorist attacks, corporate scandals and stock market declines, our economy is recovering." It's a rhetorically masterful sentence. The causes of the sputtering economy are consigned to the past, assigned no human agency, and dropped into the beginning of the sentence, while the declaration of recovery is put in the emphatic position at the end.

After conceding that the pace of the recovery is too slow, the president then tackles the unhappy news about unemployment. Again, the bad news comes in a dependent clause at the beginning of the sentence—"With unemployment rising,"—while the rest of the sentence offers a solution to the problem in a series of mounting statements that end with a vivid image and a ringing applause line—"our nation needs more small businesses to open, more companies to invest and expand, more employers to put up the sign that says, 'Help Wanted.' " The president then goes on to outline the steps that will bring about this happy result, beginning with his proposed tax cuts.

Agent and *Ethos*

The second element of any rhetorical situation is the person doing the persuading, the *agent*. The quality of any act is tied to the perceived quality of the act's agent, his or her *ethos*. Are they trustworthy people? Do they have the appropriate credentials and experience to speak to the issue? What is their "history" on the issue? Are they identified strongly with a particular interest? Agents do not arrive on the scene tabula rasa, absent prejudices, ideologies, beliefs, allegiances, etc., that predispose them to view the situation in certain ways. They arrive on the scene as members of a given socioeconomic class, gender, ethnicity, nationality, age group, and so forth. They may well have already taken positions on the issue at hand or on similar issues, and desire to remain true to their previously expressed convictions and consubstantial with those who have shared their views in the past. Their need to at least appear to be consistent and thereby trustworthy people means that their response is to some extent predictable, even inevitable. They may, after all, be required to reach certain conclusions—or rewarded, sometimes lavishly, for persuading others to reach those conclusions—by those who employ them. All of these would be considered "given" factors that influence a person's persuasiveness regardless of what he or she actually says or writes. Those same givens may also cause an agent to modify his or her usual personality and to adopt a readymade persona—bellicose leader, thoughtful statesman—more appropriate to the occasion.

But more often than not, what a person actually says or writes will probably have the greatest bearing on our willingness to credit them with a strong *ethos*. We've already mentioned some features of the message that will render it more or less effective, and we will later take up other factors that bear on the content of an argument. But *how* agents deliver the message—the tone or voice, the persona their words and/or gestures conjure up for us—is crucial to our ability to identify with their position. One of the most obvious elements of the message that influences our view of agents is their characterization of those with whom they disagree. The use of highly charged, prejudicial language on the one hand, or the failure to qualify carefully their certitude about the claims they make on the other will cause us to question whether they have "interfered" with their personal interests sufficiently to construct sound arguments. To be sure, all of the above practices may be mimicked by propagandists skillful in the art of counterfeiting the manner and arguments of reliable people. So, while absence of these practices justifies one's skepticism about agents, their presence should not render us completely credulous regarding said agents' reliability.

SIDEBAR II   SOUA and Presidential Ethos

By virtue of being the democratically elected leader of the world's most powerful nation, George W. Bush possesses a great deal of credibility. The stature of his office was dramatically underscored by the deference shown to the president when he entered the chamber to give his address, the eagerness with which legislators—who must be seated well before the president's formally announced entrance—from both sides of the aisle reached out to shake his hand. Moreover we routinely grant presidents a presumption of expertise in whatever matter is before them. To varying degrees, we also grant them a presumption of disinterestedness in their conduct of the nation's business. We hope that presidents will rise above party affiliation to do what's best for the country. While some presidents, like Richard Nixon, never managed to persuade the nation of their objectivity, others, like Ronald Reagan, managed it handily and earned enormous political capital as a result. In the case of George W. Bush, his *ethos* had suffered some blows in his early days of office, including his election. Opinion polls and a sampling of editorials of the time suggest that he was a controversial leader when he gave the address and would subsequently become an extremely controversial figure, even a "polarizing" figure in the eyes of some. Indeed, the impact of this particular speech and the subsequent questioning of it by his political opponents played a major role in his increasingly controversial reputation.

When he came into office, after a tightly contested, very heated race that required Supreme Court intervention to determine the outcome, the president was perceived to lack a mandate for his agenda. His standing in the polls inched inexorably downward, thanks largely to a bad economy, until the events of 9/11. After 9/11, the president's stature and his favorable ratings in the polls shot up. A nation was reminded that he was not only

President of the United States, but Commander-in-Chief of the armed forces. He eagerly took on a role he himself referred to as that of a "war president," promising, and delivering, bold and decisive responses to the terror attack. In short order terrorist training camps in Afghanistan were destroyed and Taliban leaders were neutralized. While many Americans had questioned his credentials prior to and during the elections, citing his relatively brief career in state politics, his spotty record in business, and his oft-questioned service in the Texas Air National Guard during the Vietnam conflict, his quick response to 9/11 and his stirring verbal challenges to the terrorists won over many Americans. He used his popularity in the months leading up to the speech to gain support for military action against Iraq. But he paid a price for his advocacy as his favorable ratings in the polls declined, in part, to be sure, because of a weak economy, but also because of the public's uncertainty about Iraq's place in the war against terrorism and their puzzlement over the failure of other world leaders to endorse our cause. By the time America actually went to war two months after his address, the president's approval ratings hovered around the lackluster 50 percent level that he had experienced prior to 9/11.

So, while the president certainly benefited from the status of his office and the trappings of power and prestige that framed his presentation, these "givens" would not by themselves be enough to persuade a skeptical electorate that an invasion of Iraq was justified. As his polling figures showed, he was not speaking from a position of strength. Many of his longtime critics questioned his objectivity, citing in particular his personal antipathy toward Saddam Hussein, who had once plotted to kill his father, former President George H. W. Bush. Others cited the fact that a number of key figures in his administration had called publicly for the overthrow of Iraq years earlier. His critics conjectured that he was using the events of 9/11 as rationalization for a war that they felt was unjustified but to which he had been committed long before the terrorist attack. Given his diminished popularity and the depth of the suspicions about his motives, the speech itself would have to compensate for a weakened *ethos*. The president would have to project a trustworthy, competent figure through his presentation and offer solid grounds for the war.

While frequently criticized for his shortcomings as a public speaker, particularly in spontaneous situations where his tendency to invent words and pretzel logic sometimes raised eyebrows and crossed eyes, the president's style served him well on TV. His flat, nasal east Texas accent marked him as a man of the people, belying his patrician upbringing and his Ivy League education. And while some commentators were exasperated by his predilection for mangled syntax and tortuous logic, many ordinary Americans were more appalled by those who ridiculed his speech, perhaps remembering their own unhappy experiences with middle school "Grammar Nazis," and identified with his plight. His unpolished speaking style was well suited to television, an intimate medium that put him directly in people's living rooms, where folksiness often works better than eloquence, and where nuanced messages may well be lost on audiences conditioned by the dynamics of television to listen for sound bites and laugh lines and to ignore the tedious middle bits.

A final note on the role of the agent in the persuasiveness of the State of the Union Address concerns questions about the way the president qualified, or failed to qualify, several of his claims about the danger posed by Iraq. A number of people questioned the claimed existence of weapons of mass destruction prior to the war. And yet, several times the president presented as matters of fact claims about Iraq's WMD and ties to al-Quaida that were later shown to be matters of conjecture. While we may never know the proper degree of certainty that should have been accorded these claims, absolute certainty seems a stretch by any reckoning. And we also may never know just who was finally responsible for overstating the certitude of such claims. Many people around the world assumed that Saddam Hussein had such weapons, and when asked by the president if such weapons would be found in the wake of a war, former CIA director George Tenet famously exclaimed that it would be a "Slam dunk!" Whatever the source or magnitude of the overstatements, they found their way into the president's address. Thus, at one point he declares that "From three Iraqi defectors we know that Iraq, in the late 1990s, had several mobile biological weapons labs." The only questionable part of this statement is the "we know" locution. We had been told by Iraqi defectors, whose credibility was questioned at the time by some in the intelligence community, that such labs existed. Unless the sources were infallible, the "we know" conclusion is unearned. Likewise the president states flatly that "The dictator of Iraq is not disarming. To the contrary, he is deceiving." Based on what was ultimately found in Iraq, it appeared that Saddam Hussein had, for whatever reason, been disarming. Almost certainly, he was also deceiving. The evident certainty of the second claim apparently led many to "deduce" the equal certainty of the first claim. While those contributing information to the speech had initially examined the record and set about "proving opposites" concerning the proper conclusions to be drawn, they eventually decided to come down on one side and ignore the other.

Offering probable truths as certain truths should certainly undermine the *ethos* of the president and would normally earn his address a place on the coercive end of our persuasion/coercion continuum. A couple of factors mitigate the severity of our judgment without exculpating his act. First of all, the State of the Union Address, for all its pomp and circumstance, is understood to be closer in spirit to a campaign speech than a speech to the nation occasioned by world events. Which is why networks who carry the address are obligated afterward to present rebuttals from the opposition party. We don't necessarily look for balanced presentations from presidents offering State of the Union Addresses. Moreover, when presidents speak on formal occasions, it is widely understood that they speak as representatives of their administration, and that the speeches they deliver are the product of many hands. Certainly they bear a strong measure of personal responsibility for the truthfulness of their remarks, but they necessarily rely on staff and agency heads to provide them with accurate information on which to base their conclusions. When faulty conclusions are drawn from information, one cannot assign definitive responsibility for the problematic statements without being privy to the information.

Moreover, even if one were to conclude that the president's address constituted a piece of propaganda, that judgment is not necessarily fatal. After all, our own Declaration of Independence, which is at one level the ringing birth pronouncement of a new nation, is at another level a first-rate piece of propaganda, a sly appeal to the world community, particularly France, to help us out in our struggle with England. Indeed, according to Jacques Ellul, one of our most astute students of propaganda, the use of propaganda is not limited to tyrannies and dictatorships. Democratic governments too will resort to propaganda in order to influence public opinion, to secure "the consent of the governed," or simply to ensure their political survival. Without popular consent, no democratic government can execute its policies. Yet policies must be stable to be effective and public opinion (as witnessed by the notable dips and surges in the president's approval ratings over a brief period of time) is famously fickle. Every democratic government will on occasion use persuasive practices from across the entire continuum, including classic marketing and advertising techniques, spin control, and, yes, propaganda, to gain support for its policies. But no president who relies heavily or even significantly on propaganda techniques to win the day with the electorate can long retain his *ethos*. So while the existence of propaganda in his speech should not be considered fatal to George W. Bush's *ethos*, evidence that he relied significantly on propaganda would be.

According to Ellul, use of propaganda to influence public opinion is especially prevalent in the area of foreign affairs. While many Americans are acutely aware of the impact that policy decisions about the economy might have on their personal lives, and most of us can judge over time if economic policies are working or not, most of us are considerably more dependent on our government to sort out foreign policy for us. We simply don't have much access to the information on which foreign policy decisions are made, and the moral and political complexity of decisions arising from that information tends to be greater by an order of magnitude than domestic policy decisions. And when foreign policy decisions involve questions of war, democratic governments are particularly prone to using propaganda. No other political decision requires a stronger public commitment or signifies a higher expression of national interest. Moreover, members of the public both care more passionately about war and feel a greater sense of personal responsibility for its consequences. Which is why unpopular wars can mobilize political opposition so quickly and so massively and why politicians take such special care to gather popular support for declarations of war. Which is also why throughout history the most egregious uses of propaganda by American administrations have been associated with foreign affairs generally and wars most especially.

Rhetorical Scene

Before there's an *agent* or a *rhetorical act*, there's a *scene*, a particular time and place and a context, that gives rise to both. The characteristics of such a scene can be articulated with reasonable clarity; but, as we shall see, determining just what elements of the scene may be relevant to one's argument and identifying the proper "scope" of the scene is a considerably more difficult matter. By its nature a rhetorical scene is one that demands a response of us. What might otherwise be heard as a straightforward descriptive statement—e.g., "America liberated Iraq"—is heard as a claim, a contention that matters to us and to which more than one response is possible. Moreover, there can be no final certainty about the rightness of any of these responses, either because there's insufficient knowledge or information to demonstrate their truth beyond all doubt, or because the responses rest on incommensurable assumptions incapable of amending one another. In many cases, both conditions apply. But for whatever reason, we feel compelled to offer up a response. Perhaps because our self-interests are threatened or served, perhaps because we feel we can construct a response not yet offered, perhaps because our position or office requires us to offer a response, perhaps because a value or belief we subscribe to strongly is challenged. Typically, the issue has about it some sense of urgency, a decision point, a window of opportunity, a recurring cost, an ongoing struggle whose outcome hangs in the balance. Whatever the goad, it is sufficient for us to overcome our inertia or our willingness to wait until a perfect and definitive solution is possible and to set about committing ourselves to a rhetorical act. The particulars of the scene will determine the particulars of that act, but in general a rhetorical scene will motivate us to seek cooperation from others in the form of identification with our views. In some cases, that may mean that we ask them to take some form of action or to change their minds radically. But in many cases we may be seeking simply to increase our audience's adherence to an attitude they hold less strongly than we or decrease their adherence to one we oppose more strongly than they.

While one may at first blush think of a scene as the most concrete, the most thoroughly "given" element of a rhetorical situation, it turns out to be extremely amorphous and highly manipulable. What is the proper "circumference" in space and time of the scene? How far back do we seek historical precedents? How far afield do we look for analogous situations? How far aloft do we pursue applicable principles? Different fields of knowledge and disciplines provide more or less readymade answers to such questions, but in many cases it's a judgment call that each of us must make anew with each rhetorical act, and seldom will an audience be privy to the criteria used to make that judgment. Our attention will be directed to some things and not to others, but rarely will the principle of selection be articulated or justified. Just as point of view indiscernibly guides our perception of events in a novel or movie, the determination of scene in a rhetorical situation indiscernibly orients our perception of the issue at hand.

On the rare occasions when a scene's scope becomes an explicit issue, it's usually because a critic has contested its scope, charging it with a failure to take the "larger context" adequately into account. A larger context, in the language of this study, refers to the choices we make in attempting to define our subject "in terms of" other matters—especially precedents, analogues, and principles. When we wrestle with the question of what is singular about this particular issue and what is connected in time and space to other matters, we are determining the proper scope of our argument.

Proponents of gay marriage, for example, will include as part of the issue's larger context the precedent of "antimiscegenation" laws that withered away in the last third of the twentieth century. Like the ban on gay marriage, state bans on interracial marriage had existed for many years in this country and over time had been normalized through custom. It was considered "unnatural" for people of different races to marry and have children. While such bans were more prevalent and more sedulously observed in some regions of the country than in others, they were widely accepted or at least tolerated. But in the wake of the civil rights movement and the striking down of many laws promoting discrimination on the basis of race, the bans on interracial marriage were also struck down, culminating in a 1987 Supreme Court decision that ended them completely. Proponents of gay marriage point out that, by the same token, many of the laws allowing discrimination against homosexuals, including laws criminalizing gay sexual behaviors, have been struck down, which in their view opens the way for same-sex couples to marry. Opponents of the measure of course stress the differences between same-sex and interracial marriage and look to religious proscriptions against homosexuality, thereby in their view "outflanking" their opponents and enlarging the relevant context even further. Whether in fact religious proscriptions trump legal tolerance is an issue that continues to play out as this is written.

Audience as Scenic Element

The most crucial element of scene is *audience*. Indeed, as we noted in Chapter 2, the most distinctive feature of rhetoric as a way of understanding is the role of audience in shaping discourse and determining truth. In choosing to treat audience as an element of scene rather than as an independent element of the rhetorical situation, we may seem to downplay its significance. In some people's eyes, all other rhetorical questions can be reduced to questions about the effect of our choices on our audience. For many of these folks, to lump audience in with other scenic considerations is to trivialize it. That's certainly not our intent.

Our approach here simply reflects our desire to balance rhetoric's concern for audience with its concern for invention, the extent to which rhetoric is practiced in order to persuade an audience to believe or do whatever is consistent with our aims, and the extent to which it is practiced to discover more and better arguments. Audience is one means, the most important means, of finally determining which line of argument to pursue, which reasons and what evidence to put forth, but it is not the only one. And more importantly, our choice is not between pandering to a "given" audience's norms and beliefs or constructing new and better arguments. Audiences too are constructed as well as given and readymade. We can appeal to an audience's basest nature or we can appeal to their "best selves"; we can challenge their most questionable assumptions or we can reinforce those assumptions. Indeed, as we've seen, those who do the most to alter their arguments to suit their audiences, who demand the least of their audiences in the way of transformation, are most likely to persuade audiences to acts and beliefs that ill-serve audience interests.

All of which is not to suggest that one ignores actual audiences. Saying that an author must modify a rhetorical act in recognition of the genre and the medium within which it operates is to acknowledge the power of audiences. The conventions imposed by genres and media are grounded in audience expectations and limitations. Audiences self-select according to the types of media they choose, the shows they watch, the commentators they listen to, the advertisements they attend to, and the books, newspapers, journals, and magazines they read. Clearly, one would have to have a death wish to ignore those audience expectations. Just as clearly, we have to determine who our primary audience might be, who has the greatest say in the outcome of an issue, and how good our access to that audience is. Not every audience will be prepared to hear what I have to say, no matter how passionate I am about an issue and even, in some cases, no matter how much I may know about the issue.

SIDEBAR III   SOUA and Scene

Some elements of the "scene" for the State of the Union Address have already been mentioned in the discussion of the president's *ethos* and the lingering skepticism about his motivations. This overlap between scene and agent illustrates the earlier noted difficulty of treating the various elements of the rhetorical situation as separable. In this case, the prior actions of the agent help construct the audience's understanding of the scene, which affects their take on the message. In what follows, the scene, or larger context for the address, will first be considered from the perspective of the president, who attempted to link his justification for military action against Iraq as firmly as possible to 9/11 even as he also supported the principle of preemptive war; it will also be considered from the perspective of the president's critics who challenged such links and questioned the wisdom of launching a preemptive war. Further, the president's strategy for dealing with a heterogeneous audience will be inferred from the manner in which he constructed his message.

In his 2002 State of the Union Address, the president helped set the "scene" for his linkage of Iraq to 9/11 by referring to Iraq as part of an "axis of evil" that included Iran and North Korea. Specifically, he cited the three countries' commitment to securing weapons of mass destruction (WMD) and the possibility that they would supply terrorists with such weapons. While this reference creates a precedent for the references in his 2003 address, it also poses a problem insofar as he now needs to distinguish the threat posed by Iraq from the threat posed by the other two nations—if we must now go to war with Iraq, why aren't we also going to war with Iran or North Korea? In his 2003 address, thus, he again mentions Iran and North Korea (he refrains, however, from naming the leader of either country, even though North Korea's leader Kim Jong Il was widely viewed as even less stable than Saddam Hussein), but only after suggesting that "Different threats require different strategies." In the case of Iran, says the president, our strategy has been to support Iranian citizens who protest their country's policies. In the case of North Korea, he says, our strategy has been to seek cooperation from other countries in the region in imposing economic sanctions and isolating North Korea from the rest of the world. But in light of the fact that we had every reason to believe that Iran and North Korea's nuclear weapons programs were far more advanced than Iraq's, the decision to single out Iraq seems puzzling. Until differences in the level and type of threat posed by the three countries have been elaborated, it's difficult to evaluate the different strategies to which they gave rise.

The above argument assumes that proving Saddam Hussein a threat to our national interest and to our security was sufficient to justify a call for war. While that may be true, it is not an argument designed to appeal strongly to American idealism. Indeed, by care-fully limiting any discussion of tangible sacrifice—the address con-tains no references to the financial costs of the war and makes only vague reference to "the brave Americans who bear the risk" of bat-tle and the "days of mourning" that war brings—the president's ar-gument appeals less to his audience's sense of nobility than to its sense of self-preservation. Certainly throughout much of his long apostrophe on Iraq, the president pays far more attention and lends considerably more presence to the threat posed by Iraq than to matters of duty and sacrifice.

Which brings us then to his conclusion and his most ambitious attempt to "ethicize" the war. In building to his conclusion, the president twice refers to the coming war in these terms: "If war is forced upon us. . . ." He immediately goes on to clarify that the ne-cessity for war arises not just from mere self-preservation, but from a higher obligation, a "call of history [that] has come to the right nation." We are the right nation because of our willingness to "ex-ercise power without conquest, and [to] sacrifice for the liberty of strangers." More importantly, we seek liberty for others in "God's" name, who has given it as a "gift to humanity." In the next-to-last line of his address, he brings this line of his argument to a swelling climax: "We do not claim to know all the ways of Providence, yet we can trust in them, placing our confidence in the loving God be-hind all of life and all of history." If much of his earlier argument constitutes a powerful secular appeal to his audience's fears and in-terests, this last appeal is designed to resonate with a long-standing and powerful national *mythos*, a belief stretching back to the Puritans, that America is God's favored land, that in realizing our "manifest destiny" we realize God's designs. Against the backdrop of this "larger context," the war in Iraq is transformed from a pre-emptive strike to a political necessity, and finally a holy obligation. To be sure, this message is more likely to resonate with some in his audience than with others; indeed, some are more likely than oth-ers to hear it all. Because religious references are quite common in the conclusion of presidential addresses, many in the president's audience doubtless heard his words as more ceremonial than sub-stantive. But the members of the president's "base," his core politi-cal constituency, may well have heard it as the most meaningful appeal of the address.

4

Rhetoric and Persuasion II

THE STASES AND TOULMIN

We've already alluded to *purpose* as a generic element of every rhetorical situation. Obviously, most generally our purpose in argument is to persuade someone of something. In slightly less general terms, we take this to mean that we wish our audience to identify with the beliefs, attitudes, and values we promote and to cooperate in the name of those beliefs, attitudes, and values. In some cases, we may achieve that end by weakening their identification with or adherence to an alternative set of attitudes and beliefs. In some cases we may wish our audience to act on this shift in attitude by, say, voting, or making a contribution, or buying a good or service, or agreeing to find the accused guilty. At the most particular level, our purpose in any given rhetorical situation would be our answer to the question, "What's your point?" Because there are as many ways of responding to that question as there are points we might be trying to make, it may at first blush seem an unhelpful one. If there are as many purposes as there are points to be made, what is there to be learned from exploring any particular point? How will it help us identify the available means of persuasion in a potential rhetorical situation? Luckily the points one might possibly make about matters that divide us can be grouped into a finite number of categories based on features that recur across multiple instances. Identifying purpose, thus, can help us anticipate lines of argument associated with the *sort* of point we're making, as well as audience expectations about the reasons and proof required to convince them about our sort of point.

So what "sorts" of points do we make? There is no official list. Different people have proposed different systems for describing them; one particularly powerful system is what's called a "stasis" approach. A stasis, for the purposes of this chapter, will designate a question that gives rise to a division among people and occasions a rhetorical act, in the form of an argument, designed to overcome that division. We designate five such questions: "What is this thing?" "How much is this thing like/unlike that thing?" "Why did this thing happen?" (Or, if we reverse the direction of the question, "What might the consequences of this thing be?") "How good or bad is this thing?" (or "Is this good?") "What should we do about this thing?" Proposing answers to these questions and responding to others' answers to these questions constitute our point; and our immediate purpose is to make that point with an audience. In turn, we may have in mind a specific hope for what our audience will do in response to our points, a hope that would also fall under the purview of rhetorical purpose. Do we want to *move* our audience to act? Or do we want to *bend* their attitude such that in the future they will be more inclined to act in accordance with the beliefs and values we've invited them to share? A conservative politician giving a speech extolling the virtues of the free market is fulfilling the latter purpose; a liberal politician writing an editorial calling for expanded regulatory powers over energy markets is fulfilling the former purpose.

SIDEBAR IV   The General Purpose of SOUA

In the case of the 2003 State of the Union Address, the question of what purpose the address serves in relationship to its audience is a particularly interesting one. For the most part, the talk seems to be designed to bend the audience's attitude toward the subject of war in Iraq rather than to get them to act. Certainly that is the case with the wider television audience, which wouldn't be directly involved in any decision about war, but whose popular support the president needs in order to persuade his immediate audience of legislators to act by granting him the authority to declare war and by appropriating funds necessary to wage the war. What the talk reminds us is that an attitude is, in Burke's words, "an incipient act." If the president's audience can be made to share his sense of urgency about the Iraqi threat and his belief that to wage war against Iraq is to wage war against terrorism, it will legitimate his own act and unite the country behind him.

By itself, the State of the Union Address could not, of course, achieve such a tall order. The case for war had been made throughout the months leading up to the speech by administration officials in their informal remarks on television and radio, their speeches around the country, and in their public testimony; in turn these remarks were reported in various media, repeated on TV talk shows and call-in radio shows, and analyzed by coworkers over coffee. Indeed, according to a Knight Ridder poll conducted just prior to the president's address, a majority of the American people believed that Iraqis had been directly involved in carrying out the 9/11 attacks, all evidence to the contrary notwithstanding. This symbiotic relationship between a specific rhetorical occasion like the State of the Union Address and less clearly defined rhetorical occasions that precede and follow it is part of a peculiarly contemporary persuasive phenomenon. In the realm of consumer persuasion, the address would correspond to an advertisement for a product, while the surrounding "buzz" of supportive statements and word-of-mouth testimonies would correspond to marketing for a product. In the political realm, these "unofficial" supportive statements that serve to market an idea or policy constitute what I like to call "ambient persuasion." Ambient persuasion occurs when proponents of a policy, a decision, or an ideology repeat, typically in the same or similar phrases, a set of loosely related claims or "talking points" that lay the groundwork for a fully articulated case. It exemplifies the old advertising adage that "repetition is reputation": Repeat anything often enough and it will be believed. It works on the same principle as Muzak or elevator music; we almost don't notice that we're hearing it but it affects us anyway. It bends our attitude in tiny, almost imperceptible increments. When the same claims that we've been hearing sporadically for months, frequently expressed not in the form of persuasive claims so much as "oh, by the way" assertions of fact, are marshaled together in a formal address, their familiarity gives them the ring of truth. Ambient persuasion is a means for manufacturing public opinion in a compressed time frame. What the Greeks used to call "doxa," the traditional wisdom and popular assumptions that develop in an oral culture over decades, and that was once transmitted mostly through stories, fables, and proverbs, can be "purpose built" in a relatively brief time in a mediated culture like ours, especially with our 24/7 news cycle. And once it's out there, it can be appealed to in a speech as if it were an assumption held by the hearers rather than a claim emanating from the speaker.

The purposes of any given rhetorical act will be multiple. A purpose can be expressed in terms of the point one wishes to make or in terms of the effect one wishes that point to have on an audience. Further, in making any substantial point about an issue of any complexity, one will have to make a number of points in support of that point. The "gist" of any argument we might make, like the gist of our identity, is a many-sided entity, not a single pointed essence. Later on we will develop a language for talking about the internal dynamic of argument and the optimal arrangement of our points in relation to each other so as to make our main point most effectively. For now we'll discuss each of the "stasis" questions without regard to their possible place within the structure of an argument. We will look at them as sources of invention, as a wellspring of cues for the construction of our argument and for the anticipation of responses to our argument.

What Is This Thing? Definitional Questions

Not every question of this sort—indeed not any of our five questions—*necessarily* motivates a persuasive response. Sometimes a noncontroversial answer is immediately at hand or can be figured out with minimal fuss or retrieved from a reliable source. And often it doesn't matter all that much how we answer such a question. Nothing much is at stake if the rugby ball I'm holding in my hand is mistaken for an American football. But if the definition of a thing, say, dictates its value or determines the way it is to be treated, and if these consequences are deemed to be significant, then the definition matters. Sometimes it matters a great deal. One of the ways definition matters concerns what philosophers sometimes refer to as "the rule of justice," which requires that members of the same category be treated in the same way. Saying, thus, that women and minorities belong to the category of "all men" that our country's founders declared to be "created equal" meant that they had to be granted the right to vote, assemble, own property, receive public education, cross state lines, sit wherever they wished on public transportation, and so forth. In many other cases, defining what something is automatically makes it more or less valuable, legal, honorable, and so forth. Is graffiti art, vandalism, or some combination of the two? Is a D and X procedure performed in the second trimester a "partial birth abortion"? Is flag burning a form of free speech? Are employee stock options an "expense"? Is the Hummer a truck?

If we attempt to resolve the question, "What is this thing?" with a rhetorical act, we can anticipate that our audience might raise a number of questions, two of which are particularly crucial: (1) an audience might question the criteria we use to determine class membership of our thing, or (2) they might ask whether the item in question actually meets those criteria. In the first case, they may doubt whether our criteria conform to generally accepted criteria or if we are adding to or subtracting from those criteria, or if we are assigning artificially high or low weights to accepted criteria. In the second case, they might agree that our thing meets many of the criteria, but with insufficient strength to make it into the class. Or they might suggest that our thing much more strongly fits the criteria of another class, mutually exclusive of the one we're trying to place it in. In reviewing these possible responses, we need to ask ourselves, "Which one would I have the greatest difficulty answering?" That is the response that requires our fullest attention. It will probably produce the greatest amount of new thinking or invention and require one to craft the most carefully worded response. (Apropos of our earlier discussion about the range of persuasion, those at the coercive end of the persuasion/coercion continuum will take particular care to ignore or divert attention away from those anticipated responses that promise to give them difficulty.)

SIDEBAR V   SOUA and the Definition of Preemptive War

Before considering a definitional question raised by the 2003 State of the Union Address, a word about how stasis questions are chosen and analyzed and their relationship to one other is in order. Typically, one works backward from what one takes to be a major claim in an argument and then considers other claims insofar as they support that major claim. In the case of the 2003 State of the Union Address, the major claim, which will be considered last, is the proposal that Iraq be invaded. While a number of important definitional claims are made in the address, the one that bears most clearly on the presumptive major claim concerns the meaning of "preemptive war." Before one can evaluate whether or not preemptive war is politically sound and ethically justifiable, one must first determine what it is. Having said that, it must be acknowledged that President Bush never uses the phrase in his address. He had earlier used the phrase, and had called on his audience to recognize its legitimacy, in a June 2002 speech at West Point. And, I would argue, he once again justifies the concept of preemptive war, without using the term, in his State of the Union

Address. Further confusing the issue is the fact that he also appears to argue that a war against Iraq would be retaliatory, a just rebuke for Iraq's putative role in 9/11, rendering his argument a two-part contention: Iraq almost certainly had a hand in 9/11, but even if it didn't, preemptive war is justified by the "serious and mounting" threat posed by a leader whose "sanity and restraint" are clearly in question. The subsequent failure to establish clear ties between Iraq and 9/11 means that this second claim becomes essential to his major claim.

Because of the president's reluctance to designate the war in Iraq a preemptive war, the criteria for determining what constitutes a preemptive war are left unclear. From what is said, certain things may be inferred: The opposing force should have manifested some signs of bad intent toward our nation and should have the means to act on that intent. The threat it poses should be of sufficient magnitude that allowing it to strike first is unthinkable. There is some reason to believe that the threat is imminent. (Here again, an issue of semantics: While the president says at one point that we cannot afford to wait until a threat is imminent, he does so only after going to great lengths to suggest that the threat from Iraq is indeed imminent. When the opposition's threat is not imminent, one may still justify what some call a "preventive" war against it, but the burden of proof for waging such a war will be greater and the alternatives to war more numerous.)

Now, whether or not Iraq actually met those criteria—the "match" of the criteria-match process of definition—remains a topic of lively debate. But assuming our inferences are reasonable and the above conditions could serve as criteria for the definition of preemptive war, we are left with questions about the soundness of those criteria, a topic that has been little debated thanks largely to the above noted confusion. Further adding to this confusion has been the subsequent shift in the administration's argument to an emphasis on reasons that loomed less large in the address (i.e., bringing stability to a volatile region and liberating the Iraqi people from an oppressive regime) so as to render them the primary justifications for the war after the fact. And this confusion matters a great deal because the Iraq War constitutes a precedent for future preemptive wars. Since there are few such precedents in our history, it will have a major impact on how we make decisions about the next candidate for preemptive war, should there be one. As we consider, for example, other nations assigned to the "axis of evil" category, what changes in their status, short of aggression against us or an ally, might justify a declaration of war against them?

How Much Is This Thing Like/Unlike That Thing? Resemblance Questions

Questions of resemblance come up all the time, most visibly in the law in the form of questions about precedence. Determining which previous cases most closely resemble the present case may go a long way toward determining the outcome of the case. The second major sort of resemblance one encounters in argument is the analogy. The distinction between analogies and precedents may sometimes be elusive. If one were to liken universities' awarding athletic scholarships to governments' hiring mercenaries, one would be comparing two phenomena normally viewed as substantially different and exhibiting no clear historical succession; hence treating their relationship as an analogy makes greater sense. On the other hand, if one were to liken bans on same-sex marriage to bans on interracial marriage, one would be comparing two acts of a similar nature that are historically linked; hence treating one as a precedent for the other makes greater sense. In neither case does one event cause the other. We are simply viewing something that's not well understood or clearly evaluated "in terms of" another thing that our audience is likely to understand better and/or accept as good or bad in order that they might transfer their attitude and understanding of the better-known thing to the lesser-known thing.

One making a resemblance argument can anticipate that audiences will resist the power of the precedent or analogy to determine the nature of the thing in question. Precedents and analogies are not fate; they can't determine an outcome with the force of a physical law (note that we just slipped in a resemblance claim), they can only suggest an outcome. Which is why in most cases resemblance arguments can't stand alone. They can serve to "frame" an issue, thereby inclining an audience to sympathize with our conclusion. And this is a very powerful move insofar as getting an audience to accept a resemblance early in an argument can strongly influence their point of view toward the subject and the acceptable scope of the argument.

Every resemblance argument calls attention to certain features of the thing in question at the expense of other things. Thus, the comparison of mercenaries and scholarship athletes ignores such salient matters as the fact that scholarship athletes don't normally kill people, are typically motivated by matters beyond money, and aren't taking the place of citizens who have a civic responsibility to perform the duties the athletes carry out—all of which blunts the negative edge of the comparison. Anyone making an analogy must be prepared to acknowledge important "disanalogous" elements in their comparison—and there can't be too many such elements—and to limit their use of the analogy to specific points that clearly do bear on one another.

| SIDEBAR VI | SOUA and Resemblance Issues |

As noted above, precedents for this Iraq War are difficult to identify and none are enunciated in the address. Operation Desert Storm represents something of a precedent in that we used that war to decimate Iraq's weapons programs. But clearly that war was not a preemptive war insofar as Iraq's invasion of Kuwait provided a reasonable *casus belli* or provocation for war whereby our national interest, mostly in the form of our oil supply, was threatened and a friendly nation was under direct attack. It should also be said that history provides examples of retaliatory wars whose putative *casus belli* turned out to be feigned or trumped up, thereby rendering the war in question in fact preemptive. Thus, for example, in Vietnam, a relatively minor incident in the Gulf of Tonkin was used as an excuse to produce a congressional resolution authorizing the use of force in the region. In retrospect, Vietnam might be seen as a preemptive war that was launched not because we had been directly attacked, or even because we were in any "imminent danger," but in order to prevent a series of Southeast Asian countries from "falling like dominoes" into communist hands. One might with some justice thus equate the current threat of global terrorism with the threat of communism then and cite Vietnam as a precedent for the Iraq War. But given the inauspicious outcome of Vietnam, no one is eager to use it as a precedent for any imaginable pending action that they support. Indeed, much of the debate in the wake of the war concerned parallels between our ineffectual and costly presence in Vietnam and our often-troubled presence in Iraq, a precedent the administration strongly rejected. The one precedent the president does identify in his address concerns the similarity between current "outlaw regimes," including Iraq's, and earlier situations in which "small groups of men seized control of great nations, built armies and arsenals and set out to dominate the weak and intimidate the world." Specifically he cites "Hitlerism, militarism and communism" as precedents for the threat posed by Iraq.

In none of these cases, however, did we launch preemptive wars. And in the case of communism, economic collapse rather than military defeat led to its downfall. Clearly the scope of these particular precedents is extremely narrow, and they were apparently invoked only to underscore the mischief that is caused when rogue individuals hijack sovereign nations. To the extent that the president's analogous elements are not on the same scale as Iraq—Hitlerism and communism were quite literally world threats while Iraq lacked the means to threaten any but the weakest of its immediate neighbors—he is guilty of exaggerating the case for war.

While the president cites no precedents for preemptive war and offers no analogies between the situation in Iraq and other situations, we later learned that his secretary of state, Colin Powell, used a particularly striking analogy to register his concerns about the proposed war. According to an account taken from Bob Woodward's book about the administration, when Powell was first told by Bush about the president's plan to invade Iraq, he reminded him of "The Pottery Barn Rule," which states that if you break something you own it. In this particular case, he was suggesting in an especially colorful way that while Iraq's armies might be easily defeated (broken), we would then assume responsibility for putting Iraq back together at enormous cost. This particular analogy was subsequently adopted by many of the war's critics for whom it proved to be a useful means of reframing popular understanding of the Iraq War. The president's argument in the State of the Union Address was especially vulnerable to the analogy, thanks to the scant attention paid to the war's costs and the absence of serious concern for the challenges posed by the aftermath of war.

Why Did This Thing Happen? Causal Questions

In asking why something happened, we are asking what *caused* it to happen or what *motivated* its occurrence. Causal questions are important because once we understand why things happen, we are better able to predict consequences and shape policy so as to prevent bad things from recurring and encourage good things to keep on flourishing. We can use our understanding of how bad things came about to reverse a trend, solve a problem, or cure a disease. Most issues arising in the sciences, social sciences, and business are grounded in causality, including the causes of crime waves, of global warming, of successful companies, of musical fads, and so forth. When something occurs only once, like a particular crime, we must operate more on the model of those forensic scientists one sees on police dramas who use a combination of science, human psychology, and intuition to bring the evildoer to justice.

Causal arguments dealing with recurrent phenomena are the most technically sophisticated of all arguments. In some cases, they rest on statistical and scientific methodologies of daunting complexity. All too often, in fact, people hide behind the technical and quantitative sophistication of causal arguments to coerce lay persons or less technically sophisticated colleagues into assenting to assertions that they can't properly assess. That said, all of us are capable of understanding causal complexities at a basic level sufficient to construct and critique most causal arguments that affect us day to day.

The first matter to be on the lookout for in causal arguments is the substitution, witting or unwitting, of correlation for cause. Correlations are statistical relationships that suggest a connection between or among phenomena. If one thing happens and another thing happens 80 percent of the time, one can estimate just how likely it is that the relationship between the two things is not accidental. That estimate of likelihood is typically expressed as a "confidence level." But note that it doesn't say anything about how or why the two things are related. Which one might be the cause and which one the effect—if they are in fact causally related in any way—is uncertain. What other conditions might have to be present or absent for the relationship to occur is not known. Why the connection does not always occur is unexplained. How one thing actually affects the other, the mechanism or process that physically links the two, is undeveloped. In short, correlations are intriguing and suggestive relationships that initiate serious study and a search for causes. But in themselves, they are potentially mischievous expressions of confidence in matters that remain mysterious. A correlation is perhaps best understood as a statistician's version of an analogy: It's a useful place to start an argument, but it shouldn't be used to finish one. And perhaps the most common form of coercive argument is a correlation masquerading as a cause.

The second common problem with causal arguments is closely related to the first. Correlations between one thing and another are frequently presented to us as causal relationships in the hopes that we will praise or blame, buy or sell, the putative cause: If only we wore the right cologne or drank the right beer, we'd be irresistible. The function of the argument is to get us fixated on *the* cause and to ignore the possibility that there are multiple causes or many uncertain links between the putative cause and the putative effect. In fact, our desire for simplicity, our strong bias toward explanations with the fewest steps—Burke refers to this prejudice as "Occamite nonsense" in honor of William of Occam, who originated the Law of Parsimony—inclines us to believe in such single-cause explanations, and to embrace the "magic bullet" solutions that follow in their wake. So, causal arguments may on the one hand be complicated artificially to bludgeon audiences into compliance or on the other hand oversimplified drastically to seduce audiences into assent.

When we seek out the causes of a single instance, we may well use causal arguments such as those sketched out above to help us solve our problem. That is, we would look at better-known situations similar to— analogous to or precedents for—the one before us, and look to the causes of the prior situation to find hints about the causes of the current situation. In the case of homicides, for example, police often look first to people close to the victim because the overwhelming percentage of murders are committed by friends, family, and associates of the victim. By the same token, when we are trying to predict the consequences of a single instance, say, a volcanic eruption, we will look at similar instances in history to guide us. But as a general rule, our ability to identify the causes of, or to predict either the occurrence or consequences of, a single instance is notoriously bad and the more singular the instance, the worse our powers of prognostication or explanation.

| SIDEBAR VII | SOUA and Causal Questions |

Again, in relation to the major claim emerging from the president's address, there is one powerful causal argument: Defeating Iraq militarily will make America and the world safer by weakening global terrorism. Little attention is devoted to any actual causal mechanisms that might bring about this end, presumably because the president believes the link to be self-evident. By the same token, even less consideration is devoted to alternative causal scenarios. While the president does not claim that Iraq is the only cause of global terrorism or the only source of our insecurity, his focus on Iraq to the near exclusion of other explanations or other "outlaw regimes," and the strong presence he lends the Iraqi threat through his presentation, renders it by default the most powerful immediate cause of our problems. In combination with the lack of attention paid to the consequences and costs of war in Iraq, the president's focus on a single cause renders military action if not a magic bullet cure, an almost inevitable choice. Given the difficulties of predicting the consequences of a single instance like a war and a historical record replete with cases in which the unintended consequences of wars have overwhelmed the intended consequences, some qualification of this bold causal claim would seem to be in order.

But the bold certitude of the president's proposal is grounded in his assessment of the root causes of the danger posed by Iraq. As the president makes abundantly clear, the threat of Iraq is the threat of Saddam Hussein. In an aside to the Iraqi people, he assures them that "Your enemy is not surrounding your country, your enemy is ruling your country." Saddam is the one who possesses the weapons with the potential to wreak havoc; Saddam is the one whose "sanity and restraint" are not to be trusted; Saddam is the one who has continually deceived the world community; and Saddam is the one who has left "thousands of his own citizens dead, blind or disfigured." The president goes on to describe in graphic detail the torture methods imposed on the people of Iraq and concludes that "If this is not evil, then evil has no meaning." Having earlier implicated Iraq in an "axis of evil," the president's citation of evil here is particularly significant in the context of causal questions. When evil is identified as the root cause of one's problems, particularly when it is said to reside within a particular person, one is relieved of the responsibility of detailing its causal dynamic. One cannot reverse or undo evil. And one does not parley with evil because its malice is "motiveless," unfathomable; one must either coerce it into submission or destroy it. And having failed at coercion in the years since the Gulf War, we appear to have only one choice left to us.

How Good or Bad Is This Thing? Evaluative Questions

There are two ways of thinking about good. One can think of it as the opposite of bad, or one can think of it as the opposite of evil. In the first case, one is thinking of good as an evaluative term, as an adjective applied to all sorts of acts, objects, entities, performances, people, and so forth. You can make a good play in baseball, you can have a good meal, you can be a good teacher, and so forth. You don't normally, of course, think of having an "evil" meal. In the second case, one is thinking of "good" as an ethical term, capable of being thought of as a noun, "the good" that stands alone, rather than as an adjective in search of a noun.

As an evaluative term, "good" means "good of its kind." One evaluates things according to the classes to which they belong, the functions that they serve. Hence the importance of making sure that before you evaluate something you have defined it correctly, assigning it to the proper class of things that will serve as a standard of judgment. Before you know if anything, be it a senator or a DVD player, is good, you need to know the purposes of the class and how well members of the class generally realize those purposes. But in making an ethical judgment, one's standard of judgment is not relative to a particular class of things; one's standard applies across classes and categories. No matter what one's profession, class, gender, religion, and so forth, one is expected, as a whole person, to do "the good." As we suggested earlier, there is no single, universally agreed-to definition of "the good," but every belief system has some ethical notion of the good that transcends evaluative judgments of various classes of things. You can be a "good" hired assassin who works hard and carries out assignments with due diligence, but that does not make you a good person by the lights of most belief systems.

As suggested above, evaluative arguments are closely tied to definitional arguments. In both cases one has to articulate criteria, often in the form of statements about what the members of a given class do, for membership in a given class. Before we can say if someone is a good or bad teacher, we have to define what it is that teachers are supposed to be and do. Since we are dealing here at such a high level of generality, we can expect dissent about what those criteria will be and which ones are most important. It is crucial, thus, to ensure that whatever class we have identified as providing the standard of judgment for our evaluation is in fact the most relevant, the smallest applicable class. Thus in the case of teachers, our standards will vary if we're talking about kindergarten teachers, high school teachers, swim teachers, or college teachers. Teachers at all levels share certain characteristics, but some of those characteristics will be unique to specific levels of instruction, and some will assume greater or lesser importance in different settings. Assuming criteria are accepted, one has to measure the degree to which those criteria are fulfilled. Again in the case of teachers, measuring teaching effectiveness has proved an elusive matter, a problem that is too often solved by tying it directly to student performance on standardized exams. As a dubious measure of learning, the standardized exam thereby does doubly dubious duty by pretending simultaneously to measure teaching effectiveness and student performance. And even assuming standardized exams were good measures of learning, how confident can we be that such confounding variables as class sizes, quality of support services, family income and levels of parental involvement, and so forth, were not at least as responsible as effective or ineffective teaching for student performance? Further, one must be careful when evaluating anything always to ask "compared to what" is it good or bad? Is the standard of comparison a particularly weak example of the class? Is it an average or representative example? One of the most common problems in evaluation occurs when one's standard is hypothetical rather than actual, particularly when one's example is fetched afar from some Platonic realm of Pure Forms. While it's fine to use a standard that has never actually been attained if one's purpose is to improve the overall performance of an entire class, it's not so fine if one uses it to make actual decisions about individual members of a class. Again in the case of teaching, one might imagine a paragon of teaching, let's call her Ms. Chips, who saves students from terrible fates, reforms curricula, publishes cutting-edge research, mentors colleagues, works twenty-four hours a day seven days a week conquering ignorance, stars in a blockbuster movie based on her life that inspires thousands of young people to enter the teaching profession, and, having taken a vow of poverty, happily spends her entire $42,000 salary on school supplies. Such a model may provide a sound starting point in determining what the limits of possibility might be in the field of teaching. But if one evaluates real teachers by that standard—implying, perhaps, as those who invoke unrealistic standards often do, that in "the good old days" one's hypothetical ideal was the norm—one may end up either with a staff of dispirited, "failed" teachers, or no teachers at all. When perfection becomes the norm by which human performance is judged, the perfect becomes a resolute enemy of the good.

Is This Good? Ethical Questions

There are two ways to form ethical judgments. On the one hand, one can base one's ethical norms on a set of principles, say, the Ten Commandments, that if violated will constitute an ethical breach, no matter what. Such principled ethics tend not to draw fine distinctions among violations and by and large ignore "mitigating circumstances" that might cause us to view an infraction more charitably. Applying principled ethics is a relatively straightforward matter so long as two or more of our principles don't conflict, as when, for example, a pacifist must choose between defending his family against a killer and prohibitions against taking another human life. The major problem facing the defendant of principled ethics is that she may be forced to take stands that will strike many as rigid and inhumane, lacking in proportion. Principled arguments often rest on variants of slippery slope arguments that transform minor violations into major infractions by equating every misstep with the first step on the road to perdition. Drinking caffeinated soft drinks will lead to coffee, will lead to over-the-counter pick-me-ups, will lead to illegal amphetamines, will lead to heroin addiction. While there are many sound reasons for forbidding kids to drink caffeinated soft drinks, treating it as a preliminary to heroin addiction may well lead to unduly harsh punishments.

In most cases, ethical arguments also take consequences into account. For some ethical thinkers, called "consequentialists," only consequences matter. The drinking of caffeinated beverages, thus, is judged according to the consequences of the act. If it is determined that caffeinated beverages negatively impact your health, the consequentialist would consider it bad to ingest such beverages and perhaps, because of the scope of the consequences, worse yet to traffic in them and promote them. But the consequentialist would likely not offer a strong condemnation of the practice insofar as consuming caffeinated beverages is no more or less harmful than the consumption of many other foods (the "compared to what" standard). The consequentialist may take the principled ethicist's slippery slope argument into account, but would demand to know how often people actually slide down the slippery slope from Mountain Dew to heroin. The less frequently it occurs, and the murkier the causal relationship between the first and last steps, the weaker the case for strong ethical prohibition by consequentialist standards.

The hardest thing for any consequentialists to know are the actual consequences of any given act. As we've already suggested, the significance of unintended and unforeseen consequences can be far greater than the significance of those we factor into our ethical choices: For example, one may make an ethical choice to save a child's life at birth at the expense of its mother's life only to have the child grow up to be a moral monster. In order for a consequentialist case to be effective, a sound causal argument detailing how things might turn out is helpful, and such arguments are vulnerable at every point that a causal argument would be vulnerable. And finally, some acts are so heinous that no positive consequences could possibly justify them. Jonathan Swift's "Modest Proposal" is a classic "consequentialist" argument that were it not for one tiny flaw—it calls upon readers to solve Ireland's chronic problems of poverty, hunger, and overpopulation by eating large numbers of Irish children—would be irresistible.

Which is why most ethical arguments are blends of principled and consequentialist elements.

| SIDEBAR VIII | SOUA and Evaluative and Ethical Questions |

When the good or bad thing one is assessing is war, the difficulty of disentangling straightforward evaluative arguments from ethical claims is considerable. Can there be such a thing as a "good" war? Some people, operating from the perspective of a principled ethical stance, might well answer, "No, never." Others, who leaven their antiwar principles with realism, might take the position that war is evil, but sometimes it is a necessary evil or the lesser of two evils. While respectfully acknowledging the first position, we'll discuss the Iraq War from the perspective of the second position. Given all the moral compromises that wars require of us, it makes little sense to talk about an ideal war. World War II, sometimes referred to as "the last good war," might serve as a model for war that most would find at least palatable, if not noble. The United States spent years trying to stay out of World War II and was brought into the conflict against its will by German and Japanese aggression. It fought in order to protect its national sovereignty and to prevent the subjugation of other sovereign countries by foreign aggressors who appeared bent on global domination and the suppression of alien peoples. Our entry into the war was not apparently motivated by a desire for material gain. It was a war against foes of roughly equal strength (at the outset at least) who were not attacked simply because they were vulnerable. For the most part, rules of war were observed and attempts were made to spare enemy civilians. (To the extent that our conduct of the Iraq War has been criticized, our failure to protect the innocent has probably been seen as our greatest shortcoming.) The "Good Guys" won and were benevolent in victory, helping to rebuild their former enemies and ease their entry back into the international community. In sum, it achieved the purpose of war, which is to restore order while inflicting as little unnecessary damage as possible after all peaceful means have been exhausted.

Any evaluation of the Iraq War would have to consider our motivations for entering the war and our conduct of the war itself. (The third criterion for evaluating the war, its consequences, are considered below in the examination of the rationale for the proposal to pursue the war.) As previously noted, the rationale for entering the war shifted over time. While the president notes most of the criteria in his speech, their relative importance changes significantly as events on the ground change. But clearly, our rationale for entering the war differs from our rationale for entering World War II in at least a couple of important respects: We had no clear evidence of Iraqi aggression against our state or against an ally. And many of our allies questioned whether all peaceful means for resolving our differences with Iraq had been exhausted. It seems clear today that Iraq did not possess WMD at the time of the address, though in 2003 many experts from many nations contended that it did. While one could argue that Saddam's subjugation of his own people constitutes a justification for military action, history provides few precedents for such a move. America has not traditionally questioned the authority of dictatorships and in fact has helped install and maintain a number of dictators in power (including Saddam) when they seemed like the lesser of two evils. Ironically, the same realism that compels us to overcome our aversion to war sometimes contributes to the very conditions that necessitate war. In the case of our World War II model, we certainly allowed Hitler to rule Germany in tyrannical fashion and to run roughshod over the rights of his people for many years before events forced us to oppose him.

In assessing the conduct of the Iraq War, indeed in assessing the conduct of virtually any war, the most difficult judgment to make concerns the degree to which innocents as well as combatants have suffered. The president acknowledges this dimension of war in his address when he declares that if war is fought, it will be fought "by just means, sparing, in every way we can, the innocent." As implied by the modifying phrase "in every way we can," some innocents will inevitably suffer. No war will spare the innocent completely. "Collateral damage" is an inevitable by-product of military action. Civilians will be killed, maimed, and injured; homes and workplaces destroyed; and people's lives thrown into chaos any time war is waged. Such consequences are unintended in the sense that no particular innocent person is willingly harmed; but in another sense, they are if not exactly intended, foreknown and tolerated. Military planners can and do build in estimates of civilian casualties and property damage to their battle plans, thereby acknowledging the fact that the suffering of innocents is one cost of waging war. Which is why there is a strong presumption that wars should only be fought when they are unavoidable, when all other means have been exhausted.

How well we were able to keep the president's pledge to spare the innocent remains unclear. Certainly technical advances in weapons systems and satellite imaging allowed us to avoid the worst sort of excesses that were inflicted on civilian populations in World War II. But reliable damage assessments are hard to come by in Iraq. While some nongovernmental agencies have tried to compile assessments of damage done to Iraqi civilians, our own military has withheld estimates of civilian casualties and nonmilitary property damage. (In withholding such estimates, the difficulty of making accurate estimates has been repeatedly cited. While this is a reasonable contention, it is also doubtless true that the military was not eager to lend presence to the suffering of innocents in a controversial war.)

What Should We Do about This Thing?
Proposal Questions

In the realms of business and politics, proposal arguments in the form of legislation, funding requests, calls for change in policy or procedure, and so forth, are ubiquitous. We put them last here because they often contain all four of the other sorts of argument. Typically they begin by pointing out a problem of some sort. This may entail defining the class of things to which the problematic element belongs—secondary schools, combat helicopters, energy programs, marketing campaigns, and so forth—and what such things are supposed to do. The proposer will then evaluate the problematic element by the standards of its class. He may then lay out a causal argument showing just how the problem came about and/or how the solution will solve the problem. And in establishing the soundness of the solution, the proposer will often cite precedents or analogous situations in other realms where solutions like this one were successful. At each of these stages of the proposal process, all the previously discussed challenges associated with the other argument types will manifest themselves.

Not all proposals, of course, begin with problems as we normally imagine them. Sometimes proposals simply stress benefits that will flow from the proposal. But insofar as the failure to act on the proposal will result in lost opportunities ("opportunity costs"), the proposal indirectly implicates a problem in the status quo. Determining the beneficial consequences of a proposal may be the most difficult task facing a proposer. First, the causal chain linking the proposed action to the promised boon may be questioned on empirical grounds. For example, one might question whether a proposal to let the dollar weaken in value relative to other currencies would help the trade in lieu of a detailed explanation of causality. And dissimilarities between the present situation and the situation prevailing in one's precedent or analogy may overwhelm the similarities. In the case of the previous example, precedents of weakened currencies helping with trade deficits had best be taken from a time when something like the current conditions of global capitalism prevailed. Second, the proposal's benefits may be insufficient to justify its risks. In any event, estimates of *net* benefits (benefits minus costs) may be extremely difficult to work out since the debits and credits may not be reducible to a common currency. Thus, for example, in judging a proposal to fund preschool programs, one must weigh the value of poor kids being healthier and better prepared for school against the dollars required to fund the program and all the other things that money might buy— missile defense systems, better highways, pay raises for government employees, and so forth. In every proposal argument one is well advised to follow the old Watergate adage: "Follow the money." That is, ask yourself, For whom is the problem a problem? Who is paying the cost of the problem? Who will benefit from the solution? And who will pay the cost of the solution?

The implied cynicism of that last piece of advice underscores the special challenges posed by proposal arguments. Anyone proposing a change to the status quo may find themselves faced with a particularly long row to hoe. Human beings are naturally resistant to changes, particularly ones they don't initiate. They are not unfamiliar with the law of unintended consequences, and what was touted to them as "progress" has not always worked out in their favor. And the more significant the change, the more resistant one can expect one's audience to be. Hence the folk wisdom, "The devil you know is better than the devil you don't know." Moreover, proposals always require action of some sort at the end of the day, and they almost always have a material effect, direct or indirect, on those to whom the argument is being made. Which is why the burden of proof for proposals is often greater than for other forms of argument and why one is well advised to give a good deal of "presence" to one's proposal argument. By the same token, when one opposes a proposal, one is well advised to include as graphic a depiction as possible of its potential negative consequences.

SIDEBAR IX   SOUA and Proposal Questions

The main claim of the 2003 State of the Union Address, the call for a military solution to the problems posed by Iraq, has been dealt with under all of the other stasis categories. At this point, considering several of these supporting claims collectively allows us to assess the validity of the major claim, the overall effectiveness of the argument, and the major "missing pieces" that supporters of the claim would need to provide to render it more efficacious. Clearly the president does an astute job of depicting the problem and lending it presence. The extent of Saddam's past wickedness is well documented and vividly presented. Unfortunately, those aspects of the problem that render him a "clear and present danger," his possession of WMD and his ties to terrorist organizations, turn out to be the least-well-supported elements of the case for war. And little is offered by way of a causal explanation for the problem in Iraq. For the most part, the cause of the problem is reduced to the evil intent of one man. Removing the man should thus solve the problem. The fact that the solution did not work suggests the need for a more complex causal analysis. And by the same token, if new justifications are put forward for the war in Iraq—e.g., a stable Iraq will stabilize the region—the causal dynamic by which they will bring about the desired outcome should be outlined.

The crucial definitional question in regard to the proposal has to do with the nature of the war to be waged. Because of the president's reluctance to designate the Iraq War as a preemptive war and to elucidate criteria for the definition of such a war, it remains an elusive precedent for future action. By the same token, no precedents are cited to justify the war, and history appears to provide few credible candidates for the role of precedent. In turn, the consequences of the war, crucial to any evaluation or moral judgment of it, get short shrift in the president's address. The costs of war are barely mentioned while the benefits are mostly implied rather than enumerated. Ridding the world of an evil and powerful man may justify the act if one's moral position is purely principled and ignores the moral costs (the harm to innocents, the diversion of moral goods from other efforts) of the act. In retrospect, this failure to discuss the costs of war or to acknowledge the uncertain nature of some of the benefits marks the most vulnerable portion of the president's argument. In the months that followed the State of the Union Address, as the costs started to become apparent and many of the benefits failed to materialize, the president's case appeared at times naive, raising questions about the administration's credibility. Moreover, one of the unacknowledged costs of the war and occupation of Iraq was the limited ability of our nation to conduct military operations in other parts of the world. For example, a humanitarian crisis in the Sudan involving millions of people went long unaddressed in part because our troops and dollars were already committed to Iraq.

The marked absence in the speech of evidences of dialectical thought, of "proving opposites" and generating novel solutions, places it toward the left end of our argument continuum, away from pure persuasion and toward propaganda. But again, pure persuasion is an ideal standard by which to measure any argument. Given the circumstances of the speech, in particular the timing involved, some use of propagandistic means seems inevitable. The purpose of the speech is not to engage in a conversation about the advisability of war, but to rally popular support for a war that has already been deemed by policymakers and some in the intelligence community to be inevitable. And if the war is to be fought, military experts argued, it must be launched within two months. As arguments go, then, the president's address clearly fulfills the function of propaganda, of increasing audience adherence to conclusions not open to question by those proposing them. The popular will is being brought into line with expert opinion. While the president has been charged with being disingenuous for not admitting that the war was already fait accompli, few in his audience were under any illusion that alternative solutions to war were being actively pursued.

On the other hand, an important question about the place of expert knowledge in a democracy remains. There are two aspects to the question: How do policymakers balance the advice of experts against the will of the people? How is expert knowledge gathered and assessed by policymakers? In the first instance, doing what is "best" by the lights of experts will sometimes conflict with what a majority of the people view to be in the best interests of the country. And while experts generally know what's best in the context of their domains, they are famously thick on occasion about what's best in a larger context. Experts often suffer from advanced cases of Burke's occupational psychosis(ROM, 133). Economists, thus, see economic solutions to every problem, while generals see military solutions, and so forth. And when occupational psychosis is crossed with what might be called "ideological psychosis," such that free-market economists only see free-market solutions and Air Force generals only see bombing solutions, the possibilities of arriving at an eco-logically balanced solution are virtually nil. Which brings us to the second aspect of the issue. To the extent that experts are involved in proposing solutions to problems in a democracy, it is essential that they represent a broad range of expertise and ideology. In the case of the 2003 State of the Union Address, even if the speech shows few signs of "proving opposites," we must hope that the process by which its conclusions were reached constituted a robust, dialectical engagement. To the extent that the process fell short of this standard, the speech represents an exercise in propaganda not unlike the sorts of pep talks Soviet leaders once gave to their peo-ple about the wonders of five-year plans dreamed up by their right-thinking economic experts.

Arguing Backward: Logic and Toulmin Schema

The next two tools of persuasion are particularly useful at the second-draft stage of an argument, after one has made a first pass at one's case and has made a series of related points aimed at winning an audience's identification with one's position. In fact, logic is only useful at this stage as a tool for "testing" one's arguments or the fully formed argu-ments of others. A Toulmin schema may serve earlier in the process, but is most helpful at this stage both to test one's argument and to build on it.

For some people, "logic" is one of those God Terms that trumps all other considerations: "Your argument is not logical" means it's done, cooked, beneath contempt. And being "logical" is the highest possible praise one can attribute to an argument or its maker. And to be sure, even for those of us who are generally less awed by the power of logic, it remains a good and useful tool. Certainly one does not set out to be il-logical or to knowingly violate logic's laws. But one does not wish to be restricted to logic in conceiving of or assessing arguments. It proves to be unhelpful in many situations and misleading in others. Sometimes arguments that are not logically sound may still prove to be effective, and not just because audiences are too dim to perceive the unsound bits. Other elements of persuasion simply matter more than logical consistency.

What logic helps ensure is that arguments are internally consistent and that the conclusions we draw do not go further than the reasons we adduce in support of those conclusions allow us to go. In its most familiar form, logic is expressed through categorical syllogisms of the type All X are Y (Major Premise), Z is an X (minor premise), Z is a Y (conclusion). Fleshed out, a representative syllogism might say something like the following: All marriages are sacred; Bob and Rosemary are married; Bob and Rosemary's marriage is sacred. Given the two premises, the conclusion is certain and inevitable. That's not to say it's necessarily *true*—Bob and Rosemary may already be in court battling over the wording of their prenup—simply that it is *valid* according to the rules of logic. For the conclusion to be true, the premises have to be true, and clearly the above premise is open to debate. Some will ask, "Why can't marriage be a serious and committed relationship without bringing religion into it?" Or, "Isn't it true that some church weddings end in divorce before the year is out while some weddings performed in the Elvis Chapel thrive for decades?" Logic can't help us formulate a reply; it can merely stand by until we've formed one, through whatever means, and then help us arrange the parts to ensure their consistency.

The problems with logic are exacerbated as the complexity of the argument increases. It not only becomes harder to translate plain English into logical statements of the proper form, but the limits of logic in helping us find the best position become even more evident. In considering the issue of gay marriage, for example, logic may in fact end the search for a best position before it ever begins. In responding to a 2003 court decision legalizing gay marriage, many pundits rejected the idea on the grounds that it was "illogical." They pointed to the many existing references, in lexical and biblical sources, defining marriage as a union between a man and a woman: 'Nuf said. Basically, they were treating the meaning of marriage not as an issue but as an imperiled fact; all one need do to prove a fact is to look it up in an accepted source. For these pundits, it was as if someone had asserted that "genuine" meant "bogus." If one starts with the premise that marriage is between a man and a woman, one cannot "logically" arrive at a position that acknowledges the legitimacy of gay marriage. In fact, logic never allows one to arrive at any conclusion not anticipated in its premises. And logic doesn't provide any means for producing or interrogating premises; it can only ensure that whatever premises we start out with, they lead to formally sound conclusions. Foregrounding the logical issues in argument may in fact serve an extremely coercive function insofar as it suppresses all questions about premises.

Which is where Stephen Toulmin comes in. In the middle of the last century, Toulmin rejected the logical model of argument sketched out above. Translating complex arguments into a series of formally correct logical structures accomplishes little, particularly given the "costs" in time and effort associated with such efforts. So Toulmin developed a model of persuasion grounded on some of the same assumptions discussed in Chapter 1 under the heading of legal reasoning. Unlike logic, where arguments are "unsituated," every legal argument is a response to another argument; the process is adversarial and requires that appeals be made to third-party audiences. In turn, the law has a store of precedents and formal principles that advocates must use to determine what "counts" as a point and what evidence is relevant. Any statement made in a courtroom is open to challenge, most especially those very premises that in logic require no support. Every field, every discipline, has similar, if less formally expressed and codified, conventions, used by practitioners to resolve disagreements arising from fundamental differences in their assumptions (i.e., differences in their arguments' premises).

SIDEBAR X   SOUA and the Peculiar Nature of Political Premises

As should be clear from our earlier discussion of the 2003 State of the Union Address as an illustration of a rhetorical situation, the conventions of sound argument in the "field" of politics are considerably looser than in the field of law. While politics, like the law, relies on an adversarial system to ensure dialectic exchange, it lacks a third party like a judge charged to rule on the soundness and acceptability of arguments based on a formal record and codified procedures. And instead of juries, bound by the conventions of the law and judges' instructions, politicians appeal to mass audiences. What would be considered "hearsay" in a court of law might count as unassailable testimony in a political debate; and economic estimates with margins of error best expressed in orders of magnitude rather than mere percentages are treated reverently by politicians as solid grounds for policy-making. Moreover, what counts as a "point" in a political argument basically comes down to whatever one's audience accepts as a point. And thanks to the highly mediated environment within which political debates play out, politicians can greatly expand the store of acceptable points to which they might appeal through the use of ambient persuasion to create "instant doxa." All of which serves to remind us that while we can fruitfully apply Toulmin to political arguments, we need to keep in mind the peculiar nature of politics as a field of argument in drawing conclusions from our applications.

Toulmin's model of argument is built around six elements, three of which are sometimes treated as exhaustive. Certainly an argument would be recognized as such if only these first three elements were known. They are: the "grounds (or data)," which is "what we have to go on," sometimes equated with the *evidence* in a case; the "claim," the contestable assertion arising from the data or grounds, sometimes equated with the *conclusion* reached in a case; and the warrant, a principle shared between an audience and the one making an argument that "warrants" the move from the grounds to the claim, sometimes equated with *reasons* in support of one's case. The warrant is often unstated in an argument, especially if it is already adhered to strongly by most audience members. Arguments expressed in the form of "grounds—therefore claim" with the warrant implied are referred to as "enthymemes."

The conclusions you are licensed to draw from your examination of the grounds can at best be reasonable, but never incontestable. Unlike logic, where your conclusions basically restate information contained in your premises, your claim has to be teased out of your grounds. And depending on the nature of your grounds, teasing a claim out of them might pose quite a challenge. Seldom will grounds in the real world readily lend themselves to well-formed statements of the sort one finds in logical syllogisms. Grounds typically take the form of isolated pieces of information or data that come without handles or labels. We have to select them out of a welter of similar information. In picking them out, we are typically guided by our warrant, which serves as our principle of selection. And the warrant one chooses is typically an artifact of the claim one is committed to making. Thus while the direction of Toulmin's schema when sketched out in the abstract appears to go from grounds through warrants to claims, in actual cases it usually moves in the opposite direction. If we care enough about a given issue to make a claim about it, it's usually because we already have a tentative position on that issue. Few of us come across an issue and, in the manner of Sherlock Holmes showing up at a crime scene, start looking around for relevant grounds without having first formed a hypothesis, a theory, a guess, or even a conclusion about the ultimate position one intends to take. Pragmatist philosopher C. S. Peirce, noting how the terms "induction" and "deduction" both missed the mark in describing this process, came up with the term "abduction" to describe what we usually do when confronted with a mystery or problem. We start out neither from a clearly stated premise/warrant that we use deductively to sort out the facts of the case, nor from purely factual grounds/evidence that we use inductively to arrive at a conclusion. Rather the first step in the process is a sudden leap to a conclusion (or claim), a guess or abduction based on our experiences—as filtered through our "orientations," "terministic screens," ideologies, belief systems, and so forth—and the unconscious associations built up during those experiences. We then proceed to test our abduction, modifying it as we go. The role of Toulmin's schema in the context of such a process is to provide a formal means for conducting one's testing.

SIDEBAR XI   SOUA and the Direction of Reason

Viewing the 2003 State of the Union Address in light of the above model of reasoning appears to take some of the sting out of many criticisms of the president. Showing that the president may have started out with a conclusion ("Let's invade Iraq") and worked his way back to the grounds justifying that conclusion ("Iraq has WMD and links to terrorist organizations") does not by itself constitute a fatal indictment. Formally at least, it's a path many of us regularly follow from our beliefs to our understandings. His tendency to view evidence through the lens of his own "terministic screen" cannot be judged categorically invalid without ruling most arguments out of play. If his approach to evidence gathering is open to criticism, let it be on quantitative grounds. Instead of claiming that the president lied or presented fatally flawed arguments because of bias—a very difficult charge to prove—a critic of the president's speech might more plausibly claim that his arguments were weakened by his aversion to self-criticism and his tendency to ignore countervailing arguments or confounding evidence. How thoroughly were his original assumptions tested, how carefully were opposing arguments attended to, and to what extent were supportive conclusions coerced in the process of gathering evidence? These are the crucial questions that need to be answered before a judgment of the president's process can be rendered.

The relationship between one's claim and one's warrant is hardly fixed. More than one warrant can be used to justify a given claim, and more than one claim can be justified by a given warrant. Thus in the case of gay marriage, one may use the rule of justice as a warrant to say that what's OK for heterosexuals is OK for gays because their similarities overwhelm their differences and hence they ought to be treated alike before the law. (In American legal parlance, the rule of justice is expressed through "equal protection" clauses in our federal and state constitutions.) Or one could use that same warrant and conclude that their differences are crucial enough in this case to justify differential treatment. Or one might invoke a different warrant, some variant of "whatever is is right," with "whatever is" taking the form of a dictionary definition of marriage, and conclude either that gay marriage is an oxymoron or a gross violation of sacred customs and traditions.

In every case, it should be noted, the terms of a Toulmin schema are not stable. They name a particular function, a place in the schema, not a particular thing or class of things. Given the same issue, one may examine different grounds and use a different warrant to arrive at a different conclusion. And the same statement that serves as a warrant in one argument may appear as a claim in another. In a sense, each of the three terms is a claim making a contestable assertion—"These are the appropriate grounds to examine," "This is the right warrant to invoke," "This is the proper conclusion to reach." Hence the need for the other three terms included in Toulmin's schema: "Backing" is whatever one uses to support the legitimacy of one's warrant. Ideally, it will have a more "fact-like character" than the warrant, though in practice it may well be little more than a principle that's more widely accepted than the warrant it supports. Thus if one uses the rule of justice as a warrant legitimating the equal treatment of heterosexuals and homosexuals, one might cite court cases, employment laws, and the like supporting that homosexuals have the same constitutional rights as heterosexuals. "Qualifiers" are those terms that indicate how confident one is that one's case is adequate to one's claim. Thus one might claim that gays "certainly" should be allowed to join in civil unions with the equivalent legal status of marriage, but only "probably" or even "perhaps" should the traditional term "marriage" be used to designate that union. "Conditions of rebuttal," meanwhile, point to exceptions or particular cases where one's claim would not hold. Thus the fact that marriage laws vary from state to state may move one to conclude that gay marriage ought to be allowed except in those states whose equal-protection clauses expressly exclude it.

Each element of a Toulmin schema is as open to interrogation as is the relationship between each of them. As such, they may serve a heuristic function, causing us to think of new ways to strengthen our case in response to challenges we might foresee in response to each one. And they may also serve as a formal check on the internal consistency of the parts of an argument: Is my backing appropriate for my warrant? Does my qualifier adequately express the degree of confidence I have in my grounds? In either case, applying the schema to an argument allows us to measure the "candor" of the argument, the extent to which it articulates its grounds, warrants, and backing or the extent to which it suppresses them. In this regard, applying Toulmin is not unlike per-

forming an MRI on an argument. And what we learn from an application of Toulmin schema is not unlike what we learn from examining
pictures from an MRI: that our argument is a whole lot more complex
than a quick scan of the surface could reveal. And sometimes when we
do articulate elements that have been left unstated, their deficiencies
become clear, the excessive burden of proof they entail becomes obvious, and the need for "surgery" is evident.

SIDEBAR XII   SOUA in the Form of a Toulmin Schema

Laying out the 2003 State of the Union Address along the lines
suggested by Toulmin's model of argument allows us to bring together in an economical way a number of points developed at much
greater length in our discussion of the rhetorical situation. The
simplicity of the final model, however, belies the complexity of the
analysis required to arrive at the model. Each of the major elements
of the model, it will be recalled, constitutes a choice, a contestable
choice. After presenting our model, thus, we'll go back and consider a few of the issues raised by our choices and what those issues
have to say about the argument from which they've been derived.

Claim: America should launch a war against Iraq.
Data/Grounds: Iraq has an untrustworthy, evil leader; Iraq has a
working relationship with al-Quaida and thus links to 9/11; Iraq
possesses weapons of mass destruction; the Iraqi people have en-
dured untold suffering under Saddam Hussein's rule; Iraq has regularly violated U.N. arms control agreements and deceived U.N.
inspectors; Iraq is an unstable country in the midst of a volatile
region crucial to our national interests.
Warrant: War is a necessary response to any hostile nation with a
capacity to do us great harm and an unwillingness to resolve differences through diplomatic means.
Backing: U.N. Resolutions 1441 (2002), 687 (1991), and 678
(1990), which call on Iraq to disarm; international law that recognizes the right of any nation to act in the name of protecting its
sovereignty; Puritan doctrine that decrees America an agent of
God and bids us to follow "the ways of Providence"; the historical
record of America's progressive realization of its manifest destiny.
Qualifiers (Q): None or few
Conditions of Rebuttal (CR): Unless Saddam "fully disarm[s] for
the safety of our people, and for the peace of the world," war is inevitable.

Let's begin our discussion with the last two elements of the Toulmin model, Q and CR, whose importance is easily overlooked. The one element of the president's argument that most clearly marks it as propagandistic is the virtual absence of qualifiers. The call for war is unqualified because the veracity of the grounds is never questioned. If the probability or improbability of several of the grounds had been acknowledged, or if their relative significance ("compared to what?") had been put into some sort of context (How much worse off were the people of Iraq than the people of North Korea? How much more or less advanced were Iraq's weapons programs than Iran's?) and appropriate qualifiers appended to the major claim, the argument's long-term viability might have been strengthened, albeit at the expense of some immediate persuasiveness. And the one act (the condition of rebuttal) Bush cites that might forestall war—Iraq's destruction of its weapons of mass destruction—would be impossible for Iraq to perform if, as it appears, it had none left to destroy.

The warrant for the president's claim is, like most warrants, implied rather than stated. In rendering that warrant explicit, war is decreed a "necessary" as opposed to a justified response to the grounds, mainly because of the lack of qualifiers or a realistic condition of rebuttal appended to the claim. This wording reflects the necessitarian nature of the argument presented here and the president's sense that war is being "forced upon us" by an implacably evil foe, the call of history, and the hand of Providence. From this highly deterministic view of the matter flows one very important consequence: If this warrant not only legitimates but requires war whenever the conditions outlined by the president are met, committing ourselves to this war will significantly lower the bar for declaring future wars. The president reinforces this possibility by failing to give serious consideration to alternative scenarios. The only mention of an alternative to war comes in one sentence— "Trusting in the sanity and restraint of Saddam Hussein is not a strategy, and it is not an option." In suggesting that this is our only alternative, the president appears to dismiss various plans put forth at the time by the United Nations and various of our allies that called for a continuation of sanctions and inspections on a significantly increased scale, while leaving open the possibility of multilateral military action at a future date.

The backing for the warrant comprises a curious mix of documents, principles, and religious beliefs, some of which are cited, others of which are implied. As is the case with warrants, backings are seldom named unless the person invoking them anticipates controversy. Thus, while the president never mentions U.N. Resolutions 1441, 687, and 678 by name, these are the agreements to which he alludes when he accuses Saddam of systematic violations of an agreement to disarm. Since these resolutions represent the one tangible sign of multilateral support for our policy toward Iraq, they receive a great deal of play in the run-up to the war. Unfortunately, they lack that factlike character that one wishes for one's backing. The oldest of the resolutions predated the Persian Gulf War of 1991 and many questioned its continued applicability to the case at hand. The second two resolutions less clearly call for the use of military force as the most obvious response to noncompliance. Resolution 1441, for example, refers to "serious consequences" that would attend noncompliance, but the document calls for a meeting of the Security Council to determine the response. And according to U.N. doctrine, any military response must meet the conditions of "necessity and proportionality." Which is to say, advocates for war would have to show at that meeting that war was a necessary response to Iraq's "material breaches" of the agreements, and that the punishment of war fit the crime of noncompliance. Indeed, a number of signatories to 1441 specifically rejected the notion that war would automatically result from noncompliance. The administration, meanwhile, took the position that any member of the U.N. Security Council could unilaterally declare war on Iraq if the U.N. agreements were not kept, a position that was not shared by most of our allies. By continuing to cite the authority of U.N. resolutions to justify its actions, even in the face of U.N. rejection of those actions, America created a good deal of ill will within the international community. The resolutions, thus, proved to be at least as controversial as the warrant they were supposed to support. One hopes for a bit more from one's backing.

The citation of Providence and, by implication, the doctrine of manifest destiny are potentially even more controversial than the invocation of U.N. resolutions as support for the president's warrant. While religious allusions are ubiquitous in American political documents and ceremonial statements, care is usually taken to ensure that they remain unspecific. In this case, the president's references to Providence and his trust that a "loving God" guides our decision to go to war will evoke worrisome echoes for some in his audience. In the past, this equation of our national self-interests with the designs of a deity has served to justify some of our most questionable policies, including our forcible, often-violent removal of American Indian peoples from lands that they had occupied for centuries in order that we might fulfill our expansionist dreams. What is sometimes referred to as "exceptionalism," the belief that we are less answerable than other nations to worldly authority by virtue of our special status as God's "chosen people," has not always served us well in the world community whose members may hear in our justification for war some unpleasant echoes of the rhetoric employed by other nations to justify ignoble wars in the name of other gods.

The major claim (America should launch a war against Iraq) and those grounds that supposedly give rise to that claim have a somewhat ambiguous relationship to one another. The claim is stated in its broadest possible form so as to connect it both to those grounds that justify preemptive war and those that justify retaliatory war. If one were to append a "because" clause to the claim stating that we must go to war "because if we don't, Iraq will soon commit a hostile act far worse than 9/11," the relevance of the various grounds to the claim shifts dramatically. Concerns about long-term stability in the region and the suffering of the Iraqi people take a step back and Saddam's instability steps forward. By the same token, if we were to append a "because" clause saying something on the order of "because if we don't, the Iraqi people will be further persecuted and stability in the region will further erode," the links between al-Quaida and Iraq recede in importance. In one sense, all the grounds cited justify a call for war. They don't necessarily contradict each other. But not all the grounds support the same reasons for war. And neither do they impart the same degree of urgency about the need for war. If we find ourselves today left mostly with the second version of the claim, we probably need a new warrant.

And so we end almost where we began. Having started out from the position that persuasion is best understood as an alternative to coercion, we have spent a good part of the previous two chapters examining a specific argument that flies in the face of that position, that calls for an end to talk and negotiation in the act of justifying war. In one sense, the 2003 State of the Union Address is a litmus test for just how far one ought to stretch the principle that persuasion is to be preferred to coercion in the face of evidence that persuasion and negotiation have failed and danger is imminent. History, which will have far fuller and more certain grounds at its disposal, including the consequences—intended and unintended—of the act, will finally judge the rightness of our decision to go to war; but in the meantime, rhetoricians need not sit idly by waiting on the historians. They can "purify" the argument for war by complicating and questioning it, forcing the conversation to continue even as the war goes on. However right or wrong the act may be, the argument used to justify the act can be questioned, critiqued, and thereby strengthened. In so doing, we enter into evidence contemporary voices that historians will ultimately have to take into account, and we increase the likelihood that the next argument for coercion over persuasion will be as efficacious as the consequences it advocates are grave.

5

Rhetoric and Interpretation

In theory, "interpretation" is an operation we might perform on anything that puzzles us, from Russian novels to bent twigs on a forest trail. Normally, however, we think of it in conjunction with a certain class of symbolic acts associated with high culture. Thus we routinely think of interpreting poems but seldom newspaper articles; paintings but not billboards; short stories but not current events; foreign "films" but not blockbuster movies; holy writ but not campaign speeches. In the minds of some, the only reason for the existence of art and literature, the most esteemed of high-culture artifacts, is to require interpretation. Those who think this way tend to view the interpretation of texts as an activity roughly equivalent to solving crossword puzzles. One doesn't have to look far for the source of such a reductive view of interpretation. Too many of us have spent too many hours in literature classes taught by well-intentioned teachers ransacking poems line by line in search of The Hidden Meaning. (And however cleverly hidden, once found, that meaning turns out to be as unambiguous as a stop sign, perfectly suited to its later appearance on a multiple-choice test.) Too bad. The sort of interpretive powers one develops from closely reading literary and artistic works can be extremely valuable in interpreting all manner of things, including everything from advertisements to State of the Union Addresses to terrorist acts.

One of the important functions served by rhetoric is to put those powers of interpretation, cultivated through the examination of high-culture artifacts, in the service of humbler ends—the understanding of everyday texts, events, and images that matter to us. So while I do spend some time in this chapter interpreting literary texts, I do so not in hopes of turning you into literary critics, but to discuss how you might translate those skills into tools for everyday use. I single out literary interpretation not so much because I believe in the privileged status of literary works—in fact I will argue strenuously against such a view—but because I believe that the art of interpretation has been most thoroughly and overtly developed by critics of literary texts, many of whose methods may be readily borrowed by critics examining symbolic acts of a less exalted status.

Keats's "Ode": Literary Interpretation

To be sure, however, literary and rhetorical criticism are *not* one and the same. Literary criticism may focus on any number of elements depending on which school of criticism one subscribes to. In some cases, literary and rhetorical critics share an intense focus on the literary act—the construction, reception, and historical consequences of texts and the scenes within which construction and reception take place. But in many cases, literary critics look elsewhere for meaning. In what follows, we'll briefly analyze a venerable artifact of literary high culture, John Keats's "Ode on a Grecian Urn," using an approach, formalism, that is distinctly literary and that the work itself seems to invite. Then, in a far lengthier discussion, we'll explore the implications of that approach for a rhetorical critic. And finally we'll extend that discussion to a contemporary event of enormous importance, the terrorist attacks of 9/11, to see what modifications must be made to Keats's assumptions about art to make those assumptions work fully for the rhetorical critic examining symbolic acts of less exalted status.

Ode on a Grecian Urn

Thou still unravish'd bride of quietness,
Thou foster-child of Silence and slow Time,
Sylvan historian, who canst thus express
A flowery tale more sweetly than our rhyme:
What leaf-fringed legend haunts about thy shape
Of deities or mortals, or of both,
In Tempe or the dales of Arcady?
What men or gods are these? What maidens loth?
What mad pursuit? What struggle to escape?
What pipes and timbrels? What wild ecstasy?

Heard melodies are sweet, but those unheard
Are sweeter; therefore, ye soft pipes, play on;

Not to the sensual ear, but, more endear'd,
Pipe to the spirit ditties of no tone:
Fair youth, beneath the trees, thou canst not leave
Thy song, nor ever can those trees be bare;
Bold Lover, never, never canst thou kiss,
Though winning near the goal—yet, do not grieve;
She cannot fade, though thou hast not thy bliss,
For ever wilt thou love, and she be fair!

Ah, happy, happy boughs! That cannot shed
Your leaves, nor ever bid the Spring adieu;
And, happy melodist, unwearied,
For ever piping songs for ever new,
More happy love! More happy, happy love!
For ever warm and still to be enjoy'd,
For ever panting, and for ever young;
All breathing human passion far above,
That leaves a heart high-sorrowful and cloy'd,
A burning forehead, and a parching tongue.

Who are these coming to the sacrifice?
To what green altar, O mysterious priest,
Lead'st thou that heifer lowing at the skies,
And all her silken flanks with garlands drest?
What little town by river or sea-shore,
Or mountain-built with peaceful citadel,
Is emptied of its folk, this pious morn?
And, little town, thy streets for evermore
Will silent be; and not a soul, to tell
Why thou art desolate can e'er return.

O Attic shape! Fair attitude! with brede
Of marble men and maidens overwrought,
With forest branches and the trodden weed;
Thou, silent form! Dost tease us out of thought
As doth eternity: Cold pastoral!
When old age shall this generation waste,
Thou shalt remain, in midst of other woe
Than ours, a friend to man, to whom thou say'st,
'Beauty is truth, truth beauty,—that is all
Ye know on earth, and all ye need to know!'

—*John Keats, 1795–1821*

Keats's "Ode" is based on a meditation over a relief on an ancient Greek funeral urn. The narrator of the poem, presumably the poet, muses over the meaning of three scenes featuring lovers in playful pursuit, a musician playing a pipe amidst blossoming trees, and a priest leading a heifer to be sacrificed on an altar. The contrasting scenes of nature bursting with life and the heifer being led to her death reflect a tension that marks the entire poem. The lovers can never kiss, but then again neither can their ardor ever fade. The melodist, meanwhile, pipes "ditties of no tone" that are "for ever new" thanks to the fact that they can't be heard. And the scene of the sacrifice, a scene that momentarily causes the narrator to lose all sense of aesthetic distance and mourn the "desolate" town to which the people attending the sacrifice will never return, is finally pronounced a "Cold Pastoral!" This climactic, oxymoronic exclamation rescues the narrator from his dalliance with what some formalists call "the affective fallacy," a strong emotional identification with the scene, reminding him, and us, that what we're seeing is a representation not of any particular pastoral scene, but of an ideal. One made of cold marble, not warm flesh. The urn's relief "tease[s] us out of thought" because, like "eternity," it has no beginning, middle, or end; rather it is frozen, a scene that repeats itself endlessly as we turn the urn in our hands or walk around its pedestal. And in case we're tempted to offer a different reading of the matter, the narrator brings things to a close with the urn's urgent and famous reminder—hereafter referred to as the "Keatsian imperative"—that " 'Beauty is truth, truth beauty,—that is all / Ye know on earth, and all ye need to know!' "

Keats's "Ode": Implications for the Rhetorical Critic

If we understand Keats's urn properly and it has spoken truly, rhetoricians would probably be prohibited from interpreting poetry or urns. By the lights of rhetoric, the "truth" of any work of art does not reside wholly within the work. While rhetoric would grant that the internal coherence of Keats's poem certainly contributes to its "truth," it would also contend that some of its truth resides outside the work in the world the work depicts (ancient Greece), the world it reflects (Keats's Romantic-era England), and the world its audiences reside in (our twenty-first century sensibilities and circumstances and our knowledge of previous readers' responses). The work is not so much a thing, like a funeral urn whose heft we can feel, whose outline we can trace with our finger, as it is a coincidence of multiple interpretations, or, in the words of Argentinian writer Jorge Luis Borges, "an axis of innumerable relationships." If Keats seems determined to escape from history through his poem, reminding us with his title that it's an "ode" to a kind of beauty and as such not to be confused with actual "breathing human passion," rhetoric is equally determined to see it as an artifact of history that both reflects and helps form the world it inhabits. What then is entailed in a rhetorical reading of the poem? At a minimum, a consideration of the circumstances of its creation and its reception over time, paying particular attention to its historical consequences.

The Circumstances of the Ode's Creation

Taking into account the circumstances of the poem's creation is clearly rhetorical. As we've seen throughout, a rhetorical understanding of any symbolic act requires an understanding of the context that gives rise to the work and the circumstances within which the work is received. In the case of literary works, the matter of genre is a particularly important barometer of circumstances. Different periods of literary history are often strongly associated with particular genres, and the reasons for that strong association can often be traced to historical circumstances. The point at which one literary era leaves off and another begins is typically marked by the rise of new genres and/or changes in the way traditional genres are conceived. A literary work, like any other symbolic act, is subject to the dynamic of recurrence discussed in Chapter 2. It both reenacts similar works that precede it and introduces some element of novelty that sets it apart from its predecessors. Insofar as a text departs significantly from those texts that surround and precede it, it represents an argument of sorts, an argument for a new—or at least amended—definition of literature.

In the case of Keats's ode, its ringing conclusion—" 'Beauty is truth, truth beauty,—that is all / Ye know on earth, and all ye need to know!' "—was certainly heard at the time as a claim in an ongoing dispute over the status of art, a claim that retains at least some currency in more recent controversies. The initial reception of a work like Keats's ode is typically a function of how radically it requires audiences to rethink their definition of literature and how persuasive it is in getting audiences to accept its argument. The stronger a work's challenge to accepted definitions of literature, the stronger the initial resistance to it usually is. Throughout history, revolutionary works of art and literature have baffled, even outraged, their first audiences. Indeed, such works are not seen initially as "bad" literature so much as they are seen as "not literature." One of the distinctive features of art and literature as a class of symbolic acts is their continual commitment to challenging our sense of what art and literature may be. But the debates arising from those challenges are not purely literary or artistic debates. As is clear from any study of a work's reception over time, the changing value placed on the work, the changing understanding of the work's meaning—and consequently the meaning of literature—reflect changes in the larger culture. Which is why art and literature provide such excellent barometers of historical, social, and cultural change. Moreover, by reinforcing or challenging the values and beliefs of their audiences, important symbolic acts can greatly influence audience attitudes toward a variety of crucial matters, including everything from gender roles and social justice to war and economic policy. And insofar as attitudes are indeed "incipient acts," those influences may ultimately prepare the ground for real acts that define the time. Which is to say that symbolic acts and their interpretations both reflect and create the times in which they live.

With regard to the circumstances in which Keats's "Ode" was created, the most notable point to be made is that it represents a revolutionary way of thinking about literature. Keats's argument suggests that literary and artistic works comprise a special class of symbolic acts capable of transforming what they represent. At the time Keats made this argument, there wasn't even a term one could use to designate such a special class (at least not in Keats's England). Art was assumed to represent life, not to transform it. In arguing for its special status, Keats was arguing for a new way of perceiving it. Art was to be viewed with what German philosopher Immanuel Kant termed "disinterested interest," a sort of impassioned detachment that allowed one to view all manner of things—even objectionable, horrifying, or distasteful things—in a meditative fashion. Thanks to the creative genius of the artist-visionary, we would be afforded glimpses of something like Plato's Pure Forms in the humblest of objects.

As rhetoricians, we might pursue any number of questions about Keats's poem as a reflection of the time in which it was created, including some of the following: Assuming that every argument is an answer to another argument, an antithesis to another's thesis, what views of art is it arguing against? What historical forces rendered the deficiencies in the other views visible and by the same token gave impetus to the Romantic response? What in Keats's experiences and circumstances inclined him toward the creation of Romantic poetry? How did contemporary audiences understand Keats's "Ode"? To what extent did Keats's poem account for its own popularity by educating its audience, instructing them how it should be read, and to what extent was the poem's reception a function of the fact that it resonated with the *weltanschauung* of the day?

The preceding list of questions—and it is far from exhaustive—illustrates the many lines of inquiry opened up by just one of those innumerable relationships for which a text may serve as an axis—the one between ourselves in the early part of the twenty-first century and Keats's poem as an artifact of early-nineteenth-century art. Through that process we come to understand the work differently than we would were we simply to interrogate it through our twenty-first-century eyes. We can *identify with* that sensibility without pretending that we can make ourselves *identical to* it. By achieving this precarious sense of identity, we put ourselves in a position to more intelligently "discount" the poem's language. Discounting, it will be recalled, is a process like translation, whereby a statement is understood "in terms of" its circumstances. To borrow a distinction from linguistics, discounting is how one gets from *langue*, or language as a system, to *parole*, or language as actual utterances. One discounts from one situation to another, from one specialized terminology to another, from one ideological system to another, from one era to another, and so on. However adept we may be at acquiring and mastering a second vocabulary, we are always natives of one vocabulary and translators of a second. And as our metaphor of translation implies, we are always trying to recover the original sense of a text in the act of interpreting it. While rhetoric recognizes the limits of our capacity to replicate the original understanding of a text, it demands that we pursue it. Failure to do so will result in a zero discount—Burke refers to such discounts as "massacres"—of the meanings it held for its original audience.

To read Keats's poem without attempting to understand its original context would be like translating the dialogue from a French film into English subtitles without bothering to learn French. One might be able to pick up enough clues from the expressions, tones, and actions of the characters to make a stab at translation, but one's subtitles would in all likelihood parody the film's action more than they would illuminate it. Rhetoric of course recognizes both the futility and inadvisability of "immaculate recuperation," the perfect translation of a text's original meaning, and leaves that sort of task to the Serious Folk who would strictly construe the Constitution. Even native French speakers bent on remaining faithful to the film's dialogue would offer a range of interpretations for the subtitles to our hypothetical film. But that range would be far more acceptable to most of us than would the monolinguists' wild stabs at interpretation.

The Ode's Reception and Consequences

Over the years, Keats's poem, and the aesthetic that it embodies, has experienced its ups and downs in its influence and its reception. When I was in college, for example, Romanticism and lyric poems of the sort

Keats wrote were particularly esteemed. Popular music lyrics drew heavily on Romantic poetry, while rock musicians often cast themselves in the role of Romantic visionaries, and classes in Romantic poetry were typically filled to capacity. And the aesthetic assumptions underlying Keats's "Ode" predominated. In terms of my education, that meant that many of my literature classes comprised strenuous exercises in "close reading" of lyric poems and short stories. The key to close reading, we were taught, was not to read things "into" the works (that would constitute an "interested" reading), but only to read things "out" of the works (which constituted a "disinterested" reading). The "truth" of the works was there on the page; one read the work's patterns of imagery, meter, rhyme, and so forth, the way soothsayers once read the entrails of birds. One did not, above all, extract any "gists" from the works; prose paraphrases were profanations of the original word. Meaning was largely a matter of self-canceling ironies mounting up until the scales were tipped, ever so slightly, toward one shade of meaning or another. And politics were irrelevant to literature. Only American Marxist critics, of whom there were very few, and Europeans, whom we seldom read, insisted on dragging their ideological baggage into discussions of works that were, we were taught, unsullied by political ramifications.

From my present perspective, my early training in interpretation seems decidedly odd, however faithful to the generally accepted meaning of the Keatsian imperative and the countless rules, principles, and fallacies it spawned. It resulted in a claustrophobic understanding of literature, and largely ignored one of Romanticism's most crucial dimensions—politics. Even as Keats and his fellow Romantics were turning out their extraordinary lyric poems about ordinary matters, much of the Western world was embroiled in revolution. And the root of both the political and aesthetic revolutions was the emergence of individualism out of the last remnants of those fixed orders discussed in Chapter 3. However scrupulous our avoidance of politics in our endless classroom *explication de textes*—and in truth, my professors were forever smuggling things "into" the works we read, often apologetically, if for no other reason than simply because endless discussion of texts' inner workings makes for pretty thin gruel—the political implications of Romantic individualism were being widely recognized and acted out across America. The Romantic celebration of the artist as visionary—Keats, who wrote beautiful poems on profound themes and died young, was the exemplary poet-visionary—sent many of us off on vision quests of various sorts and inclined us to listen more sympathetically than our parents' generation to those with visions to offer. Bureaucracies, systems, organizations, institutions, technology—anything that fettered the natural growth and expression of the individual was open to critique. Thus when Dustin Hoffman, playing Benjamin, the hapless protagonist of Mike Nichols' 1967 film *The Graduate*, is advised by one of his parents' friends that the future lay in ". . . Plastics," his puzzled frown is the response of a generation. And the movie's Simon and Garfunkel soundtrack was full of lyrics that could have been lifted directly from Keats.

Though I remain forever unsure exactly how to read Keats's imperative, I keep coming back to it to ponder it and appreciate it. While I eventually distanced myself from what many of my teachers and the critics we read took it to mean, I don't regret the years spent learning to read texts in the manner implied by the imperative. It's a useful beginning point for any interpretive act. What it excludes, however, is the significance of one's interpretation, a way of saying not only what a work means but why that meaning might matter. In the end, to leave the question of significance out of one's understanding of literature, to declare literature apolitical, is to say it is incapable of equipping us to live more mindful lives or of critiquing the systems within which those lives are led. To say literature is apolitical or ought not to be read for political inflections is to make a powerful political statement. To deny the political implications of literature is to silence it. And when literature can't comment on issues of social justice, it means that the status quo, no matter how heinous, is protected from one of the most useful, most broadly available sources of critique in our culture.

That said, it is probably not surprising that the first group of American critics to translate the spirit of the Keatsian imperative into a categorical imperative for interpretative practice was a dreamy coterie of political reactionaries bent on the restoration of *antebellum* Southern aristocratic values to American society. According to these forerunners of what would come to be called "new criticism," the knowledge that truth and beauty are synonymous meant that truth was an epiphenomenon of beauty, not something one went looking for but something that one received, like Puritan grace, by fully appreciating the finely wrought inner workings of great texts.

It is probably equally unsurprising that the same Romantic individualism that lent itself to the rejection of authority and materialist values in the 1960s turned out to lend itself equally well to the embrace of rugged individualism and a virulent materialism in the 1980s and 1990s. After all, if one's model of interpretation derives from the view that texts are autonomous, wholly self-contained entities that must not, at any cost, be "read into," it seems natural for one to understand individuals and economic markets in the same way and to be equally vigilant about protecting them from human tinkering and government regulation. If the individual is the source of all value, and a few extraordinary geniuses are responsible for all the best that's been thought and said, bought and sold, why shouldn't they be compensated accordingly? And having once called upon political leaders to shift "power to the people" in acknowledgment of the people's inherent right of self-rule, isn't it logical to call on them now to rescue essential government services from collectivist thinking and bureaucratic control by "privatizing" them?

The movement of the Keatsian imperative through the twentieth century, from its use by reactionaries in the 1920s and liberals in the 1960s, to its use by libertarians in the 1980s and 1990s, is in many ways exemplary. This dynamic whereby principles are translated into policies and general terms are extended to specific cases is sometimes referred to as "casuistry," a word that has, like the term "rhetoric," fallen on hard times. But as we use the term, once again following Kenneth Burke's usage, we are simply stressing the shared root of "casuistry" and "case." Any time the circumstances change, casuistry is required to get from an established principle to a new case. If the circumstances change a good deal, "casuistic stretching" will be required to get there. And the circumstances are always changing. About-faces in meaning like the one seen above are a regular feature of this process. (In fact the nineteenth-century understanding of the term "liberal" closely resembles our contemporary understanding of "libertarian," which is today viewed as an extremely conservative position.) When such reversals occur over a relatively short time span, the proponents of the original understanding of the term may complain that the opposition has "hijacked" their vocabulary. To which the proponents of the reversed meaning of the term(s) inevitably reply that they are simply applying the general principles in a more rigorous and consistent manner than their slapdash opponents. And so it goes.

We've once again followed the same sort of circuitous path that we describe others following. We've gone from propaganda to poetry and eventually found ourselves back at propaganda. And if the connections drawn here between the otherworldly poetry of John Keats and the open market economic views of contemporary neoconservatives strike some as implausible, the source of their anti-rhetorical skepticism may well lie in the very Keatsian imperative that began our circuitous journey. The prevailing reading of that imperative during my formative years would have forbidden the sorts of connections between life and art, politics and poetry being drawn here. Governments should take a

laissez-faire approach to human affairs and readers should take a detached, objective, and, most especially, apolitical approach to literature—and God forbid anyone might confuse art and life, cool marble
urns, and the "breathing human passion far above." But if followed out
to its logical conclusion, the Keatsian imperative inevitably confuses
art and life—indeed art swallows life—in ways our anti-rhetorical skep-
tics might find most disquieting.

9/11 and Some Further Consequences of the Keatsian Imperative

If that last judgment seems a bit harsh, consider the case of one Karlheinz
Stockhausen, a German composer of some note who was quoted in the
September 25, 2001, English-Language Edition of the *Frankfurter
Allegemeine Zeitung* claiming that the attacks of 9/11 constituted "the
greatest work of art imaginable for the whole cosmos." Stockhausen went
on to grant that the act was also criminal because "those involved didn't
consent" to participate in the performance. But this disclaimer is a mere
qualifier appended to his major claim, the assertion that the attack went
"beyond the limits of what is feasible and conceivable, so that we wake
up, so that we open ourselves to another world."

Rhetorically speaking, one might attribute the flaws in
Stockhausen's thinking here to a tendency Burke, borrowing from John
Dewey, refers to as "occupational psychosis." So obsessed is Stockhausen
with his professional objectives that everything is filtered through the
lens of musical composition. Two planes full of hundreds of people flying
into skyscrapers filled with thousands of people and setting off a 2,000-de-
gree inferno becomes a piece of performance art to be judged by appropriate aesthetic norms, in this case its capacity to "wake [us] up" to other
worlds. Formally, Stockhausen's argument is a first cousin to Swift's eigh-
teenth-century argument in favor of cannibalism: "Ignore the fact that
this scheme is morally monstrous, because it's a really terrific idea." Minus
the irony. Viewed from a "stasis" perspective, Stockhausen is offering an
evaluative claim (The attack was a good or bad piece of art.) that begs far
more compelling issues of ethics (Was the attack good or evil?) and definition (Can evil be art?).

The most obvious candidate for a warrant that might license
Stockhausen's evaluative claim that 9/11 comprised the "greatest work
of art" ever is his definitional claim that art is that which "wake[s us]
up" to new possibilities, new worlds. Certainly this is a venerable notion in aesthetics, the idea that art is visionary, allowing us to see the

world anew; Keats and his fellow Romantics are closely associated with this very notion. And while one can accept this as one possible criterion—even a necessary condition—for membership in the class "art," few people would grant that this criterion is the "essence" of art, the one and only necessary and sufficient condition for membership. Moreover, many would argue that a number of things that "wake us up"—various calamities and crises, sudden changes in scene, etc.— would not qualify as art because of their direct effect on us and the difficulty we have reflecting on them. And as previously noted, that overly narrow aesthetic norm makes for an even more lamentably insufficient ethical norm.

Stockhausen's infamous response to 9/11 is clearly based on assumptions that comport nicely with the Keatsian imperative. What, after all, is Stockhausen doing but looking at the images of 9/11 in a "disinterestedly interested" way, objectifying and thematizing the carnage as if it were a scene on an urn. For him it is a self-contained vision, and those who would judge it in the light of political or ethical standards would be as guilty of the "affective fallacy" as Keats's narrator mourning an imagined empty town. The image of the planes flying into the towers is not a literal representation of a real event for Stockhausen; it is a simulacrum, an image for which there is no original referent. In Stockhausen's world, the imperatives of art trump the principles of law and ethics so soundly that the latter can be consigned to the realm of illusion. If something is beautiful, it is true and as such resides far above "all breathing human passion" in the realm of the eternal beyond the reach of the legal and ethical standards of mere mortals.

However morally repugnant Stockhausen's remarks may be, we need also to reserve some of our obloquy for the woefully inadequate view of interpretation they represent. If one is to interpret the events of 9/11 more fully and satisfyingly, one must leave behind Stockhausen's overly narrow aesthetic understanding and embrace a more robust historical view. Which is not to say that one might not *start* where he starts, with that by-now-iconic image of the planes slamming into the World Trade Center towers. Like the image of the mushroom cloud rising up from Hiroshima, the image of those planes flying into the towers forever altered the consciousness of those who witnessed it. The term "9/11" almost surely evokes that image for most people. And one of the things that makes the image so powerful, and here Stockhausen must again be given his due, has to do with the fact that it is so anomalous. Standing in the TV room of my university's Memorial Union building seeing it for the first time, I turned to my wife and said, almost against my will, "My God, it's like a bad movie." The only "genre" within which symbolic actions of this sort took place in my experience was the Hollywood action film, and it seemed grotesquely inappropriate, a meager and impoverished vehicle for understanding the catastrophe I'd just witnessed. I badly needed to put a frame around this monstrous experience (in German, the word for "monster" is *Ungeheur*, which literally translated is "without limit"), "tame" it by enclosing it, place it in a context that would give it proportion, keep it from escaping and spilling over into daily life. But I couldn't. Stockhausen apparently experienced a similar overwhelming of his cognitive abilities and deemed the experience sublime. Casting about for some term I might see the event "in terms of," I could only imagine something like a Bruce Willis movie.

In the wake of the attack, the media repeatedly, almost obsessively, featured the scene as a lead-in or trailer to their coverage of 9/11. Isolated like that, often in slow motion, the image took on a life of its own, that of pure spectacle detached from history, an image in keeping with Stockhausen's aesthetic vision of the event. In retrospect, it seems probable that the predictable media response to 9/11 was part of the rhetorical design of the attack. It helped solve for the terrorists the crucial problem of audience access, the amplification of their symbolic act. If military strikes are typically designed to maximize the destruction of enemy resources, terrorist attacks are designed to maximize news coverage. Lacking the resources to win a conventional war, terrorists design their acts so as to weaken the will of the domestic population and to win converts worldwide to their cause. Creating attention for the act and controlling the interpretation of the act are critical elements of terrorist strategies, which are based as much on rhetorical as military principles. Hence the IRA practice of timing their attacks in Northern Ireland so as to ensure front-page coverage in the next morning's papers. Ensuring TV coverage of a rhetorical act requires more than the good timing adequate to ensure newspaper coverage; it also requires visually spectacular footage. Spectacle hypes ratings, as acknowledged by the local news mantra "If it bleeds it leads." In a twisted bit of irony, thus, the terrorists used our endless appetite for spectacle and sensationalism to help us terrorize ourselves.

While the 9/11 attacks surely accomplished the first end for al-Quaida, their attempts to achieve the second end, controlling the interpretations of the act, appear to have met with limited success. To be sure, those already inclined to be sympathetic to the al-Quaida cause, their "base" if you will, appear to have been galvanized by the act and took to the streets in celebration and support. To the extent that the act might be termed successful, thus, it achieves its success through a rhetorical strategy known as "merger by division" whereby an attack on a mutual opponent (division) is used to strengthen the bonds (merger) among loosely affiliated parties. In ancient times, scapegoat rituals and tragic dramas followed the logic of merger and division to bring people together. In the twentieth century, the practice has been more thuggishly and less imaginatively employed in various acts of genocide around the world. The shortcomings of the strategy are self-evident and in the wake of the attack created a backlash that made it virtually impossible for the terrorists to maintain control over interpretations of the act. While the targets of the attack, the Pentagon and the World Trade Center, had been carefully chosen so as to signal the symbolic import of the attack—"global capitalism and American military might are bringing ruination to our culture"—the vast majority of people in the world refused to separate the institutional symbols from the thousands of ordinary people who inhabited those buildings.

In this regard, one of the most effective rhetorical responses to the attack took a very simple form that on the surface may not appear to be at all rhetorical. The New York Times, the "local" paper, responded to the dehumanizing of 9/11's victims by giving them all faces in the months following the attack. Not only did the paper limn the heroic deeds performed by police, fire department personnel, and ordinary citizens on 9/11, it featured brief bios on every one of the nearly 3,000 victims, often with pictures and anecdotes from relatives and friends. These weren't obituaries stressing the accomplishments of the deceased so much as tributes of the sort people read at funerals. Such homely accounts gave enormous "presence" to the human, nondoctrinal consequences of the event. Individualizing the victims transformed an abstraction, an anonymous, unthinkable number, into thousands of anecdotes, and turned the terrorists' B-movie cardboard villains into rounded characters of the sort one might encounter in a good book, or in one's own life. Moreover the ethos of the New York Times, a paper frequently critical of Bush administration policies, lent credibility to its interpretation of the event. It seemed unlikely that the paper had set out to "spin" the event so as to help unite the country behind the administration, though their reporters' accounts may well have had that effect. Rather these thumbnail sketches of the victims lent 9/11 a sense of proportion and helped put readers in touch with its tragic dimension, a dimension obscured by its pure spectacle.

The struggle to shape the meaning of 9/11 in its immediate aftermath continues, and promises to continue for a long time. In this regard, the competition to determine what building might replace the World Trade Center constituted a friendly debate among those attempting to eulogize the dead in the most appropriate way. All of the more than 5,000 building designs submitted for consideration were intended to serve not just as spaces where people would live and work, but as rhetorical acts, pieces of ceremonial rhetoric that would help all who contemplated them better understand the significance of 9/11. Thus the design ultimately selected, "Reflecting Absence," eschews monumental structures and instead features two reflecting pools in the spaces where the towers' "footprints" were located in order to make palpable the enormous sense of loss associated with 9/11. The struggle to make sense of this overwhelming event, on the one hand to turn it into a piece of visual propaganda, a recruiting poster for a terrorist cause, and on the other hand to recover a sense of individual suffering and dignity for the victims, underscores a fundamental principle: At the end of the day, those who initially construct rhetorical acts have less say not only about the meaning of their acts, but also about the impact of those acts, than those who interpret them.

How You Construct (an Argument) Is How You Construe (Any Symbolic Act)

The dynamics of interpretation as sketched out above in our discussion of Keats and of Stockhausen's aesthetic response to 9/11 features an eternal tug-of-war between rhetorical readings of poetry, propaganda, history, and so forth, and narrower sorts of reading that would exclude much that rhetoric takes into account. In particular, rhetoric interprets its subjects "in terms of" matters both intrinsic and extrinsic to a text or event while alternative ways of interpretation tend to stress intrinsic matters and to downplay, or even to explicitly exclude, extrinsic matters. These narrower modes of interpretation are comparable to essentialist views of identity discussed in Chapter 2. In that light, what we've been calling the Keatsian imperative can be understood as an essentialist doctrine, an attempt to limit the identity of a work to what it *is*—not what it isn't or what it's like, what it's related to, when and where it exists, or any of the other "innumerable relationships" for which it might serve as an axis. And the struggle between rhetorical and essentialist interpretations of things is not limited to the special category of objects collected under the name "literature." The same struggle goes on in virtually every discipline and knowledge domain including, as we saw in Chapter 1, the law. Always on one side of that struggle are the objectivists or literalists, or formalists, or originalists, those who would limit truth to some one thing—beauty, or whatever is, or math or logic or tradition or an original intention or a singular purpose or the word of one person, institution, or ideology, and so forth—while on the other side are arrayed the tribes of rhetoric and their cousins, those who understand truth as a kind of tenuous balance among multiple forces and perspectives, constantly evolving in response to changes in place and time. By the lights of the latter orientation, truth might be likened to an ecosystem whose survival relies on the maintenance of balance among perspectives within the system and of openness to new forces from outside the system. On the other hand, those who attempt to establish the absolute truth of one element of an interpretive system, subordinate all other elements to The One True Element, and then seal off the system from outside influence are setting up an ecological disaster. Like any closed system, it will eventually succumb to entropy through the dissipation of difference. And while the absence of difference in the physical world leads to energy loss and eventually heat soup, absence of difference in an interpretative system leads to loss of meaning. When everything is X—with X being The One True Element—one's interpretive system is rendered as useless as a one-word dictionary.

Avoiding this fate requires us to seek new perspectives in an intentional and systematic manner. To this end, the approach we use to interpret texts and events in a rhetorical manner is not unlike the approach we used to analyze the rhetorical situation for arguments. How we go about constructing a persuasive case for our view of the world is, inevitably, a creature of the same sensibility and the same procedures that we use to make sense of the world. Or as Ann Berthoff has more economically stated it: "How you construe is how you construct." Not surprisingly, thus, there is a fair amount of overlap between the tools we use to interpret the world and the ones we use to make our case for those interpretations. But whereas the starting point for persuasion is the perception of a difference in understanding between ourselves and another, the starting point of interpretation is the perception of uncertainty in our own understanding. To be sure, the two are sometimes indistinguishable. In cases where our uncertainty arises from an encounter with an interpretation that differs from our own, for example, our first response may be to hear that interpretation as a rival claim and to construct a persuasive response. On the other hand, if an encounter with a different interpretation causes us instead to reexamine our own interpretation and to modify it in order to diminish the sense of uncertainty that the differing interpretation has given rise to, interpretation and persuasion remain distinct activities. Then again, at the limits of persuasion, when it is "pure" it once again becomes indistinguishable from interpretation. In sum, whenever one wrestles with the meaning of a symbolic act and sets out to lessen one's uncertainty rather than to trump a rival or to win over an audience, one is engaged in interpretation. Whatever the source of our uncertainty—be it an interpretation that challenges our own, an encounter with a novel act that does not readily fit any of our mental schema or is not fully explained by our existing interpretive frames, or a change in circumstances or perspective that casts a familiar act in a new light—interpretation is a way of reducing that uncertainty.

The Imperative to Create Uncertainty

Before we set about using interpretation as a means of diminishing uncertainty, we must overcome an even more difficult challenge—recognizing and forcing ourselves to acknowledge that uncertainty actually exists. Until we overcome our powerful resistance to this acknowledgment, the admission that we do not completely understand or comprehend something, our interpretive model cannot be set in motion. And the lessening of uncertainty we obtain at considerable cost through interpretation is readily available to us on the cheap in the form of willful ignorance, denial, and false innocence. So why expend interpretive labors to purchase the comforts of certainty when one can simply refuse to acknowledge challenges to one's assumptions and common sense in the first place? Raising awareness, thus, is the first responsibility of our interpretive model. Occasionally, of course, such an awareness may be involuntarily raised by a drastic challenge from the outside. The Great Depression, thus, forced many people, albeit with great reluctance, to reassess their assumptions about the economy and the role of government in people's lives. Others, however, accept the responsibility to be self-critical, to deliberately and regularly challenge their assumptions about the meanings of things and to remain open to contrary interpretations. And this is not an easy thing to do, not just emotionally as we've already suggested, but cognitively. Some critics, in fact, argue that we are incapable of stepping outside our normal ways of seeing things and adopting an alien perspective on them.

But that said, the costs associated with a failure to modify our interpretations are too high not to try. Otherwise, to paraphrase a memorable line from George Bernard Shaw's *Man and Superman*, we may find that in our blind effort to live, we may be slaying ourselves. Or to borrow a less dramatic, but perhaps more telling version of this sentiment from the field of critical thinking, we may find ourselves being "blocked by openness," whereby the ready availability of a perfectly plausible or workable solution/interpretation prevents us from discovering a better solution/interpretation. Whatever our interpretive model may be, it must raise doubts and initiate self-criticism as readily as it diminishes uncertainty. An interpretative model that lacks the capacity to generate complexity, ambiguity, and other forms of uncertainty would be as unsatisfactory as a persuasive model that lacks the capacity to generate multiple opposing positions on issues. More than a *methodological* imperative, this requirement that our persuasive and interpretative models produce complexity and novel insights even as they also produce efficacious arguments and clarifications is an *ethical* imperative, one whose entailments will be examined shortly.

The dangers of ignoring this imperative can be illustrated with an example from the previous chapter. According to the 9/11 Commission, the interpretation of crucial data in the years and months leading up to the attack was hampered by the fact that the intelligence community engaged in "groupthink." Because of the strong presumption within the community that Iraq possessed and actively sought to expand its store of WMD, they tended to stress evidence that supported that presumption while dismissing or downplaying evidence that disputed it. Because there was no active, systematic challenge to these interpretations from the outside and strong incentives to support them from within, conclusions that at some point in the process may have seemed shaky were eventually promoted to statements of fact. To borrow a term from literary criticism, the intelligence community lacked the means to "defamiliarize" the material they were interpreting, to see it, as it were, for the first time rather than as the fulfillment of well-defined expectations. Like the philosophy of Parmenides, the beliefs of the intelligence community obscured the new, the uncertain, the unfamiliar, or anything that might cause them to question their assumptions. The meaning of what they read was evident the moment their eyes encountered it, and the case they constructed from their reading wasn't so much an interpretation of the material as it was a reiteration of their expectations. In the world of interpretation, thus, familiarity doesn't breed contempt so much as it produces the false innocence of unearned certitude.

All those "innumerable relationships" that our interpretive model invites us to explore should serve simultaneously as a means of creating and diminishing uncertainty. Each relationship for which the text/act serves as an axis marks a difference, and difference gives rise to meaning by requiring us to create a synthesis that reconnects the terms and establishes a new common ground between them. This active model of meaning making is, as always, at odds with the "single-vision" model of interpretation touted by originalists and foundationalists. If, for example, a nineteenth-century text/act is seen connecting a nineteenth-century audience and a twenty-first-century audience, the originalist would simply assimilate the latter to the former, assuming that how the work was understood by the creators/actors and their audience is the one true understanding of the work. To the extent that a twenty-first-century reading might "deviate" from this reading, the originalist would "correct" it. Our own model of interpretation would suggest that twenty-first-century readers should enlarge their understanding of a work by taking earlier interpretations into account and attempting where possible to reconcile the different perspectives and where not possible to at least account for the differences. To paraphrase an earlier account of this process, the meaning of any given text is in part a function of the words on the page and in part a function of every "performance" of those words by a reader with a different set of relationships in mind. Since the relationships for which any text/act may serve as an axis are literally "innumerable," we'll name only a couple of them. Once one understands the basic dynamic, one can readily generate other relationships. But before we examine some specific instances of these innumerable relationships, some clarification is in order.

Tweaking the Text as Axis Metaphor

Up to this point, we've discussed these relationships as if they were binary. And while it's true that these relationships are always reducible to a pair of terms, any given relationship that forms around a symbolic act must finally be understood as a *complex series* of relationships. In this regard the terms connected by a text are like the elements of a rhetorical situation; one can think of them as distinct, like separate fingers, or one can think of them as one interrelated whole, like a hand. Thus, for example, a particular reader's relationship to a particular text is necessarily a relationship as well between the time and place of the reader and the time and place in which the text was written and, if the time and place in which the text is set is different from the time and place in which it was written, that third temporal dimension will also figure in. Which is precisely the relationship that exists when a twenty-first-century American reads a nineteenth-century Englishman, John Keats, writing about a fifth-century B.C. Greek urn.

A second possibly misleading aspect of our "text-as-axis" metaphor has to do with the presumed passivity of "axes," which are generally conceived of as lines around which other elements may, literally or figuratively, be arranged. In the case of symbolic acts, that characterization misses the mark. When symbolic acts serve as axes, they don't simply *describe* connections between points, they *generate* connections and actively influence our understanding of the connected points. They are simultaneously objects of our perception and ways of perceiving or "equipment for living," instruments through which objects are examined, interpreted, and understood. They cause us to see things—including themselves—differently. In order to interpret a truly original symbolic act, we have to learn how to read in a new way, a way that the work itself must teach us to perform. And that new way of reading will inevitably carry over into our perceptions of ordinary life. An extreme version of this process was spelled out by Oscar Wilde, who has a character in "Decay of the Art of Lying" declare that London's "brown fogs" did not exist until the Impressionists painted them. Most rhetoricians, while admiring Wilde's use of hyperbole to gain attention for his point, would "get off before the end of the line" that Wilde journeys to. It smacks too heartily of subjective idealism to meet rhetoric's realistic, socially based standards of truth. In the case of Wilde's "wonderful fogs," Impressionism would certainly receive credit for getting people to notice them; but industrial pollution should get at least some of the credit for coloring London's actual evenings. While the world that lies beyond our perceptions, our imaginings, and our language is impossible to articulate and is knowable only through its immutable recalcitrance, it still demands our attention in the same way that the actual lives lost on 9/11, known to most of us only secondarily through unthinkable images, demand our attention. The manipulation of physical reality solely through the medium of language is a trick rhetoric leaves to magicians.

Text-to-Text and Text-to-Type Relationships

With these caveats in mind, let us return to the basic dynamic of interpretation as it is expressed through innumerable relationships. We'll begin with a relationship of one text to another. By looking at Keats's poem "in terms of" other poems, those that are part of his own oeuvre and those of other poets from other times and places, we change the valences of both, causing some elements to stand out and others to recede in importance. If we were to look at his poem in relationship to a poem by, say, Alexander Pope, who less than a century earlier wrote odes of his own, what would stand out would be differences—in shape and length of the poems, scansion and meter, point of view and tone, and most importantly "gist." To call Keats's poems revolutionary is in one way simply a summing up of all the important differences between Keats and Pope and those of their respective ilk. What makes such a comparison especially meaningful, however, is their relative proximity to one another in time and geography. While we expect to see differences between texts widely separated by time and space, we don't expect to find such striking differences between texts originating in the same place over a relatively brief time span.

A second relationship involves a fairly straightforward extension of the relationship of one text to another. In addition to one-to-one relationships, groups of texts may be "typed" by virtue of their numerous shared traits. The typology that has perhaps the greatest influence on interpretation is that of genre. Because the conventions of textual genres are more overt and codified than the conventions of other typologies, they shape our expectations of what will be said and how it will be said in particularly powerful ways. These generic expectations may then interact with expectations derived from less formalized categories—for example, historical and geographical proximity, ideological similarities, shared subject matter—to reinforce particular interpretations.

In the case of Keats's poem, for example, its generic typology as an ode and its ideological typology as a Romantic poem interact to reinforce one of the major themes of Romanticism. Or, more precisely, by confounding certain of our expectations about the generic conventions of the ode, Keats calls attention to an important thematic novelty in the poem that is in turn symptomatic of an important ideological shift that we've come to call Romanticism. As contemporary readers, we may not be familiar with the poetic conventions that Keats was manipulating here, so we need once again to identify with the time and the place of the poem's origin and ask ourselves what his contemporary readers might have expected of something called an "ode." It is an ancient poetic form, one that can be traced back to Pindar and the sixth century B.C. Traditionally it was a very formal, highly conventional verse associated with important public occasions and celebrations of illustrious personages. What is surprising about Keats's ode, and the odes written by his fellow Romantics, is the shift from a public to a private focus. They used the form not to honor royalty but to mark existential moments of great stress or epiphanic moments of personal revelation. These "deviations" from the conventions of the ode called nineteenth-century audiences' attention to a meaningful difference—the Romantic shift of the reality principle from outside to inside the mind. By using for the celebration of private moments a form traditionally reserved for the celebration of public events, Romantics construct a formal analogue for their epistemological, ultimately social revolution.

Because we always attend more consciously to the unexpected and the strange than to the predictable and familiar, one of the surest ways of redirecting audience attention is to judiciously violate familiar generic conventions. And when, as in Keats's case, an individual author's deviations are taken up by contemporaries, the thematic implications of the shift are further reinforced. In fact, what we've just described is the dynamic whereby literary epochs, like Romanticism, are distinguished from one another. Each epoch privileges certain genres and certain ways of departing from the earlier conventions of those genres, teaching us new ways of seeing in the process.

Specialist and Nonspecialist Strategies of Interpretation

The sort of interpretive strategies implied by the above relationships requires at least a rudimentary knowledge of literary history and criticism. Genres are not, after all, intuitive categories; they are self-consciously constructed and sedulously maintained by members of communities sometimes referred to as "interpretive communities." Knowledge of genre is just one example of the sort of thing one has to understand before one can claim membership in such a community. When "interpretive communities" form around a well-defined corpus of texts and subject matters, one is typically required to know a stock set of interpretive strategies and basic historical information that might serve as the basis of interpretive claims within that community. Literary criticism and the law are obvious examples of such communities; in fact every academic discipline comprises such a community. Or, more precisely, "communities." No such community can long remain monolithic. Because of class differences among members arising from their varied socioeconomic background, gender, ethnicity, national heritage, and so forth; because of differences in education and training; and because of purely idiosyncratic personal differences among community members, different schools of interpretation and competing theories of meaning inevitably arise. Unless one has mastered a broad understanding of a given community's requirements and the specific approach of a given subcommunity, usually through extensive formal training and apprenticeship, one will have difficulty finding a voice within that community.

But many of the "innumerable relationships" that one might explore by way of interpreting a symbolic act are accessible without specialized knowledge or membership in a formally constituted community that prizes such knowledge. One can interpret all sorts of symbolic acts, even literary texts, without formal training or the assistance of highly restricted interpretive communities. Many of the interpretive communities we inhabit—groups of people talking over coffee after they watched a movie together, families sitting around a dinner table remembering a favorite book; students in a college dorm room arguing about an essay in their econ class or a presidential candidate's campaign speech—are not formally constructed and require no specialized knowledge of their members. In such settings we may rely on relationships between the object of discussion and recently shared personal experiences or public events, other works known to the group, or even analogies and hypotheticals to better understand the work. By these less formal means, we may well reach conclusions and explanations not unlike those reached by members of more formalized communities using more esoteric tools.

Undoubtedly the most common relationship each of us uses to make sense of the texts we read is their relationship to other texts that we've read. And to be related, those texts need not belong to any of the standard typologies invoked by literature professors. Or if they do, we don't have to know the names of those categories in order to find salient points of contact between the two. Personal experience, even if it is highly idiosyncratic, can serve a function similar to that of a shared text, providing we can construct a shareable narrative account of that experience. And all of us draw on personal experience, including our own idiosyncratic reading history, to help us diminish our uncertainty over a new text that puzzles us. Thus, for example, when I saw the film *Cold Mountain*, I kept flashing back to Homer's *Odyssey*, a work I have not read since high school. Seeing Anthony Minghella's film "in terms of" Homer's epic strongly influenced my interpretation. It helped me place the film in a particular emotional register, to render plausible some of its more magical moments, and to accept the loose, episodic nature of its plot. And the conclusion of the movie, by deviating from Homer's epic, puzzled and engaged me and forced me to refocus my interpretation on differences between the two texts. OK, I am an English professor and this is the sort of thing I'm trained to do, but I don't think my training had much to do with my recognition of a story I haven't read since high school or the simple pleasure I took in recognizing patterns, or the more complex pleasure I experienced when my expectations weren't met and I was forced to construct an explanation for the deviation. (*Cold Mountain*'s darker conclusion has, I think, to do with the changed nature of war and the changed attitudes toward war and warriors from Homer's time to ours. The particularly violent, notably unheroic battle scene that opens the movie anticipates the hero's more or less random death in the film's climactic scene, underscoring the futility of war. The real heroes of the movie are the women who wait for the hero's return, the latter-day Penelopes who outwit rather than destroy the enemy and reclaim the neglected land for fruitful uses.)

In a similar vein, all of us have the experience of reading a book at one point in our lives and responding to the same book very differently when we encounter it later in life. More often than not, we find ourselves less enamored of books the second time around. They don't "hold up" for us. When I first read Ayn Rand's *Atlas Shrugged* as a high school student, for example, I thought it both fascinating and profound. But when I reread the book many years and many novels—not to mention many works of politics and economics—later, I found it contrived and mean-spirited. The novel's hero subscribed to once-unpopular beliefs that had achieved respectability—indeed among a hard-core constituency, those beliefs constitute a sort of religious orthodoxy—during the interval between my first and second readings; and as is so often the case with once-subversive beliefs that become mainstream, they had lost their edge and struck me as highly inflated. The many public figures who now echoed the hero's sentiments looked and sounded less like him than like the book's altogether disagreeable villains; and the triumph of his ideology seemed to be having the most baneful consequences for the least-fortunate among us. Moreover, the hero's love interest now seemed cloyingly unreal, and his antagonists appeared to be made of cardboard.

The foregoing is less a professional judgment than a personal observation. I offer up no support for my dim view of this perennial bestseller and seek no one else's endorsement of it. I cite it merely to illustrate a general point: How we read a given text is a function of the other texts we've read and the experiences we've had, and as the latter change over time, so will the former. (In fact, I chose this example to illustrate this particular point mostly because I was reminded of it by another book I was reading, Tobias Woolf's *Old School*, which recounts an incident in the life of a young man similarly infatuated with Rand's philosophy who is abruptly disenchanted after a disastrously funny encounter with the author.) This shifting relationship between our histories and our interpretative acts means that we may find it necessary to discount our own earlier interpretations of a text just as we discount others' interpretations. Indeed, one of the most interesting of the "innumerable relationships" that one establishes through reading texts is the one we maintain with our earlier selves. Who, I wonder, was that young man who thought so highly of Ayn Rand's political potboiler? In some cases, I've found that my disagreements with my own earlier reading of a text are stronger than any disagreement I might have with another reader over the same text.

This last example calls attention to another crucial nonspecialist relationship fostered by texts: the one that forms among readers of texts. In this regard, the British writer C. S. Lewis once said that "We read in order to know that we are not alone," a statement that can be understood in at least a couple of ways. In the first, the reading of texts is an important way for us to reaffirm that our silent inner world of unexpressed observations, understandings, judgments, and so forth, is shareable and real, having found expression in the texts that we read. In texts that affect us most profoundly, we may sometimes feel as if we are reading ourselves, as if voice were being given to feelings and ideas that we possess—or that possess us—but that we could not articulate. This sort of intimate relationship between readers and texts is probably not the norm, however. For most readers, Lewis' statement suggests a different sort of relationship, a relationship that the text enables with other readers. Such relationships are formally established in classes where all of us read and discuss the same works, or less formally in book clubs or discussion groups where texts are discussed for pleasure or personal development or simply camaraderie. Or sometimes in connection with our work, we may read books about the things we do and discuss them with colleagues, formally or informally, by way of seeing how they might apply to our own situation. When we read others' reviews or criticisms of texts we ourselves have read, we are in a sense in conversation with them about the text. And we may be so moved by others' remarks that we feel compelled to respond in writing and give voice to our agreement or disagreement.

When we relate to other people through a text, it can serve as a touchstone by which we measure their perspicuity or character or gauge their potential compatibility. (I recall a friend and former colleague who once opined that people claiming to find Jane Austen boring should never be invited for dinner.) More often, influence flows in the other direction, such that our relationships with other people cause us to modify our views of texts. When people we like recommend books to us, we may read them more charitably than we otherwise might. And vice versa. Or when friends explain their view of a book, they may force us to rethink the particulars of our own view. Also, our responses to characters in a text may well be influenced by their similarities to people we've encountered in our own experiences. If the protagonist of a text bears a striking resemblance to the tenth-grade math teacher we loathed, we may find it difficult to identify with her point of view. And if the figure of fun in a text looks uncomfortably like ourselves in some of our lesser moments, we may forgive him in ways the author cannot. We are not, to be sure, prisoners of our personal histories, our reading experiences, or our sundry idiosyncracies, but inevitably we will be influenced by them. They mark the starting point of our conversation with the text before us and ultimately with others with whom we've shared the text. Through that conversation we may come to understand both the text and ourselves differently.

Ethics and Interpretation

The history of ethics is deeply intertwined with the history of rhetoric in Western culture. Both ways of thinking are born out of the emergence of philosophy from myth, and both ways of thinking, initially at least, encourage an iconoclastic turn of mind. Whereas myth privileges piety over criticism and tradition over novelty, rhetoric and ethics celebrate the power of critical thought as a means of freeing ourselves from the notion that history is destiny. Thus it is that one of the first important rhetorical works takes the form of a heterodoxical reading of Homer. And so it is also that several of the most important ancient Greek playwrights delighted in challenging the ethical assumptions of Greek myth by revising the traditional stories (mythoi) and by shifting audience sympathies to figures and viewpoints shortchanged by myth. Connections between rhetoric and ethics remain visible even today, though ethics, by virtue of its greater respectability and tendency to "bureaucratize" into ethical systems and dogma, may not always retain its iconoclastic edge. But in the area of interpretation one can still recognize the interdependence of ethics and rhetoric insofar as both struggle to increase the scope of human freedom by distinguishing between myth and practice, between what *must* be done and what *ought* to be done, between "the way things are" and "the way things might be."

When discussing ethics and interpretation, we need first to distinguish between an ethic of interpretation and interpretation as a tool of ethics. We already touched on this first relationship when we underscored the interpreter's obligation to resist "single-vision" readings resting on one-to-one correspondences between words and truths and a belief in the absolute and eternal certainty of those correspondences. However reassuring the certitudes promised by such approaches, they foreclose all possibility of further conversation about the significance of whatever has been definitively interpreted. And once the conversation ceases, as we have argued in previous chapters, peaceful means of bringing about change or extending awareness are rendered impotent. When we refer to an ethic of interpretation, thus, we are referring mostly to the obligation placed on interpreters to keep the conversation alive by resisting closure and absolute certainty even as they work to diminish uncertainty.

In some sense, the shift from an emphasis on an ethic of interpretation to interpretation as a tool of ethics is simply a shift from seeing interpretation "in terms of" ethics to seeing ethics "in terms of" interpretation. In making this shift, there is necessarily a corresponding shift in emphasis from a stress on the symbolic character of the acts being interpreted to their existential character. There are symbolic associations with any human act and real human consequences to any symbolic act. The two dimensions are, as we saw in the case of 9/11, inextricably bound up with each other. To ignore either one impairs both one's interpretation of the act and one's ethical judgment of the act. When Karlheinz Stockhausen ignores the human consequences of 9/11, he illustrates one version of this fallacy; but focusing on human consequences of an act without fully exploring its interpretive possibilities can be equally harmful. Sound ethical judgments rest on thoughtful interpretations as surely as rich interpretations take ethical implications into account.

To illustrate the importance of sound interpretations to ethical judgment, we return to 9/ll and consider the act from the perspective of those who chose to crash planes into buildings. To understand that act fully, we must first try to identify with the actors as best we can; given the heinous nature of their act, this will be difficult. But ethics and interpretation alike require some sort of imaginative identity with the object of attention, be it a passage in a novel or a terrorist act. We have to suspend judgment long enough to size up the event properly, understand it in terms of as many other relationships as we can muster, and consider it as one of many choices possible within a field of choices. What is the act in response to? What motivated the actors? How is the act like/unlike other acts of its kind? What other options did the actors have before them? To what in my own experience can I liken the act? What conclusions have others who have examined the act reached about its meaning? These are just a few of the questions one might put to the event by way of interpreting it fully.

Let us take up the question of motivation as we consider the process of interpretation that brought the hijackers to choose their course of action. In response to what was the act committed? One of the difficulties of understanding terrorist acts as opposed to warlike acts of nation-states has to do with the causes and motivations of the act. Wars between nations are usually preceded by lengthy periods of negotiation over specific sets of issues and a gradual escalation of hostilities. While nations are not always forthcoming about their real motives for risking war, there is usually some rational pretense for war. This is not always the case with terrorist acts. While some are explicitly designated as responses to actions taken by the targeted state, many are not. The attack of 9/11 falls into the latter category. While our military presence in the Middle East is often cited as a concern, many of the manifestos issued by al-Quaida point toward more fundamental concerns—religious, cultural, and economic—underlying their hostility. It's not altogether clear how those differences might be peacefully settled. As indicated by the extremity of the act—the scale of the destruction and their own willingness to die in the process—and the targets of the act, the actors' sense of grievance is profound. We are seen as a threat not just to the sovereignty of their region but to their very way of life, most specifically to their religious beliefs.

But assuming that their interpretation is accurate, that their way of life is indeed threatened by American hegemony, what ethical system justifies their response and their slaughter of so many innocents? As many Muslim religious leaders were quick to point out in the aftermath of 9/11, there is little support in Muslim doctrine for acts such as these, and the few interpretations of the doctrine that might justify it are not widely shared. In the language of international law, the terrorists' might argue that some sort of response was "necessary" to the group's survival, but was it "proportional" to the grievances they suffered? Does 9/11 represent the best of all possible ethical choices for those nineteen men who hijacked the planes and their collaborators? Certainly some ethical systems would be more tolerant of such acts than others. For example, an ethical system based on the principle of "an eye for an eye, and a tooth for a tooth" might be invoked to warrant such an act. But before that principle could be invoked, one would need to size up the situation fully. One would need to link the suffering of those in whose name the nineteen men claimed to act to American policies and actions. The more tenuous those links, the less clearly the principle applies.

By the same token, one wonders what, if any, alternatives warranted by their own ethical code the terrorists might have considered.

In this regard, we return to one of those fundamental rhetorical questions mentioned in Chapter 2: " 'Compared to what' was the destruction of the World Trade Center the best choice?" Certainly history provides alternatives to massive carnage for the liberation of oppressed peoples. A little over a half century ago in India, Mahatma Gandhi combined nonviolent, passive resistance with an active program of economic reforms to rid his country of colonial domination. To be sure, his model would require significant modification to meet the different circumstances facing Muslim countries. But that's the very sort of "discounting" that rhetorical interpretation prepares us to do.

When sound rhetorical practices are combined with a strong ethical commitment—an ideal that Aristotle cited to justify instruction in rhetoric—the result will be the triumph of virtue. Or at the very least, a stalemate with unscrupulous but skilled rhetoricians. But just as surely as a weak moral commitment can result in efficacious but corrupt arguments, too strong a commitment to overly narrow principles can result in inefficacious arguments with horrifying consequences. This second case is of greater interest to rhetoric in part because it is more prevalent. Few people, after all, set out to be evil; more often, evil is the unintended consequence of people's unswerving allegiance to rigid and flawed ideals. When people's guiding ethical principles are so clear and unambiguous that their choices are never uncertain, alternatives are obscured and moderation is ruled unnecessary. Interpretation in such cases is reduced to little more than information processing. In the case of terrorists, one sees an extreme instance of this habit of mind.

For all the overlap between ethics and rhetoric, they remain distinct activities. The rhetorical imperatives to test out incongruous perspectives, to find the available means of persuasion, and to keep the conversation alive are both more specific and less binding than ethical imperatives to "Do unto others" or to "Act as you would have all others act." The rhetorical imperatives are more specific in that simply imagining ourselves in another's shoes, feeling their pain as it were, is not enough; we are required to think like others, multiple others, for extended periods of time, long enough to arrive at some conclusions about what interpretations they would find plausible and why, what claims they would find appealing and why. But the rhetorical imperatives are less binding in that we may in the end choose not to act on our identification with others when it comes time to offer our own arguments or interpretations. To the contrary, I may choose to use what I've learned about others to deceive them or to offer them a view that appeals to their least-noble impulses. There is, in sum, no rhetorical imperative to *be* ethical.

Before concluding with an extended examination of an issue lying at the intersection of ethics and interpretation, we offer a reminder of the trait that most clearly links the two activities: their mutual rejection of a necessary vision that dictates what "must" be in favor of a plausible vision of what "can" or "ought" to be. The inability to escape from or even to challenge a single vision of religious texts precludes terrorist entry into a conversation where war might be "purified" into persuasion. In lieu of dialogue, they can either secede from civilization or issue proclamations and launch violent attacks. Unwilling to discount their own or others' interpretations, they can only defend themselves by force. Terrorism is, in sum, a dramatic instance of what happens when one party tries to impose its vocabulary, its interpretation of the world, on everyone else. What we turn to next is a less dramatic, but more pervasive example of a similar phenomenon.

Political Correctness—Spawn of Doublespeak

In the context of this discussion, political correctness (PC) refers to a form of disputed language use. But unlike disputes about definition discussed under the rubric of persuasion ("What does it mean?"), the PC dispute concerns an entire vocabulary associated with an ideology—albeit a very loosely defined one. Those who protest PC—we'll call them PC-protestors for convenience's sake—reject the ideology and argue that describing the world in the language of PC gives rise to wildly misleading interpretations involving the systematic substitution of euphemisms for perfectly workable terms in the name of not offending some popular belief or class of people. Commit a questionable breach of linguistic etiquette, PC-protestors complain, and some self-appointed guardians of political correctness—we'll call them PC-proponents for convenience's sake—are sure to cry "Gotcha!", thereby derailing a potentially substantive discussion and leaving everyone who used or condoned the offending language feeling annoyed, or guilty, or both. PC-proponents, in the view of PC-protestors, would be assigned the same level of hell as those Grammar Nazis (itself a term unlikely to pass muster with a moderately diligent PC-proponent) who correct our split infinitives midsentence.

At least that's the currently dominant view of PC's pernicious effects. And like most popular conceptions, it's not without a basis in reality. Many of us have found ourselves at various times criticized for failing to observe some piety we didn't know existed until we'd violated it. Clearly these more heavy-handed attempts at imposing a PC vocabulary on conversations are worthy of PC-protestors' scorn. And for people presumably sensitive to the impacts of language on our understanding of the world, PC-proponents have been slow to acknowledge how decisively the adoption of their vocabulary would prejudice the outcome of a discussion. We'll return to the share of culpability properly owned by PC-proponents in this dispute later in the discussion. But for now, we shift the critical focus of this discussion to the foibles of the PC-protestors. The latter group, it will be argued, is guilty of many of the same transgressions that it charges against PC-proponents, and the vocabulary it uses to interpret the world is no less misleading—often, in fact, it is more inaccurate and more misleading.

Popular acceptance of the viewpoint promoted by PC-protestors, the general scorn for attitudes considered "PC," and the tendency to overlook PC-protestors' foibles and inaccuracies are at least partly attributable to their alignment with a traditional view of language that has long dominated our culture. That tradition privileges "common sense" over subtle (i.e., casuistic) analysis and "plainspokenness" over complexity of language. In opposition to pettifoggers and trimmers, blusterers and bafflegabbers who would dazzle us with verbiage or mislead us with jargon, Americans have long esteemed those who speak clear and simple truths from their hearts. One of our most cherished novels, *Huckleberry Finn*, embodies this theme in a particularly acute and humorous way. But the tradition extends far back in time beyond Mark Twain. The British preference for simple Saxon words over a more "Frenchified," Latinate vocabulary has been pronounced at least since Chaucer's day. But in the interest of brevity, we pick up the tradition in nineteenth-century England and a figure whose hostility to euphemism anticipates the fiercest of PC-protestors.

The redoubtable utilitarian philosopher Jeremy Bentham certainly deserves pride of place in any discussion about the triumph of the plainspoken man bent on "telling it like it is" (a phrase popularized in the early 1970s by sportscaster Howard Cosell, who was, ironically enough, a blustery self-promoter of Barnumesque proportion) or, in Bentham's own language, on preventing "unearned increments" of meaning from being smuggled into the language. (Unfortunately, given his commitment to transparency, Bentham's own prose is famously opaque.) What Bentham sought from language is what people of his ilk have always sought from it—absolute clarity. He was as vexed by metaphors as the earlier mentioned Sprat, who attempted to have them outlawed in

Parliament. By conjuring up associations, metaphors surreptitiously load the dice, inclining readers' sympathies one way or another without ever stating one's position on a matter. He refers thus to "question-begging appellatives" that possess either "dyslogistic" or "eulogistic" connotations that assume what remains to be proved—the goodness or badness of the idea or person modified by the appellative. In response, Bentham set out to develop a purely neutral language with no "unearned increments" of meaning. To that end he constructed an elaborate table, featuring three sets of terms that might be substituted for one another in given circumstances: dyslogistic terms, eulogistic terms, and neutral terms. Thus one might describe a six-foot, 145-pound male as "skinny" or "bony" (dyslogistic), "lithe" or "fit" (eulogistic), or "slender" (neutral). Depending on one's choice of terms, one's seemingly innocent descriptor will prejudice one's audience for or against one's subject.

From the vantage point of the present century, Bentham's table may look more than a bit goofy, a wondrously complex mechanism that accomplishes little. Or, conversely, the table may put some in mind of a more sinister resemblance. Bentham, it will be recalled, also designed the "Panopticon," a prison in which a single observer could maintain constant surveillance of prisoners without himself being observed. His table could serve the role of the tireless, all-seeing observer of the Panopticon, a figure with a number of unhappy associations for denizens of an age in which privacy is an increasingly prized and threatened commodity. Just try to smuggle some dyslogistic or eulogistic meaning past Bentham's table! But who gets to create the table and determine the valences of every word? (Or who gets to determine who is the prisoner and who is the observer?) Language is a creature of a community, a social construct, and is gloriously unstable, undergoing constant evolution through actual usage in changing circumstances. How can one person be arbiter of its infinite inflections and faithful recorder of all its changes? The fact that many terms in Bentham's table have disappeared from usage while many more have changed valences testifies to the futility of Bentham's project.

All that said, Bentham's attempt to put the matter of usage on a scientific basis, as if words were like elements in the Periodic Table, is not to be dismissed out of hand. He is calling attention to an important, and easily overlooked, rhetorical principle that we've already encountered: terminologies are lenses through which we see the world. Inevitably they serve both to express and to shape our valuation of matters even if we don't intend them to. His mistake, and it is a hardy perennial, was to believe in the existence of a neutral language, an ideal language in residence elsewhere, not one in actual use, available for describing the world. Meanwhile Bentham himself was blind to the "unearned increments" of meaning that permeated his own utilitarian vocabulary, whose systematic bias caused him to privilege quantifiable measures of human happiness over qualitative measures, a prejudice that, for example, caused him to rate the game of pushpin over poetry as a source of happiness. (Charles Dickens' novels feature a number of characters, notably the schoolmaster Gradgrind in *Hard Times*, who richly illustrate the defects of a Benthamite vocabulary in the everyday world.)

But the mistake Bentham makes is not simply hypocrisy or logical inconsistency. In setting out to unmask a world full of "question-begging appellatives," Bentham sets a standard for usage that no one, including he, could meet. All language, particularly all language that matters to us, requires discounting and interpretation that takes actual usage into account. A neutral language without connotation or emotional coloring, without ambiguity, never in need of discounting or interpretation does not exist. Technical-scientific language comes as close as we can to such an ideal (if one can think of this goal as an ideal), but the stringency of its denotation is purchased at the expense of its scope. Few people can use the language, and its application to significant human problems by those who can use it has had some disastrous consequences.

In the twentieth century, Bentham's dream of a neutral language faded, though it never disappeared. While there appear to be few active attempts to create something like his table, the possibility of a neutral language exists as an unstated assumption or belief in the minds of many. Perhaps the most famous twentieth-century attempt to expose the presence of unearned increments of meaning in language came in the form of George Orwell's novel *1984*, a look (in 1948) at a futuristic dystopia marked by "Newspeak," a government-imposed language that reflected orthodoxy and rendered critical thought impossible. Newspeak is a transcendently euphemistic language that makes palatable even the most objectionable government actions. A forced labor camp, thus, is termed a "joycamp," a "question-begging appellative" if ever there was one. In an earlier essay, "Politics and the English Language," Orwell makes clear that language can't be completely neutral—he admits committing some of the very sins against language that he assigns his enemies—but he does believe it can be more transparent. The problem, according to Orwell, is that in the twentieth century, governments are often in the position of "defending the indefensible" and must themselves use propaganda on their own people. (In *1984* there is a "Ministry of Truth" with a "Fiction Department.")

Consequently, governments use language primarily to obscure reality and reinforce political orthodoxy. So, like Bentham, Orwell sees language abuse on a massive scale; unlike Bentham, he does not promote the possibility of neutral language and he emphasizes the use of what Bentham calls "eulogistic coverings" (singling out the most positive possible motive to "cover" for many complex motives), almost to the exclusion of "dyslogistic" elements.

The concept "doublespeak," meanwhile, which Orwell did not coin, is strongly associated with the philosophy of language articulated in 1984 and in "Politics and the English Language." Doublespeak is evasive language, language that gives every appearance of imparting information without actually doing so. It's typically inflated and euphemistic and in its most egregious forms, the product of some large institution frantically covering its derriere. Thus, for example, many terms of art from contemporary management, terms like "rightsizing," are used to cloak brutal business practices in the mantle of pseudoscientific terminology. In the wake of Watergate and Vietnam, two avoidable catastrophes that led to derriere-covering on a massive scale, it was difficult to ignore countless examples of doublespeak. Once government proved to be less trustworthy than we had long assumed, we began actively to seek in its bureaucratic jargon the more sinister motives we now suspected it of. Annual awards were given facetiously for the most heinous examples of doublespeak culled from news sources.

Clearly, doublespeak and political correctness name similar sorts of linguistic chicanery. The shift from one to the other is largely a shift in ideological emphasis. When more liberal commentators catch a more conservative source in some presumed linguistic evasion, they will probably label it "doublespeak." When more conservative commentators catch a more liberal source in some presumed linguistic evasion, they will probably label it "political correctness." The fact that doublespeak "plays" less well and less often these days, the fact that even egregious instances of doublespeak slip by unchallenged, while the mildest instances of PC are relentlessly rooted out and condemned, has mainly to do with politics. The fate of the two terms reflects shifts in America's political landscape. Over the past thirty years, conservatism arose from its previously moribund state to become a powerful political force with a clear message; liberalism meanwhile became a less powerful political force with a less clear message. Ironically, it has gotten so bad that many erstwhile liberals have taken to calling themselves "progressives," itself arguably a move open to the charge of doublespeak, in hopes of distancing themselves from a term identified with numerous unpopular causes, including political correctness. And the fact that even liberals themselves, sometimes at the expense of their professed political ideals, charge others with PC underscores the conservative victory in the "vocabulary wars."

The direction of causality is probably two-way here. Charges against PC-proponents broadly resonate because more people share the assumptions of those who file the charges. But PC-protestors have won many of those same people over by invoking the powerful rhetorical strategy that underlies their campaign. One of the major rhetorical advantages enjoyed by PC over doublespeak has to do with the subtlety of its critique. Whereas the charge of doublespeak suggests that one has committed a sinister offense against language to cover up a grave reality, the charge of political correctness suggests that one has clouded a serious issue with trivial language. The insistence, for example, on the part of those who support a woman's right to an abortion that they are "pro-choice" is rejected by those who oppose abortion on the grounds that a woman's right to choose pales in importance next to a child's (not the "fetus's") right to live. Those who uphold PC are thereby doubly guilty of distortion and insignificance, of deceiving people about a substantive matter in the name of a bloodless orthodoxy and a commitment to mere "correctness." Hence the desirability of being "politically *in*correct" insofar as it marks one as a bold soul, independent and iconoclastic, above any concern for mere linguistic etiquette. (There is no comparable virtue attached to using "*single*speak.") PC-proponents, in the language of Chapter 2, don't *act* on behalf of their beliefs as do the politically incorrect, they *behave* in conformity with those beliefs. Or at least in theory that's how it works. In fact, the assignment of the politically incorrect epithet is determined by the orthodoxy of the act more than by its boldness. Take the case of Bill Maher, host of a television show called *Politically Incorrect*, who suggested that the 9/11 terrorists had displayed "courage" in carrying out their mission. His bold, plain-spoken remarks raised such a firestorm, in particular from those on the right, that his show was canceled. He was guilty, in short, of the wrong sort of bold plainspokenness, and had offended the wrong set of pieties. More recently, University of Colorado professor Ward Churchill, who characterized the victims of 9/11 as capitalist tools and "little Eichmann's," similarly failed to earn the politically incorrect epithet.

Not only is a charge of PC more dismissive than a charge of doublespeak, it is considerably vaguer. Whereas doublespeak always refers to specific acts of language use, PC is often invoked to critique attitudes, behaviors, and policies at a more general level. I've heard the term applied to everything from the University of Michigan law school's commitment to diversity, to a colleague's insistence that search committee members quit referring to female job applicants by their first names and male job applicants by their last names. All of which makes it devilishly difficult to refute a charge of PC. In defending oneself against a charge of doublespeak, one can limit one's argument to the particulars of the case in which the disputed language was used. In defending oneself against a charge of PC, meanwhile, one is also required to defend one's motivation, which inevitably makes one look defensive, and to persuade people that the language we use to describe the world has real effects on our perception of the world, which is not a widely understood or popular notion. If doublespeakers are charged with evasion, PC'ers are charged with a deeply flawed, and worse yet, a relentlessly shallow worldview.

When charging someone with PC, we are doing three things: (1) we are "unmasking" putative descriptive terms, revealing them to be persuasive claims; (2) we are establishing a binary opposition between the offending term and what it "really says," such that the second completely negates the first, thereby rendering the speaker guilty of bad faith at best, downright deceitfulness at worst; (3) we are implying that the particular offense is part of a larger ideological agenda. (The charge of doublespeak seeks to achieve the first two ends without necessarily seeking the third.) This process can be seen perhaps most clearly when the terms that draw the ire of PC-protestors refer to race and gender. In the early days, even before the rhetorical ploy of PC was available for use, the substitution of "person" for "man" as a universal referent galled nascent PC-protestors. The word "chairperson" would be spoken sneeringly, and if one were to say, for example, "repairperson" as opposed to "repairman," it would be drawled back at one ensconced in scare quotes. More recently, the use of the term "people of color" has raised the ire of PC-protestors. Those who used the term to refer to large groups comprising multiple races were seen as ideologues using trendy jargon to cover up a reality better captured by a more traditional term. The fact that new terms were in every case more faithful to the reality they represented than were the traditional terms did nothing to stop the criticism. While at one time those who chaired departments, committees, and programs were indeed overwhelmingly male, a growing number are now female, just as those who repair things are increasingly female. And in contemporary America, the rich racial mixtures represented by many of our citizens often elude traditional labels even when referring to a particular individual. When talking about large groups of individuals who are African-American, Middle Eastern, Asian, American Indian, and Hispanic, and all possible mixtures of races, none of the traditional terms is adequate to the task. The sometimes sinister consequences of PC-protestors' vocabulary choices are more clearly seen in the case of words used to describe people's "sexual orientation." The latter term, the term used by the American Psychological Association to describe "enduring emotional, romantic, sexual or affectional attraction to another person," is, as it turns out, contested by PC-protestors, who would rather we refer to gay and lesbian sexuality as a "sexual lifestyle" rather than a "sexual orientation." While the word "orientation" may or may not connote choice, the word "lifestyle" is highly associative of consumer matters and free-market choices. Our choice, for example, of Ralph Lauren's "Carib" paint in a semigloss enamel over Martha Stewart's "Belize" in a flat latex, is an exemplary lifestyle choice. And the matter of choice is exactly what PC-protestors would like to underscore. Only if one's sexuality is a matter of choice can gay and lesbian behavior be deemed deviant, a disorder rather than, well, an orientation. But the American Psychological Association and the American Psychiatric Association removed homosexuality from their lists of mental and emotional "disorders" not just because they found no mental or emotional pathologies associated with sexual orientation, but because scientific evidence did not support the belief that we can choose our sexual orientation. The question of treating a condition that was neither debilitating nor corrigible was thereby rendered moot.

In words taken from the American Psychological Association Web site, ". . . human beings can not choose to be gay or straight," a conclusion that most of us can probably validate in our personal experience. In all likelihood, few heterosexuals awoke one morning at age fourteen or so, looked in the bathroom mirror, and announced to the world that they, by golly, had chosen to pursue a "heterosexual lifestyle." And probably fewer yet were sufficiently emboldened by their pronouncement to further suggest that they might even pursue a "heterosexual agenda." But if one chooses to be gay or lesbian, surely heterosexuals (including those who reject the notion of sexual orientation) must also have chosen in some fashion to be straight. And who could blame them for choosing to be straight? Why, one wonders, given the widespread homophobia in American society, would anyone choose to be gay or lesbian given all the stigmas, penalties, and dangers attached to that choice? To insist that sexuality is a choice flies in the face of scientific evidence, ignores most people's experience of not making a conscious

choice, and justifies unequal treatment of a whole class of human beings. Far more is at stake, in short, with one's choice of terms in this
case, than mere fussy "correctness."

From the above, we can offer some conclusions about the three-
part nature of the "politically correct" epithet. In the matter of "unmasking" the PC term to show its "real" intent: The terms in all three
cases cited above are more faithful to the reality they represent than are
the traditional terms. The fact that one term is more familiar than another term does not render it the best term for accurately "sizing up the
territory" in question. Its familiarity, the fact that it's camouflaged by
"the film of custom," simply means that its inaccuracy and ideological
bias are easier to overlook. The traditional beliefs that human beings
choose their sexuality, and that males are in charge of all organizations
and do all blue-collar work, are the contemporary equivalents of the belief that the sun goes around the earth, irresistible in part because they
are so thoroughly embedded in our language.

In the case of the third charge implicit in the epithet "politically
correct," the suggestion that its substitutions are part of a larger ideological campaign, we need to go beyond the substitution of single terms
such as "person" for "man" or "orientation" for "lifestyle" to the matter
of vocabulary. Viewed on this scale, the conflict between PC-protestors
and PC-proponents can be understood as a flat rejection on the part of
PC-protestors of an alternative vocabulary; or in Burke's language, opponents propose a "zero-discount" on terms from that second vocabulary. The premise underlying this rejection is a first cousin to Bentham's
"neutral language" ideal; the PC-protestors' reject PC-proponents' language because it is unnecessary, because it proposes to do badly work
that is already being satisfactorily performed by traditional terms with
which everyone is familiar. Adopting these new terms is hence considered inefficient and "uneconomical." The latter judgment constitutes a
broader indictment of the PC vocabulary than the charge that it is motivated by the wrong ideology.

The warrant for this charge is what might be called the "economical language" ideal: The clearest, simplest language performs the most
work for the least effort and is hence a better buy. Again in Burke's parlance, the PC-proponents have, in the name of the Law of Parsimony,
reduced the qualitative to the quantitative. Or in slightly different
terms, they have equated effectiveness with efficiency. And this bias toward efficiency in language isn't simply a means for *expressing* a political
ideology, it is *part and parcel* of that ideology. And the PC-protestors are
surely right that the vocabulary of PC-proponents is less efficient than

their own. Like the language of metaphor, the neologisms of political correctness devised in response to perceived changes on the ground call attention to themselves. They call on us either to re-vision our experience or to explicitly reject such a re-visioning—either way, an uncomfortable business requiring mental effort. Meanwhile, invented terms from the other side of the political spectrum open to charges of doublespeak enjoy a distinct advantage over PC neologisms insofar as they are often the coinage of experts in a given domain and hence are more likely to be taken as "technical terms" rather than as metaphors. Business and the military are particularly rich sources of doublespeak—think "embedded reporters," "collateral damage," "outsourcing," and so forth—while the language of PC is largely the work of amateurs acting in their capacity as citizens rather than experts.

In Conclusion

Our goal in the preceding section has not been to demonize PC-protestors or to ethicize critics of doublespeak. The two practices are more alike than different. They both offer categorical condemnations of singular acts and rule out of play language practices and rhetorical moves necessary for any persuasive or interpretative act. As such, they are both guilty of "debunking." Debunking, according to Burke, is a sort of "perfectionism in reverse" whereby nothing is what it appears to be and the debunker reveals a sinister truth behind every sunny appearance (GOM, 100). Debunking does *too thorough* a job of refuting the opposition. Not content to question or "cajole" an opponent's representation of things, we demand they represent things "the right way" in our vocabulary. We declare them guilty of the sin of orthodoxy and set things right by substituting our orthodoxy for theirs. But of course, like Jeremy Bentham, the one orthodoxy none of us can ever see clearly is our own. Our partisan vocabulary seems to us the neutral language that Bentham labored so mightily to create. We dream ourselves back in time, before the time of "Babel after the Fall" when words could be perfectly innocent, perfectly clear, and there was no need for interpretation or rhetoric and deplore rather than discount the scandalously partisan language of our foes. Like all utopian schemes, it's a futile enterprise, one with an unfortunate tendency to debase civic discourse, create social injustices, and in extreme cases to start wars.

6

⚛️

Rhetoric and Everyday Life

With this final chapter, we return to our discussion in the first chapter about rhetoric as a "way." In that earlier discussion, it will be recalled, many of the standard criticisms of rhetoric were rehearsed—it is amoral and relativistic, it promotes linguistic chicanery of various sorts, it lacks the rigor of more scientific disciplines, and so forth—prior to mounting a defense of rhetorical practices. In Chapters 2–5, we extended that defense of rhetoric by demonstrating its usefulness as a tool of identity formation, persuasion, and interpretation. In this chapter we will be concerned with the usefulness of these same tools, but this time in a variety of situations, not all of which may appear to be "rhetorical." In this context, those putative defects of rhetoric bemoaned by the more Serious among us, particularly its decidedly eclectic approach to understanding and its aversion to formal methodology, turn out to be its greatest strengths.

In real-time, seat-of-the-pants applications as we're trying to make sense of our lives while they unfold, trying to formulate responses to immediate challenges, trying to express and protect our identity in everyday interactions—in sum, whenever we're functioning in our capacity as citizens and ordinary people rather than as specialists of some sort—the more "rigorous approaches" touted by Serious Folk prove to be far too cumbersome. That is not to say that we cannot use the fruits of such approaches in our own work—the methodological imperative of rhetoric is, after all, "to use all that is there to use"—but we are not bound by the methods that bore those fruit. Much of what follows, thus, is informed by research from various disciplines, though its conclusions are typically arrived at following the more circuitous path of the rhetorical way than the straighter and narrower paths of the more rigorous disciplines.

The Peculiar Relationship between Rhetorical Theory and Practice

One of the distinguishing characteristics of rhetoric as a discipline is in fact the singular nature of the relationship between rhetorical theory and rhetorical practices, between principles and application. In the physical sciences and in disciplines that aspire to the status of the physical sciences, those who theorize about the field and those who operate within the field's theories mostly belong to two distinct castes. Scientists who theorize set up the problems to be solved and direct the attention and priorities of scientists who subscribe to and operate within the theories. Those who do not theorize, meanwhile, use methods of testing and probing—"scientific methods"—that are relatively unaffected by the particulars of the prevailing theory. The latter group has been dubbed "normal scientists" by Thomas Kuhn, while those who question and probe the inadequacies of theories and work out new paradigms for the normal scientists to operate within he dubbed "creative scientists." What is unique to the physical sciences is the extent to which at any given time one dominant paradigm prevails and guides the practices of normal scientists, who cannot long operate under conditions of uncertainty or dissensus. They require a stable paradigm in place, a unified set of assumptions and principles and ways of looking at the world, in order to carry out the exacting, highly specialized work of articulation and puzzle solving that is their raison d'etre. Which is why change in science tends to be sudden and revolutionary rather than gradual and incremental. Extended uncertainty about the validity of a guiding paradigm leads to paralysis among normal scientists.

There is no such single paradigm to guide practitioners in the human sciences. Rhetoric is distinctive among these sciences not in its failure to achieve the status of a "monotheistic" enterprise, but in the degree to which it acknowledges and accepts its "polytheistic" nature. Multiple theories, principles, and "paradigms" (if we may be allowed some license with the import of that overused and much-abused term) coexist in our field—and are borrowed liberally from other fields—even when they dispute and contradict one another. It is difficult if not impossible to falsify a rhetorical theory, and so ancient theories mingle happily with postmodern theories; it is not unusual to find several applied within a given analysis by a single rhetorical practitioner, including, in earlier chapters, this one. While some in the field declare their fealty to one theory or another, most rhetorical practitioners "muddle through," borrowing from this theory or that one when the occasion calls for it.

And what is borrowed from the various theories are not methods, techniques, or principles so much as "terms." Terms are in fact so central to rhetoric that the word "theory," normally used to designate the bundles of linked concepts that guide practitioners' inquiries, should probably be eschewed in favor of "terministic screen" (LSA, 44), the rhetorical term Burke uses to designate vocabularies that serve a theory-like function. In "applying" Burke, thus, one is not obligated to impose his entire "system" any more than one is obligated to apply a nonexistent "rhetorical method." Rather Burke is applied one term, or one small bundle of terms, at a time. Those who apply the terms of his "pentad," thus, will discover different things in different ways than those who apply such Burkean terms as "representative anecdote" or "occupational psychosis." In justifying one's use of a term and exploring its implications, one will of course find oneself pulled further afield into other Burkean terms, "in terms of which" the single term makes sense. In a single rhetorical critique, thus, one may find Toulmin's "backing" mingling with Aristotle's "enthymeme" and Burke's "discounting." The choice of terms that one employs and the manner in which those terms are applied are determined by the particulars of the rhetorical situation one addresses.

This muddled relationship between theory and practice lies behind a fair amount of Serious People's displeasure with rhetoric, particularly their concerns about the relativistic, subjective nature of our work. The individual rhetorical practitioner has to make and justify choices that are predetermined for the typical normal scientist. To put the matter in Toulmin's terms, there are none or few indisputable warrants in our field to justify or license the most fundamental move a practitioner might wish to make—the one from data to claim. While normal scientists are able to carry out their work free of contentious disputes about their assumptions, to operate in an "objective" fashion, the rhetorical practitioner's methodological choices are open to dispute and charges of bias at every turn. There is no fire wall between rhetorical theorists and rhetorical practitioners such as the one that compartmentalizes the activities of normal and creative scientists. Every practitioner is at least a seat-of-the-pants theorist—even those who don't wish to claim the mantle—who must be prepared to justify application by appealing to principles that are almost certainly contested. And what passes for application in rhetoric isn't so much an autonomous activity carried out in support of a theory—it is theories, or more precisely pieces of theories, that get applied. In what follows, thus, there is no "top-down" application of a single methodology. Each case determines which theoretical borrowings, which terms, provide the best vocabulary for articulating the matter and which of the various methods that comprise the "way of rhetoric" will best serve us in inventing new insights, complicating our understanding of things, and finding the best arguments in the given circumstances.

The Rhetoric of Cell Phones

Any time something is being communicated, rhetoric can help us understand it, critique it, and formulate a response to it. And something is being communicated almost all the time. Take, for example, cell phones. In and of themselves there is nothing necessarily rhetorical about cell phones; but there is definitely a rhetoric of cell phone usage. Beginning with the obvious, cell phones are a medium of communication. As a medium, cell phones play a role in the rhetorical situation, influencing our choice of message and our manner of delivering that message. They have opened up new possibilities for conversation and, arguably, whole new genres of communication. Specifically, their portability makes them an ideal medium of communication between close friends and family during moments of idleness, or, to use the language of the first chapter, when we are going through routine motions. Consequently, an exceptional amount of "phatic" communication, messages intended mostly to "touch" other people, goes on via cell phones.

For example, my office is near the exterior doors of a classroom building and each day at sixty-minute intervals I can hear people entering and exiting the building. Many of them are carrying on cell phone conversations. Their end of these conversations goes something like this: "Hi, I'm just walking into my class." "*Dude*, hey, what's up?" "Hi, I just got out of class." On the face of it, this is pretty inane stuff. Little information is exchanged and what little there is of it is decidedly low grade; intelligence analysts would probably classify it as "chatter" or "static." But clearly it serves a rhetorical purpose; people are reminding other people of their existence with the verbal equivalent of a nudge, a pat on the back, a wink. Still, not so many years ago, this form of communication would have made no sense to most of us. People would have been puzzled to receive calls like this, out of the blue, virtually devoid of information from people they may have just spoken with. And if callers had to interrupt their progress to class, locate a pay phone, insert a perfectly good quarter, and actually punch in an entire seven-to-ten-digit number—as opposed to hitting speed dial without breaking stride—so they could tell a friend that they were en route to their two o'clock class, few of them would probably have bothered, and those who did would probably feel more than a bit silly.

Then too, cell phones have also altered the nature of long-distance calling. In years past, long-distance calls were, for many of us, momentous events. In the not-too-distant past, one's long-distance calls were reserved for important business, duty calls to important relatives, or calls to friends to exchange significant information. In the remote past, meanwhile, long-distance calls were viewed as the equivalent of "oral telegrams," conversational snippets intended to impart only essential information. I can remember my grandparents' calls from Portland, all of thirty miles away, to inform my parents when they would be arriving for their regular Sunday afternoon visit. Whichever parent answered the phone would invariably lapse into "telegraphese," an elliptical, urgently clipped mode of speaking that made me wonder if perhaps the phone company was charging them by the word.

Now thanks to an oversaturated market and a bewildering array of call plans available from wireless carriers, long-distance calls cost a fraction of what they used to. Which doesn't mean that because calls are cheaper, our talk is necessarily cheaper. A whole new genre of calls has emerged, a looser, baggier, and less urgent genre perhaps, but far from a trivial one. We may now carry on soulful exchanges while we bathe our dogs, fix dinner, or drive to the store. We can multitask, doing intimacy and drudgery simultaneously. We can realize, effortlessly, in our everyday lives the goal of Dylan Thomas, who through his poetry sought "in my intricate image / to stride on two levels." Now long-distance cell phone conversations may sound like "voice-overs" of the callers' lives, or like oral journal entries people use simultaneously to share and to work out their sense of everyday existence. (That these changes in our rhetorical practices can in part be traced back to changes in the economies of communication is hardly surprising. Money and language serve nearly identical functions. Both are purely symbolic media without intrinsic value and both are infinitely fungible. Everything imaginable can be converted to a monetary or linguistic equivalent, allowing us to assign a meaning to it and to understand it "in terms of" something else. Both words and currency must be discounted/translated when they are used in circumstances different from their origins. And the choice of currency or vocabulary to serve as the standard for a community will go a long way toward determining the value of things within that community.)

The above examples of how the cell phone medium affects cell phone messages only begin to scratch the surface of cell phone rhetoric. Cell phones, after all, are more than merely devices we talk through; they are important props that the more imaginative among us wield deftly in their everyday dramas of self-presentation. If, according to Freud, hats were once the accessories that most acutely symbolized our identities, cell phones may well be the contemporary version of the hat. And because they have an aural as well as a visual dimension, they are doubly powerful symbolic expressions of identity. Whereas old-fashioned phones all looked remarkably alike and revealed little about the personality of the phone's owner (technically the phone's lessee), and only those who knew the owner well enough to enter the owner's home would ever see the phone in the first place, cell phones offer one a much broader range of expression and a much wider audience. The look of a cell phone, its size, its visible features, its color and composition, its place on our person—the businesslike belt loop phone holster, the more hip zipped cargo pant pocket, the casual poking-out-the-pocket look, the purse phone, the backpack phone—all have something to say about us and our perceived place in the world. In the movie *Zoolander*, for example, a vacuous male model played by Ben Stiller brandishes a trendy cell phone so tiny that it's nearly useless, the perfect objective correlative for its pea-brained owner. And the rings programmed into cell phones—passages of classical music, pop tunes, college fight songs, and so forth—and the volume at which they are set are palpable signals of the owner's character and taste, signals that hundreds, even thousands of people may be exposed to in the phone's lifetime.

The Cell Phone as Theatrical Prop

Perhaps the most important rhetorical function of the cell phone is its capacity to facilitate three-, possibly even four-way communication. Direct, two-way communication between cell phone users represents minimal symbolic use of the phone and a failure to exploit fully the dramatic potential of the medium. Adroit cell phone users can transform simple exchanges into theater at one and possibly both ends of the line. Two people *hear* each other over their phones, but they may be *overheard* and observed delivering their lines by dozens of people. A recent ad illustrated the theater of cell phone usage nicely. It featured a man walking into a fancy restaurant, talking animatedly into his phone about the closure of a major movie deal while diners around the room interrupted their conversations to listen in. Then in print at the bottom of the screen it was revealed that no one was on the other end of the line. It was, quite literally, pure theater. At other times, the theatrical gesture may preclude the actual call. Thus, for example, there are those poseurs one encounters in public places who love to pluck their ringing cell phones off their belts, glance disdainfully at the caller ID, and ostentatiously drop their phones back into their pockets without bothering to answer. Clearly, the gesture says, this is one very important person.

More typically the theatrical dimension of a cell phone call is in addition to rather than in lieu of a communicative exchange. In the earlier mentioned case of the people phoning on their way to and from class, the calls may in some cases serve both to put the callers in touch with someone and to enhance their self-presentation. Because the call typically serves no substantive purpose, callers are free to improvise lines and play to their secondary audience of fellow classgoers and -comers. Walking to class, after all, can be a moderately uncomfortable experience if that's our sole activity. To make eye contact or not, how long to hold such contact; what to do with our hands; to look genial and inviting, cool and aloof, or grim and forbidding; to greet or to not greet people we know slightly . . . the walk to class can entail an exhausting series of decisions. And why, after all, are we walking to class alone, absent the company of friends? A cell phone conversation instantly transforms us from silent, lonely pedestrians unsure of and anxious about our bit part in a crowd scene into "players"—actor/authors inventing our roles, writing our lines, scripting our gestures, exploring our character's range, experimenting with various facial expressions and turns of phrase, laughs, and exclamations—reassuring our audience that while we may be going to class alone, we are not without friends, caring friends anxious to know our every move, amusing friends capable of eliciting wild laughter from us in the middle of a crowded hallway.

At other times the cell phone user's performance may be aimed entirely at the person to whom the user is speaking, in which case those of us observing or overhearing the call will, through our interpretation of things, be the ones primarily responsible for constructing an identity for the cell phone user. In this regard, we've probably all been forced to listen to people saying things on cell phones that are so embarrassing it's hard to believe they intend anyone other than the person to whom they are speaking to be privy to their words. We must of course be cautious about judging when we are in fact seeing a performance "backstage" as it were, and when we are witnessing a well-staged moment of faux authenticity. As the recent rash of "reality" TV shows—many of them apparently patterned after William Golding's *Lord of the Flies*—might suggest, some people seem to revel in sharing humiliating moments with millions of viewers who are in turn persuaded that they are seeing the real thing precisely because they assume that no one would fake something that made them appear to be such a gormless cretin.

Cell Phones and the Problematic Audience

Arguably the most useful skill we've been forced to develop thanks to our exposure to the rhetoric of cell phones is our capacity to distinguish between dialogue designed to be overheard and words aimed only at the hearer. Thus the young woman I heard tearfully arguing with her parents about her credit card bills was, I'm convinced, totally concerned about the effect of her words on her parents. And to cite a more complex example, I am ultimately persuaded that an extremely dramatic piece of self-presentation that I witnessed at, of all places, a spring training baseball game was aimed solely at the person being spoken to and not at the dozen or so people listening wide-eyed to the call. The circumstances were these: For several innings I had been seated next to an engaging middle-aged man, a remarkably fit-looking fellow, with short gray hair, stylishly dressed in slacks and a black T-shirt. The only slightly unsettling notes were the scar over one eye and the coiled snake tattoo wrapped around the words "Semper Fi" on one muscular forearm. He was a motorcycle enthusiast and a lifelong Giants fan, with a seeming photographic memory and a rich store of funny anecdotes about road trips to exotic places and perplexing Giant collapses in tight pennant races. Toward the end of the game, his cell phone rang. He glanced at the caller ID and his whole countenance changed. His smile vanished, he hunched forward, and without waiting for a greeting from the caller, he began speaking in a low growl. The gist of the call was that my neighbor was in the process of collecting a loan from the caller, whose finances were sufficiently troubled that he'd been ordered to forfeit the title to his car. He'd failed to comply with the order and was requesting an extension, which my neighbor was in no uncertain terms declining. If he didn't have possession of the car within twenty-four hours, dire things, it appeared, would be happening to the caller. It was a brief call, and as soon as it was over, my neighbor—I now thought of him as "the collector"—was cheerful as ever, picking right up where he'd left off in his latest story.

I'm relatively sure the performance I'd witnessed, and a most persuasive performance it was, was mostly if not entirely for the benefit of the caller. Had he taken the call alone in his car, I'm convinced he would have responded in exactly the same way, falling into his "collector" persona without missing a beat. In other words, the two versions of my neighbor to which I had been privy were equally real. My view of him changed as a result of seeing him in action in his "collector" role, but it wasn't as if this second version proved the first version of him false. As we suggested in Chapter 3, each of us comprises a collection of selves—a corporate self—and whichever of our selves is presented to the world is a function of the circumstances surrounding our presentation. My memory of the collector, the "gist" of him I took away from our encounter, in particular my memory of his scar and his tattoo, reflects the tenor of that encounter, the circumstances of the rhetorical situation, not necessarily any privileged glimpse I'd been afforded into his essential self.

Much of the difficulty of interpreting cell phone rhetoric lies in making the determination of where we may be situated in relation to the user. Are we the primary audience, a secondary audience, or an entirely accidental one? One of the "innumerable relationships" that bears most strongly on the interpretation of any symbolic act, including cell phone usage, is the audience's relation to the agent who performs the act. Where we place ourselves in relationship to the agent determines our point of view toward him and our evaluation of his rhetorical act. When the agent's reliability is in question or his intent is ambiguous, our own ability to interpret the act is impeded. The problem we face here might be likened to the difficulties facing the reader of a postmodern fiction such as John Barth's *Lost in the Funhouse*, a "collection novel" consisting of connected stories that comment on each other, though not in any immediately apparent way. In turn, the stories often feature storytellers telling stories about storytellers telling stories. It's difficult to know who is talking to whom or where we stand in relation to the events of the story. In one particularly dizzying story, the only way the reader can know who is talking is by counting the quote marks around each statement. From the beginning to the middle of the story we go from zero to seven quote marks around each statement, and then from the middle to the conclusion we work our way back to zero. Depending on who's talking and who's being talked to, the statements can take on totally different meanings. Luckily, life does not present us with perspectival challenges quite that daunting. But some come close.

Take for example the case of the NFL wide receiver who immediately upon scoring a touchdown ostentatiously whipped out a cell phone and (it would appear) mimicked a congratulatory phone call to his family. It was such a theatrical gesture and it followed so closely on the heels of another wide receiver's much-publicized touchdown gesture of pulling a Sharpie out of the goalpost padding, autographing the ball, and giving it to a fan that it was hard to believe that the putative recipients of his call were more than an accidental audience. Clearly the cell phone was a prop for his enactment of a groundbreaking scene from the genre "touchdown celebrations"; just as clearly his primary audience comprised the thousands of people watching from the stands and the millions watching at home.

But the complexities of the gesture don't end there. The wide receiver was already a performer, after all, already on stage before he invited us to watch him go through his cell phone pantomime. In effect, he wasn't just creating a role for himself with his cell phone, he was also "breaking role," a role that gave him access to his audience in the first place and that carried with it an implied obligation to observe the script and conventions appropriate to that role. And in breaking the latter role he incurred the wrath of many traditionalists, old-time football fans, and former players who interpreted his act as disrespecting the script and conventions that had until recent years governed players' behaviors and fans' expectations. He was in their eyes calling attention to himself and his individual achievement at the expense of his teammates' contribution to that success. In flipping open his cell phone, he was establishing a link to the world beyond the game and shutting the other players out of his script. His feigned "private moment" dispelled for some fans an illusion necessary for their full enjoyment and investment in the proceedings, the illusion that the game, and who wins or loses it, is all that matters; for these fans it was as if the player were a Shakespearian actor who after delivering Hamlet's soliloquy stopped to chat with a friend in the audience about his recent Tony nomination.

On the other hand, many younger fans, or simply edgier, hipper fans more comfortable with postmodern conventions of performance, including the belief that *everything* is a performance and the firm conviction that only the delusional believe in some reality beyond quote marks or outside the lines, were quick to defend the player's cell phone act. (To qualify as a postmodern sophisticate, one need not be a reader of John Barth's fiction, or a student of avant-garde theory, architecture, or fiction—a few years watching MTV or *Ally McBeal* reruns can suffice.) It's all entertainment, so the rejoinder went, and the player—get it, he's a "player" not an "actualer"—was just expanding the stage, offering a bonus moment of theater, as continuous with the action on the field as the exclamation mark at the end of a sentence.

In an odd way, the argument in defense of football celebrations as spectacle resembles the argument in defense of the World Trade Center attack as spectacle. The cell phone act was defended in part because it was novel and creative; so long as one begins from the premise that "it's performance all the way down," that art swallows life, an act's novelty trumps its consequences. What distinguishes the two arguments, of course, and what renders the touchdown celebrant's performance more defensible, is precisely the seriousness of the consequences; it's one thing to destroy an illusion, however pleasurable to thousands of people, and quite another to destroy thousands of lives. So, while rhetoric may on the one hand celebrate the capacity of cell phones to smudge the line between art and life, it never loses sight of the fact that the consequences of symbolic acts matter and that designating an act symbolic does not render it immune from ethical judgment or professional censure.

Travelers, Commuters, Explorers, and Tourists

To travel is to commit a rhetorical act. If rhetoric is a "way," travel is an obvious means of enacting that way. But before we elaborate on analogical connections between traveling through the world and traversing a rhetorical way, we need to distinguish "travel" from some related terms that less fully exemplify the rhetorical way. Among the most significant terms mistaken for travel would be "touring," "exploring," and "commuting." Commuting, the sort of routine shuffle back and forth between two familiar points—home and work or school and back, the home office and a regional office and back, home to the mall and back, and so forth—is to travel as motion is to act. It is habitual, a routine movement typically performed with minimal attention to the task at hand, following a route that one may know in one's sleep. One may react to a traffic problem—slam on one's brakes, change lanes, get off the freeway—but one rarely acts with a sense of purpose and never produces or learns anything novel. Travel is something we do to escape commuting.

At the other extreme, exploring, a once-dominant mode of travel and genre of travel writing that has largely disappeared, is less about perception and reflection than about collecting. Explorers functioned more methodically, more scientifically than rhetoricians, gathering information in the form of data, specimens, images, maps, and the like, which they could then take home and study systematically with the intention of using their knowledge to eventually return and take control of the territory explored. If commuters fail to notice much of anything as they pass through the overly familiar terrain, explorers purposefully looked beyond their immediate experiences, however novel, toward the ends to which their collecting would be put. And if commuters are res-olutely unheroic souls, explorers were heroes and risk takers—at least their often-unsubstantiated accounts of personal exploits were the stuff of legends—extraordinary people easier to admire than to identify with.

Tourists are closest in spirit to travelers. For both tourists and trav-elers, as opposed to commuters and explorers, movement is more an end in itself than it is a means to an end. They go someplace to take it in, experience it, and getting there is part of that experience. Both fa-vor exotic though not dangerous locales, foreign but not alien. The dif-ferences between travelers and tourists are subtle and center on their varying tolerance for novelty. While both tourists and travelers are, in comparison to explorers, risk-averse and unheroic (and therefore easier to identify with), travelers display a greater tolerance for novelty than do tourists. Tourists often travel in homogenous groups and follow common agendas set out for them by guides or agencies. If tourists travel alone, they are inclined to seek out sites notable for being typical or representative of their destination, the sorts of places other tourists are likely to visit. If they go to Paris, they will surely go to the Eiffel Tower, perhaps take a boat ride down the Seine, or pursue one of the other dozen or so activities described in any respectable Paris guide-book. There are of course guidebooks that promise to point one toward a road less traveled, to places where mere tourists never go, a prospect guaranteed to please those tourists who famously dislike others of their ilk and carefully time their trips to, if at all possible, avoid encountering people like themselves wherever they go. But judging from the popular-ity of such books, it seems highly probable that one following their rec-ommendations will encounter many like-minded souls, looking and acting suspiciously like tourists, eagerly pursuing the same formerly ob-scure paths.

Travelers may do many of the same things that tourists do. The dif-ferences lie in how and why they do things. They pursue, as it were, dif-ferent rhetorical purposes. While a tourist may be disappointed if a site lavishly described in the guidebook turns out not to correspond to the description, the traveler may well find the differences between the de-scription and the experience fascinating. For the traveler, the experi-ence of defamiliarization brought on by thwarted expectancies or by an absence of expectations can be a gift. When everyday life is rendered problematic, one's attention is intensified. One can't know the mean-ing of anything automatically, so one must interpret everything. One must understand one's new experience "in terms of" one's old experiences, one's destination in terms of one's origins. And in the process of weighing the differences and similarities, one gains access to a new perspective, an incongruous one, for reflecting on one's origins. In their appreciation for novelty and their use of travel as a means of gaining perspective on themselves, travelers can be likened to those adventurers of an earlier age for whom journeys served as rites of passage or initiation into a new stage of identity, a tradition still maintained in some aboriginal cultures in the form of the "walkabout." Tourists, meanwhile, in their devotion to canonical sites, monuments, and must-see attractions and their commitment to buying mementos of their journey, mark themselves as descendants of the early-day religious pilgrims, travelers of a decidedly Serious sort, who traveled afar to view holy sites and to purchase religious relics, thereby placing themselves in direct contact with the roots of their faith and reaffirming an essential, central self.

In sum, travel, as we've defined it here, is a branch of the same dialectical way of knowing that Burke describes in the formula "act-suffer-learn." By acting, as distinguished from merely moving, we introduce novelty into our lives, an unpredictable, uncontrollable piece of experience. We "suffer" from that act, in some cases slightly and momentarily (say, we take our first trip on the British Underground and end up on the wrong line) and in other cases grievously (we unwittingly violate a local law that carries far harsher penalties than similar laws in our native country and we end up in court). But assuming we survive the experience, we've learned how to do it better the next time. That's pretty much the rhythm of travel, a word, it is useful to recall, with its roots in "travail."

Travel and Identity

As noted above, travel and tourism have traditionally been linked to identity formation; more specifically, travel, in the form of a rite of passage, has long served as a means of identity construction or reconstruction, while tourism, in the form of the pilgrimage, has served to reaffirm one's commitment to a given identity, a soul. Today, travel can still serve as a sort of "liminal" experience where we cross or expand the boundaries of our identity by undergoing an immersion in unfamiliar geographic and cultural territory. For most of us, however, the experience today is less akin to a rite of passage than to a small-scale experiment in identity expansion, a microcosmic reenactment of the earlier discussed shift in identity formation that took place at the beginning of the modern epoch. During this period of history, it will be recalled, one's identity went from a largely given matter to more of a project, something one could construct oneself or supplement by choosing from among a stock of readymade identities. So it is when we travel. To the extent that we are able and willing to leave behind the givens of our existence—our language, our community, our history, our family—new possibilities for identity open up. As the writer Alain de Botton notes in *The Art of Travel* about the relationship between travel and identity: "It is not necessarily at home that we best encounter our true selves. The furniture insists that we cannot change because it does not; the domestic setting keeps us tethered to the person we are in ordinary life, who may not be who we essentially are." Without necessarily seconding de Botton's suggestion that there is some essential or true self waiting to be discovered in our journey, we can endorse his notion that travel gives us the freedom to seek out different selves, experiment with identities that are, if not necessarily "truer" or "more authentic," perhaps better suited to our current circumstances and our stage in life than the one we leave back home "tethered" to the familiar, the given, the routine, and, most importantly, to others' expectations of us.

People's capacity for such experimentation varies greatly. The most Serious of Folk, those afflicted, say, with a particularly acute case of occupational psychosis, may find it quite difficult to leave their established selves at home. Others of us, meanwhile, will happily shed our domestic identities like a snake shedding its skin in the spring and "go native" almost the moment we arrive. The majority of us fall somewhere in between these extremes. While we are certainly influenced by our pasts, we are not determined by them. We are capable of moving about anonymously, temporarily assuming the role of a person with no obligations to fulfill, no place to be, no role to play, no past to live up to, no future to disappoint. And while we may not choose to be utterly transformed during our untethered stay, we will perhaps push the envelope in significant ways. The more timid among us may choose to be uncharacteristically adventuresome while the more outgoing among us may opt for a more introspective persona. Ordering items off a menu we're not sure we've read correctly or entering a strange city at night without a hotel reservation can seem pretty reckless in the moment to a normally timid soul. And sitting alone on a train, ignoring the people around you while you stare out the window taking in the novel sights sliding past, and writing in a journal can make a normally sociable person feel downright rude. However small our experiments in identity modification, the fact that they are consciously chosen and monitored reminds us of our own sense of agency, a sense that is all too easily lost in the urgent, repetitive rhythms of everyday existence.

Now, all of this can backfire on us as well. In an environment where we have no established identity, we may—particularly if we are American—sometimes find ourselves vulnerable to "identity theft." Those we encounter, instead of making no assumptions about us, may feel free to make all sorts of assumptions about us and to make their attributions known to us. Upon hearing us speak, noting our clothing, observing our hesitancy in some routine matter, "locals" may jump to any number of conclusions about our politics, our cultural sensitivity or lack of same, our attitude toward everything from gender roles to money, our knowledge of food and wine, and so forth. Before we have an opportunity to fill in the blank of our identity, we may find others filling in the blank for us with readymade identities lifted from reruns of American sitcoms. So, with the heightened freedom to construct one's different identity comes the increased danger of having a readymade identity thrust upon one. But in either case, the consequences of our constructions and others' impositions are short-lived and at the next stop, we are free to start over again.

The Art of the Journey

One of the reasons that travel is so readily identifiable as a rhetorical activity has to do with the fact that it occurs in highly visible, discrete episodes—the trip or the journey. Most of us do our traveling in carefully delimited interludes of one, two, three, or four weeks, depending on how much vacation time we may have from our work. And even if the trip lasts longer—a summer vacation, a year off between finishing high school or college and starting a career, or between one job and the next—it is clearly marked off from our normal routine. A trip is a vacation, which derives from the same Latin word, *vacare*, that also gives us the word "vacate." We vacate our normal premises, leaving our occupation(s) and webs of relationships behind, board some magical mode of transportation that hours later delivers us to a location sufficiently different from our point of departure to evoke our curiosity and raise our anxieties. We stay in that location for some predetermined amount of time, acting, suffering, and learning, often forced to resort to metaphoric language in order to capture the gist of our foreign adventure in terms of our familiar world. Then we repeat our journey in the opposite direction. In the language of Aristotle, a journey, like any poetic work, has a definite beginning, middle, and end and is "of a certain magnitude" such that we can see it as a recognizable whole and connect its end to its beginning. Set off from ordinary life like plays with their stages and curtains, or paintings with their frames and museum settings, our journeys invite narrative accounts. Which is why so many of us keep journals when we travel, and collect stocks of representative anecdotes that will encapsulate the experience for imagined audiences back home.

And it's also why there is a genre of prose known as travel writing that includes a broad variety of forms, ranging from guidebooks that catalog the dates and the facts of all the obligatory sites and monuments; to magazine articles, often little more than infomercials, which extol the virtues of tourist destinations in extravagant terms; to nonfictional literary accounts about what an author may have discovered about herself in the process of discovering a place. Over the years a number of important writers, from Nathaniel Hawthorne, Henry James, and Charles Dickens to George Orwell, Paul Theroux, and Jan Morris, have written travel books and essays that inspired others both to travel and to write about their travels. Collectively, travel writing in all its forms, along with travelogues, travel sections of newspapers, geography texts, and so forth, have an important impact on how we travel and what we see.

In the case of guidebooks, for example, their often-peremptory judgments ("The monastery is worth a visit . . . the market is a shopper's paradise . . . the unspoilt town is not to be missed"), their admonishment to see this church or that town hall when visiting X echoes the language of pamphlets published in the middle ages by monks promoting pilgrimages. Such pamphlets, like their latter-day guidebook counterparts, were part informational and part promotional, descriptions of things for pilgrims to see and hyperbolic pitches aimed at persuading pilgrims that the promised sights would justify the substantial cost of their journey. (The monks who published these pamphlets, it should be noted, profited from the pilgrimages by selling religious relics to the pilgrims and renting them rooms.) Today, guidebooks come in every imaginable form and size and are as carefully targeted at specific demographics and "psychographics" as the most intentional of advertisements. High-end travelers can find guidebooks that direct them to only the most canonical of sites, hotels that "meet the most exacting requirements," and restaurants with much-coveted Michelin stars. Other guidebooks cater to the middling traveler concerned mostly with cleanliness, safety, and reasonable cost; still others direct their readers to the cheapest hostels, street markets where lunch may be purchased from a vendor, and prime spots for hitchhiking. Each guide prescribes a distinctive agenda and a different regimen for their very distinctive audience. But in every case, travel is a commodity pitched to consumers who are concerned to maximize their investment. The guides meet this need by reducing the readers' uncertainty, filtering out possible bad choices for them and "their sort," and by enhancing their appreciation for sites the guides promote with exhaustive lists of facts and dates. Guidebooks prescribe journeys that will hopefully satisfy our tastes and meet our expectations, but not necessarily change or challenge us.

While travelers will certainly avail themselves of guidebooks, they are more likely to seek out travel narratives both to inform them about the region where they intend to travel and to find models for ways to experience the region. For all the guidebooks' gushy judgments about things—as one moves from low- to high-end guidebooks the prose grows ever more purple, the praise ever more hyperbolic, in order, one supposes, to justify the ever escalating cost of the journey—they leave one with little sense of an individual sensibility. Their judgments strike one as anonymous, hegemonic—common sensical, traditional, and unquestionable, with no arguments or justifications required. They contrast sharply with judgments of the sort one encounters in travel narratives that are often quirky (cranky even), unabashedly subjective, and largely grounded in and justified by the traveler's immediate experiences. If one thinks of a guidebook as an axis of innumerable relationships, primary among those relationships is the one between the book's descriptions of reality and the traveler's experience with the reality described. Next in importance will be the traveler's experience in relation to the experiences of all those who have preceded her in the journey described by the guidebook. The countless travelers—of the sort appealed to by the guidebook—who've gone before the reader have been gratified by the guidebook's recommendations, and it's that weight of collective experience that lends the guidebook its air of authority.

The most obvious relationship established by the travel essay, meanwhile, is the one between the reader and the writer. The voice of each travel essay is distinctive and the essayist's point of view will reflect the actual circumstances of her journey. If it was raining the day she saw the Eglise Notre-Dame in Provence, and her nerves were a bit frayed because of a tense relationship with her travel companion, and she was unhappy with a turn in world events, the reader will be informed of her circumstances; and her account of the event might consequently neglect the standard guidebook's chirpy details about the Eglise's fourteenth-century tower and its 124 steps that lead one to a view of the sea that is, the reader is assured, "breathtaking." The travel writer's trek to the top of the tower might take on the character of a 124-step forced march that left her without any spare breath to be taken by the view, an occasion for a lengthy meditation on the vanity of human wishes, including those of fourteenth-century monks, and the ridiculous lengths to which we'll go in order to look down on the rest of the world. It is largely left to the reader to determine if she ought to go out of her way to take in the Eglise Notre-Dame.

As the above example suggests, the tone of a travel narrative will almost certainly be less effusive than that of the average guidebook. But even the gloomiest of travel writers, and there is an entire subgenre of travel books and essays devoted to the humorous debunking of facile guidebook optimism, will report bright moments along the way and sights worth seeing. Few are unrelentingly gloomy. That said, however, travel narratives would certainly occupy a position considerably removed from guidebooks on any travel literature continuum one might construct. The travel essay is a record of individual experience, typically constructed scene by scene rather than site by site. It offers representative anecdotes about a place rather than encyclopedic details about the place. It shows us how one person made sense out of the journey and encourages us to do the same, by paying attention to the particulars of our experience and not allowing ourselves to be bullied out of our impressions and feelings by some anonymous guidebook arbiter of good taste.

A travel essay is to a guidebook as a photograph of a site is to a snapshot of a site. A photographer is concerned with the light and composition of the shot and may well spend hours waiting until just the right moment to shoot. A snapshot, usually taken with a camera that leaves little latitude to the picture-taker about nuances of light or depth of field, ignores local circumstances and records the fact that we were there. In *National Lampoon's Vacation*, the obligatory two or three seconds that Chevy Chase spends on the rim of the Grand Canyon looking down into its vast chasm is plenty of time for a "snap" that would prove he was there—then again, why bother, when he can pick up some postcards of the same view in the souvenir shop. When we see a photograph of a site, meanwhile, we see it through the eyes of the photographer, not the camera. If the snapshot is a "fast-food" version of our trip's reality, a photograph is a distinctly "slow-food" version of our journey. And that's the basic difference between traveling rhetorically, a journey in which "circumstances alter cases" and circumstances are in continual flux, and following a path prescribed by a guidebook that banishes circumstances and flux from its account. The mood of the journey, the writer's changing attitude toward her subject, will inevitably be visible to the audience. The assumption underlying the guidebook notion of travel is that what is most important about a place is factual and objective. All of us will have approximately the same experience and places can be adequately and exhaustively described without having to resort to interpretation or metaphors (excepting those that are safely dead). Like strict constructionists and originalists in the field of law, who argue that the law is already made and the task of judges is simply to discover what's already there and waiting, guidebooks would restrict our experience of a place to what's always been there and waiting to be recognized by travelers cued by authoritative sources.

To sum up, travel essays and rhetorical journeys are about acting, suffering, and learning, though not necessarily in equal parts. As noted above, some travel essays emphasize the suffering of the traveler, whose woes often result from naive faith in guidebooks and travel brochures. Like one of the earliest travel writers, Don Quixote, who fed too long on quest romances before embarking on his own mock-epic journey, the protagonist of the humorous travel narrative is often the victim of guidebooks' and brochures' sanitized versions of travel and the false expectations to which they give rise. In some cases, the lesson the protagonists learn is a mostly cynical one: Don't trust these sources. In a few cases, they may also learn ultimately to trust their own capacity for critical experience.

Other travel narratives, meanwhile, focus on the learning phase of the "act-suffer-learn" scenario. In recent years, for example, a number of travel books have taken the form of memoirs about the authors' attempts to adjust to a new culture as they struggle to establish residence in a foreign country. While the authors of such works, people like Peter Mayle and Frances Mayes, are not technically in motion, they still qualify as travelers (and their books will be found in the travel section of most bookstores) because the experience, even if it eventually becomes permanent, concerns the transition to a new place. What are normally routine motions at home become problematic acts in this new environment. The web of relationships that holds us so firmly (and often comfortably) in place at home must be reestablished in this new place. One must learn how to shop for food, how to negotiate the local bureaucracies to acquire building permits or driver's licenses, how to deal with local tradespeople, and how to sort out the competent and honest ones from the inept or shady ones. One must learn an entirely new rhetoric, new persuasive skills, a new vocabulary, new interpretative skills, and an appropriate persona for such dealings.

And finally some travel books are all about the act, the initial break from the dull, daily round and an immersion in a culture far removed, often far riskier, than the one from whence one came. The adventurer/traveler may journey through war zones or politically volatile environments where the price paid for an injudicious act can be one's life. In the end, it isn't so much what one learns from one's acts that counts in the travel adventure as it is the act itself. Like the action movie, the adventure/travel narrative treats acts as spectacles, extraordinary and anomalous events that rivet our attention without inviting reflection. Though superficially like the explorers of old, today's adventurer/travelers collect little on their journeys other than really great yarns to mesmerize the folks back home.

No matter what mode we choose to travel in, what lens we choose to view our journey through, there is a besetting irony underlying nearly all journeys, an irony originating in our motivation for undertaking them. Whether we choose to travel as tourists, adventurers, prospective settlers, or any of the other available modes, we all go, at least in part, in search of immediate, unfiltered, "authentic" experience, an escape not only from the routine of our daily lives, but from the overwhelmingly mediated nature of that routine. We spend our days talking on phones, fiddling with PDAs, and staring at computer screens, TV sets, and video games, reading texts in print or digital form, processing and playing with information packaged so as to render it easily manipulable. We are inundated with advertisements promising us some better self in some vague, but near-at-hand future. And we devour books and articles about exotic locales. Some part of us longs for something more palpable, the original stuff on the other side of all those representations we entertain all day long. We want to feel the recalcitrance of things, the resistance of experience to our wishes, the capacity of the world to intrude on our awareness and to reassure us of its difference from us.

The central attraction of travel for many of us, thus, is the opportunity it affords us to cross over to the other side to a world we've often experienced in mediated form but never firsthand, never with all five senses involved. We want to feel the cobblestones under our feet and to catch the locals unaware, seeing them as they actually are offstage. Even tourists who celebrate the correspondences between their mediated expectations and their actual journeys long for some tingle of immediacy, of authenticity that will in a visceral way distinguish the mediated from the real experience. But one of the things all of us learn when we travel is that unmediated experience is hard to come by, that in its pure form at least, it's probably illusory. Try as we might, all of us, as more than one traveler has remarked over the years, inadvertently bring ourselves along to the places we travel. We bring our biases and our prejudices, our beliefs and obsessions, our habits, and the sum of all the knowledge we've accumulated about the place through our mediated experiences with it. Consequently, any insights we may have about aspects of the place are purchased with blindness to other aspects. As Burke reminds us, "a way of seeing is also a way of not seeing" (P&C, 49). The differences between the rhetorical traveler and the unrhetorical one have to do with the proportion of blindness to insight and the capacity to nudge the limits of sight by reflection and self-criticism and to acknowledge differences between our expectations and our experiences. Indeed, the "travail" of travel turns out not to arise from the inconvenience and strangeness of the journey so much as it does from the demands of remaining vigilant and self-critical while we're journeying.

The Rhetoric of Advertising

While cell phones and travel may not immediately leap to mind as rhetorical activities, advertising is widely seen as the quintessential rhetoric activity. Indeed, rhetoric's strong identification with advertising and politics accounts for much of its unsavory reputation. Advertising is the primary medium through which unwholesome ready-made identities are promoted; and frequently the means used to promote those identities are even less wholesome than the identities on offer. Taken as a whole, advertising acts as an immensely powerful propaganda tool for a consumerist ideology that may impoverish our psyches almost as readily as it empties our wallets.

To date, rhetoric has played a far bigger role in producing questionable advertisements and defective identities than it has in construing and critiquing advertisers. In fact, rhetorical critics of advertising have been remarkably ineffective at limiting the influence of advertising in our culture. Rhetorical critics frequently come across sounding like their ploddingly ineffectual Serious counterparts when they set out to critique advertising. Part of the problem, I'm convinced, comes from our failure, particularly in introductory textbooks, to clarify the place of advertising in American culture and history. Typically the "circumference" assigned to the rhetorical situation of advertising is too narrowly drawn. Too much rhetorical analysis of advertising focuses on this ad or that ad and on techniques for teasing meaning out of single ads. Like any other persuasive claim, advertisements are best understood as responses to other claims and as continuations of ongoing conversations. They are best understood as expressions of their circumstances, the time and place they are enacted, and the medium of their enactment. In fact, like political cartoons, advertisements are especially dependent on an understanding of the historical context they participate in and the anxieties and desires peculiar to their audiences. By way of understanding the peculiar logic of advertising, then, we will step back and consider the broader context within which advertising takes place and the origins of its present role before offering a close examination of contemporary advertisements.

A Brief History of Early Advertising

Advertising is largely a twentieth-century phenomenon. As noted in Chapter 2, it began to flourish at the turn of the last century as a means of promoting readymade identities to consumers new to city and suburban life and to an emergent middle class whose identities had been traditionally rooted in the givens of family and locale. Unsure of who they were supposed to be, they looked to models offered them by their employers (and these models were mostly male) and by advertisers (and these models were mostly female). What did people who lived in the newly burgeoning suburbs wear? What cleaning products did proper suburbanites use? What cars did they drive? How would they combat those lower-class maladies—body odor, dull, lifeless hair, or, most insidiously, "halitosis"—that followed them into their new station in life and threatened to betray them to their ever-vigilant arriviste peers? Advertisers were there to counsel and advise them—after they'd first alarmed them about the problems they promised to solve—in the dozens of new mass-market magazines, most notably the freshly revived *Saturday Evening Post*, targeted at America's budding middle class and their countless insecurities.

As the role of advertising expanded, it also changed. In its earliest forms, advertising had relied mostly on outlandish promises to hawk the various medicinal elixirs that comprised the first goods to be heavily marketed to national audiences. Such nostrums as Lydia Pinkham's cure-all for "female complaints," a potion consisting largely of opiates, became a household name by promising to cure virtually any human ill. A drawing of the company's venerable monarch, accompanied by a lengthy list of ailments the product would banish and the occasional testimonial from a prominent citizen or a blurb from a satisfied customer, was all it took to hype sales. Later, advertisers developed a more sophisticated "reason-why" strategy, sometimes known as "salesman-ship in print," and attempted to distance themselves from the snake oil promotions of advertising's early days. Such ads named a problem and then offered a product that solved the problem, along with an explana-tion, a "reason why" this product would be efficacious. These were often very "talky" ads and included minimal, if any, graphic help. They sim-ply transposed the salesman's pitch from the showroom or store to the print medium. These new-style ads represented, the populace was as-sured, a belated recognition on the part of manufacturers and advertis-ers that the consumer was no rube—and increasingly audiences of first-generation urban dwellers viewed the image of the rural bumpkin as something to be put as far behind them as possible—who could be fooled by the sort of puffery and pseudoscience that early advertisers en-gaged in. (Over the years, advertisers have gone to extraordinary lengths to shore up their questionable *ethos*. Thus, like the products they tout, advertisers perennially sell themselves as ever more scientific, not to mention ever more respectful of their audience's intelligence and tastes, ever more concerned to meet their needs, and ever more disdain-ful of the crude machinations engaged in by their predecessors in the advertising profession. What has changed over the years is the increas-ing tone of self-mockery with which such apologia are delivered.)

So long as advertisers saw their rhetorical purpose as straightfor-ward persuasion, getting consumers to act, in particular getting them to choose one product over another, their little causal arguments were a perfectly adequate vehicle for their claims. But by the second decade of the twentieth century, the rhetorical purpose of advertising began to shift dramatically. Rather than being seen as a means of "moving" peo-ple to act, ads were increasingly understood as a means for "bending" people's attitudes. Advertisements were seen less as inducements to buy a company's goods and more as a means of "giving the company a soul," a personality that resonated with potential buyers. In turn, advertisers understood their audiences differently. Instead of seeing them as cus-tomers for their product, their audiences were increasingly seen as con-sumers of goods. Whereas customers bought products that answered their needs, consumers bought goods that served their desires, that made them feel better about themselves.

The convergence of at least two phenomena drove this shift. On the one hand, as we've already noted, consumption began to rival pro-duction as the primary means by which people established their identi-ties. In a world where one was increasingly surrounded by strangers, one increasingly relied on the visible signs of identity, most notably clothing, cars, and homes, to get a fix on people. As advertisers began to exploit this phenomenon ever more consciously, intentionally, and effectively, they also came to realize something else: When goods were used to fill needs, demand remained relatively inelastic, but when goods were used to establish identities, demand was suddenly very elastic. To put it simply: Needs are finite, desires are infinite. If one bought a car to get to work and said car got one to work reliably, one had no need of a new car until the first one wore out; but if one's car was an indicator of one's taste and income, or if one bought a car because of how it made one feel—pampered, cosseted, carefree—one might well be moved to purchase a new car whenever one's status or mood changed. In theory at least, customers would quit buying goods when a need was filled, while consumers would quit buying goods only when they ran out of money. And customers would continue to use a good until it no longer fulfilled the function it was designed to serve, while consumers might be persuaded to replace a still-functional good as soon as it no longer suited their fancy. As credit gradually became easier to obtain and eventually when credit cards came into near-universal usage, consumers' capacity to fulfill their desires and replenish their self-esteem by purchasing goods expanded exponentially.

By way of illustrating this cultural sea change and the much-expanded role it afforded advertisers, consider a case involving our old friend the phone. The telephone industry, as it turns out, was a bit slow in responding to the new marketplace realities. In part because it was both a well-protected and heavily regulated industry, not to mention a monopolistic one, the telephone industry responded timidly to the new challenges and opportunities afforded by consumer society. Traditionally, phone manufacturers produced one sort of phone until technology advanced to the point that it was economical to produce a new sort of phone. Wall phones with cranks prevailed until phone networks grew in size and complexity and required a new sort of instrument to perform the telephonic function: Voilà, desk phones with dials were born, making it possible to give people telephone numbers with ever more digits. Each home needed only one phone because calls were expensive and the idea of "reaching out and touching someone" with a social call was considered frivolous. (Listening in on party lines to pick up tidbits of gossip, which was seen as a minor sin, anticipates later, more frivolous patterns of phone usage.) And all phones were black because that made them cheaper to manufacture and a phone's color was, after all, irrelevant to its function.

And then in 1928 an AT&T vice president put forth a bold proposal to get his company to change their thinking about phones. Instead of seeing the phone as a utilitarian device, he suggested that it be seen as a convenience. Having phones throughout the home would enhance that home's "livability and smartness." And having multicolored phones would mean that the phone could be used to accessorize the home. After rejecting the notion of colored phones as too radical, AT&T did attempt to market multiple phones for the sake of convenient access. But it would not be until the breakup of the phone industry and the explosion in wireless communication that the full rhetorical potential of phones could be realized; with the advent of cell phones, as we've seen, the desires phones might satisfy—including the desire to transmit visual images in real time—and the rhetorical purposes they might serve multiplied exponentially.

The exemplary case of the phone, which figures prominently in Roland Marchand's remarkable history of early-twentieth-century American advertising *Advertising the American Dream*, could be replicated endlessly. Even Henry Ford, who for years assured the American buying public that they could have a Ford in any color, provided the color was black, was forced to change his thinking when his upstart rival, Alfred Sloan of General Motors, produced multiple makes and models of cars in multiple colors and instantly snared a huge portion of Ford's market share. The idea of buying "this year's model" of car in a color that one fancied was anathema to Ford and many others who had not yet succumbed to the new consumer ethos. The idea of paying for things one did not need violated the Protestant ethic and called the American character into question. An obsession with style and aesthetic matters was generally viewed as a European affliction. But once the genie of consumerism was out of the bottle, there would be no hope of putting it back. And the rhetoric of advertising was interwoven with the logic of consumerism for the rest of the century.

The Logic of Consumerist Advertising

The traditional reason-why advertisement might be viewed as a truncated version of a proposal argument: Describe the problem/need; show how the product solves or fulfills the problem or need. With the advent of the consumerist age, this form of advertisement did not disappear overnight. It was, however, adapted to the new medium for advertising, the mass-market magazine, with its glossy pages and its ever more sophisticated layout and colorful design. In particular, newer versions of reason-why arguments were given considerably more "presence." Consider an early 1920s ad for the mouthwash Listerine. It presents a problem that previous generations had failed to acknowledge (bad breath, puffed up with the long-neglected medical term "halitosis"). It presents the unfortunate consequences of the problem in the form of a little dramatic narrative illustrated with a drawing of a young woman—"a beautiful girl and talented too"—taking up half the ad space. She is depicted gazing wistfully into a mirror, lamenting the fact that she can't find a mate. The reason for this failure, we're told in that omniscient narrative voice still favored by advertisers, is because she has bad breath, a condition that not even her best friends dare tell her about. It offers a solution to the problem (regular gargling with Listerine). And it offers a causal explanation for the success of the product (it "halts food fermentation in the mouth"). There's still an abundance of text here, and the spine of a proposal argument still serves as the organizing principle of the ad. What is different is the prominence given to the visual element of the argument and the parabolic structure of the text—it tells a little story whose moral is to buy and use the product. Not incidentally, that story line follows the same romantic story line used in much of the fiction featured in the magazine, so that what passes for reality in the magazine's short stories is of a piece with the reality reflected in the ad. Any audience that finds the former plausible will likely find the latter persuasive.

Advertisers of the day labeled this new sort of advertising "suggestional" advertising. And before long, arguments were out, suggestion was in. When appealing to people's desires and fantasies as opposed to their reason, advertisers explained, arguments were a crude and ineffective tool. Argument invited skepticism and counterargument. Suggestion invited identification. The favorite suggestive tool of advertisers was the graphic, whether in the form of the highly stylized line drawing, the blurry watercolor, the modern art piece, or knockoff of same. By convention, art of this sort was understood by readers of the day not to be representative of how things actually were. Modern art was supposed to disrupt realist conventions of proportion and linearity. If advertisers borrowed this new genre of art—not only its forms but its prestige and its license—to depart from slavish realism, to present idealized depictions of their products and those who used their products, well, that all seemed innocent enough and in fact flattered audiences that they were hip enough to understand avant-garde art. What could never be *claimed* about a product—"Use it and you'll soon resemble the elegant person depicted in this ad," "Use it and you'll soon be living in an English country estate like the one you see above"—could be *shown* and merely *suggested*.

Over time, the ratio of print to graphics in ads changed dramatically, reducing the function of print to amplifying and underscoring what was artfully "suggested" in the graphic. The rhetoric of advertising became a much more visual than verbal rhetoric. Which is one of the reasons why rhetorical critics, traditionally focused on textual matters, have been unable to get much traction in their critiques of advertising. Early on, for example, one of the favorite pastimes of advertising critics was to point up all the "logical fallacies" one could find in ads. Insofar as the text message was typically the least-important, least-persuasive element of the ad—a point intuitively and universally understood by nonrhetoricians who comprised most of the critics' audience—these critiques tended to fall flat. It would be as if a literary critic, a terminally Serious One, decided to devote all his time and energy to lecturing lovers about the egregious logical fallacies in love poetry.

The analogy between the rhetorical critic of advertising and the literary critic of poetry is not entirely fanciful. The eminent critic Leo Spitzer once referred to advertising as "Gebruchspoeisie," or "poetry of use," insofar as advertisers, following the lead of John Keats with his funeral urn, transformed ordinary objects of everyday use—breakfast cereal, kitchen cleansers, underwear, shampoos—into idealized objects worthy not just of our attention but of our veneration. The process by which advertisers effect this transformation is primarily visual with text supplying critical support for the visual message, amplifying or ironizing it. Still, for all advertising can manage such transformations, there remain significant differences between poetry and advertising—and hard as Spitzer works to treat advertising as a distinctly twentieth-century art form worthy of aesthetic attention, he never quite manages to persuade either us or himself that it is so.

To be sure, the logic of advertising resembles the logic of poetry insofar as both equate different *kinds* of things (old men and trees, cars and social status) and parts with wholes (this urn is all of art, Andie McDowell is every woman who uses this shampoo). But the nature of the transformations effected in advertising are more magical than metaphorical. Words instantaneously animate inanimate objects within a magical space where one image transfers meaning to another merely by their proximity to one another. And against all odds, these transformations are always to the good. In order to inoculate itself against the sort of skepticism that these patently implausible claims give rise to, advertising has come to rely increasingly on irony and humor. In this regard, think for a moment about the countless images of the American family one sees in advertising: What distinguishes one from the other is mostly the degree to which the stereotypes of Mom and Dad, their relationships with each other and with their children, are exaggerated. The degree of exaggeration, and these degrees are carefully calibrated and signaled mostly through visual cues, tell us how to respond to the depiction. While the slightly exaggerated family melodrama (for example, Dad taking his kids to a ballgame) calls for a bathetic response that celebrates the mythical norm depicted in the ad, the grossly exaggerated parody of family life (for example, Mom assuring a friend that she and her spouse bought a new car for its swell styling in scene one, Dad bragging to a friend that he's sold his spouse on a new car because of its powerful engine in scene two, Dad screwing up the grilling of meat in scene three) calls for laughter that reaffirms the same mythical norm from which the depiction has deviated. For the most part, advertising works as hard at remaining familiar and comfortable to its audiences—with some notable exceptions to be discussed—as poetry works at challenging its audience's assumptions and beliefs.

Finessing the Fundamental Contradictions of Consumerist Advertising

Advertisers' persistent attempts to emulate art, to have their audiences respond to ads as they would to works of art, derive in part from their desire to have poetic license extended to their work. In particular, they seek relief from the Law of Contradiction, a law from which only art is consistently granted dispensation. And we don't mean at the simple level of logical fallacies buried in the text of the advertisements. The contradictions of advertising are more fundamental than this. Take, for example, the primary mode of address used by advertisers. The omniscient narrator of the Listerine ad is still the most prevalent voice found in print advertising (though to be sure the know-it-all text is given considerably fewer lines to recite in today's ads). In TV advertising meanwhile, the aural equivalent of the omniscient narrator, the voiceover, often a recognizable, trustworthy celebrity voice, tells us what to think about what we're seeing, foresees the outcome of the scene in progress, or offers a critique of the action. Directly or indirectly, in what has been called a "buttonholing" style of address, such ads speak to each of us individually as "you." As in, here's what "you" ought to conclude about what you're seeing, here's what "you" ought to feel about it. Ironically, of course, the ad is speaking to millions of us as if each of us were the only audience. In the early days of radio advertising, when the irony of this intimate form of mass address was more readily apparent to audiences still new to advertising's conventions, the practice of the singular/universal "you" was referred to as "crooning." Advertisers, like crooners, appeared to pitch an intimate message to a particular person even as millions listened in. Beyond its use in intimate situations, the second-person mode of address is most commonly used in asymmetrical situations. "We" becomes "you," thus, when we're receiving instructions, commands, and imperatives. These two modalities cross when "you" is the child being spoken to by parents, when authority affectionately tells us what to do for our own good, and we are happily infantilized.

The singular/plural, personal/en masse contradiction mirrors an even more fundamental contradiction, the one lying at the heart of identity. As we noted in Chapter 2, an identity can be thought of as that which is most unique about each of us or it can be thought of as that which we share with others of our kind or some combination thereof. Most consumer goods are pitched as if their consumption would help us make manifest what is unique about ourselves. Hence, for example, the beer commercial featuring a barmaid visibly warming to the customer who rejects all the "usual" brews in favor of Samuel Adams—the choice, it is clear, of her most discerning customers. (In ads, the actors are always customers, never consumers, and so too for the duration of the ad are all who identify with those actors.) Here is the fundamental irony of advertising. Looking good in the eyes of another, especially an attractive other, is one's reward for defying convention and selecting a beer that, we are led to believe, is the exclusive choice of those like our hero, who appears to be some metrosexual variant of the Rugged Individualist.

The preceding irony is compounded of course by the fact that the beer in question is sold in massive quantities to millions of people each year. Which brings us to the third contradiction that advertisers must finesse: Not only must they convince millions of people that advertisements are addressed to them in confidence—in the process using consumers' concern with appearances and with fitting in to persuade them that in choosing the advertiser's product, they are choosing to become singular selves—they must also convince consumers that their product, which looks remarkably like many other mass-produced products of the same kind, is the *genuine* article capable of imparting that unique air, that *je ne sais quoi* that will separate them from the herd. In previous eras, before mass production, the authentic version of something was the prototype, the original that spawned imitation. In the late nineteenth and early twentieth centuries, thus, just when mechanical reproduction replaced the work of artisans on a massive scale, wealthy Americans like Randolph Hearst and Isabella Gardener sacked European shrines of their treasures and bought up family collections from impoverished European aristocrats, establishing a monopoly on original works and the aura they imparted. Today, one can still go to a museum (like Hearst Castle in California or the Gardener Museum in Boston) or to a cathedral to see the original work that one has only seen reproduced in books or on art posters, prints, videos, and ads and experience the frisson of authenticity; but actual ownership of an original anything is beyond the reach of all but the very wealthy.

In the realm of commercial products, however, there is no original to be owned. It's imitation all the way down. Authenticity, thus, has to be defined anew by advertisers. Most commonly, this is done by endowing the product's "brand" with the aura that was once the exclusive property of the original. It is the name that is the product's soul, a point made graphically by Andy Warhol's depictions of Campbell's soup cans in the 1960s. Hence the willingness of big businesses to buy up once-prestigious companies with lousy bottom lines. Through association—the basic logic of advertising—of a high-end brand name with their own less prestigious name, they reason, their products are automatically endowed with some of the superior product's aura. For example, in a move that would doubtless have caused Henry Ford considerable consternation given his anti-consumerist outlook, Ford Motor Company in recent years bought the financially troubled Jaguar Motor Company, whose sleek, if mechanically suspect, cars had for nearly a century been the choice of second-tier British patricians unable to afford a Rolls Royce. They then proceeded to turn out a line of Jaguars that looked remarkably like their most popular model of sedan, the Taurus. The danger of such a move, of course, is that the association could work as readily against Ford as for it. Rather than lending a much-needed soupçon of aura to the dowdy Taurus, the move might end up resulting in the fatal demystification of the numinous Jaguar name.

A cheaper and more common way of realizing the same end is to associate one's brand with a celebrity figure who epitomizes the qualities that one wishes the public to perceive in one's product. Again, the basic logic is magical. If you "wanna be like Mike," you ingest the very breakfast cereal that he ingests and endorses. Or you wear the same shoes. Thus in a classic ad campaign from the 1990s, Nike, one of the first companies to perceive the heightened value of celebrity, presented Jordan, along with filmmaker Spike Lee in the role of "Mars Blackman," a geeky Jordan wannabe adamant about the fact that Mike's extraordinary accomplishments were all the result of his shoe choice. "It's gotta be the shoes!" he would exclaim hopefully after watching some transcendent piece of Jordan court magic, obviously hoping that buying the shoes would magically compensate for his deficiencies in height, talent, and commitment. Jordan, meanwhile, would smile indulgently at Mars's clearly fallacious, magical reasoning, without confirming or denying its efficacy.

It's an exemplary ad on a number of scores. Jordan's celebrity, lent presence by visuals of his court performance, is certainly key to the ad's persuasive appeal. But Spike Lee's performance adds a critical touch as well. Lee has produced, directed, and starred in a number of edgy films on racial themes. In his own way, he's as much an icon as Jordan. But if Jordan is the mainstream hero, Lee is the more hip figure in popular culture, a fact that's underscored by his playing against type in the person of Mars. The confluence of mainstream (as measured by purchases of the product) and hip (as measured by disdain for those who purchase a product because everyone else does) is every advertiser's dream. Moreover Nike's target demographic had to believe either that the shoes by themselves might turn them into virtuoso basketball players—a delusion ironized but not refuted in the ad—or that wearing them would mark them as a "player," someone serious about the game of basketball like Mike but not delusional about their effects like Mars. As is often the case in advertising, the ad anticipates a hostile response to what's being suggested in the ad, an illogical identification of product with celebrity, and neutralizes it by parodying those who would believe such a preposterous thing in the person of Mars. In the process, it invites us to identify with Mike, to be as savvy as he about the origins of basketball talent, while at the same time joining him in his affectionate indulgence of Mars. And when we later learned that many poor kids were engaging in criminal activity to get the extremely expensive shoes, and that Nike relied on cheap foreign labor to make the shoes, the warm, friendly ads doubtless went a long way toward defusing public animosity.

The Benetton Effect

Other companies have dealt even more imaginatively with the problem of authenticity. Take the case of Benetton, the maker of high-end casual clothes. During the 1980s foreign manufacturers began producing massive numbers of Benetton knockoffs at bargain prices. They began finding their way into European and American marketplaces and severely hurt Benetton's sales. Benetton's imaginative response to all this was to emblazon its name on everything it sold. Its name became part of the garment—a veritable branding nirvana. Those who bought their goods became walking advertisements for the company. And while their designs, which were fairly standard, could be easily copied, putting the Benetton name on the clothes would violate trademark law, at least in Benetton's biggest markets. Here is the "real" Benetton, their sweatshirts announced, not a set of cotton swatches sewn together in an easily replicated pattern, but *The Brand*. In due time, Benetton's advertising campaign, under the direction of the mercurial Oliviero Toscani, took a very different turn that reflected their shift in marketing strategy.

Benetton became well known in the decade of the 1990s for a series of ads that seemed to defy advertising logic. They seldom depicted the product and they did not feature celebrities or models endorsing or wearing the product. What was depicted was typically controversial and almost wholly unrelated to, indeed antithetical to, the wearing of expensive casual clothes. And the manner of depiction was decidedly edgy. To understand Benetton's thinking here, one has to keep in mind that in their marketing they had already shifted the emphasis from the actual Benetton product to the Benetton name. Anyone could make a sweatshirt exactly like the ones they made, but only Benetton could outfit you in a "Benetton" and in the process let everyone you came in contact with know that you were a "Benetton" sort of person. So the task of advertising was no longer to move audiences to buy sweatshirts; advertising now focused exclusively on bending an audience's attitude toward the Benetton name. The more puzzling the ads, the more remote they appeared to be from casual clothes or the ads produced by other manufacturers of casual clothes, the more buzz the ads created, the better for the name. The product, in the ultimate consumerist inversion of traditional thinking, became a medium for advertising the brand.

Typical of the ads produced by Benetton in recent years is this image of a burning car shown on the next page. Only the boxed, green-lettered notation in the upper right of the photograph, "United Colors of Benetton," tells us it's an advertisement. In the code of visual rhetoric, the fact that the image is (or is made to resemble) a documentary photograph tells us it's "real," as surely as the colorful, airbrushed photographs of models wearing sports clothes in trendy locales tells us we're viewing an ad, an idealization of the sort Toscani dismissed as "banal." The image is as gritty and realistic as a newspaper photograph. What, one wonders, makes it worthy of journalistic attention? Is it part of a protest? A terrorist attack? An act of random violence? Did people die in the car? If so, were they public figures? But there are no answers and very few clues about the time and the place of the burning car. It's

pure spectacle, an arresting image lacking an explanatory narrative. It's left to the audience to create its own connections to the Benetton line of sportswear. In the language of metaphor, the ad is a "conceit," an equation or comparison of two impossibly remote terms.

The puzzlement one feels upon seeing the ad is not unlike the puzzlement one experiences when viewing some "serious" films that eschew high production values, big-name actors, and traditional narrative in favor of a montage or the juxtaposition of compelling but mysterious black-and-white images and unexplained events. The defamiliarization one experiences in both cases heightens one's attention to the images and sets one's mind to work providing an interpretive framework. For example, one might well be moved to ask in the case of the Benetton ad why the company chooses to refer to itself as the "United Colors of Benetton," with the suggestion that it is a political entity of some sort, a republic of diversely colored sweatshirts. Do the united colors of a global corporation represent an instructive alternative to the burning cars of mere nation-states? There isn't enough information to reach any sort of satisfactory closure on the spectacular image of the burning car. Which is, it would appear, pretty much the point. The image gets attention, stirs up controversy, gets criticized in some quarters for being provocative if unhelpful; and is then reproduced and written about by semioticians, rhetoricians, and English professors. It creates buzz about Benetton, and associates it with countercultural, subversive values and strong commitment to . . . something, we're not sure what, that has nothing to do with leisure wear. It is an instance of what Toscani has referred to as "the platonic sale," a pitch that eschews customer seduction in the name of arresting her attention. So those who choose Benetton are reassured by the ads and the buzz the ads create that by donning Benetton goods they are marked as out of the mainstream, serious, hip, perhaps even slightly dangerous, folk. And as Malcolm Gladwell argues persuasively in *The Tipping Point*, this is the very sort of buzz best designed to generate the spread of infectious consumer interest.

The Miller Man

The last ad we'll consider combines the sort of high-concept edginess of Benetton ads with the more classic approach of Nike. A series of ads that Oscar-winning documentary filmmaker Errol Morris created for Miller Beer combine: (1) numerous reassuring stereotypes from American myth; (2) state-of-the-art film techniques of documentary production; and (3) perhaps the ultimate ironizing voice-over. So popular was the series of ads that Morris was asked to develop a weekly sitcom series based on the "Archie Bunker-like" escapades of his Miller Man creation. But for all the aesthetic quality of the ads, they serve a clear rhetorical purpose in relation to a carefully delineated audience. Morris manages to do in these ads what advertisers often strive to do—make a virtue of a necessity. He does so by creating a niche for a product that could not win in head-to-head competition with the mainstream beer and that lacked any unique qualities that might be used to distinguish it from mainstream beer. Morris took a bland, "auraless" product and transformed bland into a mystique. He created ads that would appeal to people who were resolutely not hip, who would never resonate with the sort of ads that appealed to the younger consumers of Miller's sister beers, MGD and Miller Lite. So how does he do this?

We never see the face of the middle-aged white protagonist of the ads, who may or may not be the same person as the person narrating the voice-over. We see him fuzzily at a distance, heading out from a diner to call his "little lady" on the pay phone (the *lack* of a cell phone in this case is an important rhetorical element of his identity); we see his hand reaching to take a beer from a fridge full of beer out in the garage; we see a hand placing a rose in an empty Miller bottle; we see a hand with a fork in it bringing food to an invisible mouth. The camera angles are often odd, off-kilter, distorting proportions. The camera lingers on objects a bit longer than any inherent interest in the object would seem to justify. The colors are washed out and pale, almost like old-fashioned tinted photographs. White is the dominant color of the ads and one in particular pays tribute to a white plate heaped with monochromatic foods—mashed potatoes and milk gravy, corn and fried chicken—that Miller Man muses just might be the ultimate in culinary presentation. All the while, the voice, warm and husky, a blue-collar voice, full of certitude, sings the praises of "the high life" represented by these relentlessly bland, but slightly mysterious scenes. Clearly, the voice has it mostly wrong. It's the cocksure voice of the provincial, whose certitude is a function of ignorance rather than experience and introspection. But it's a warm and lovable voice whose foibles we chuckle at rather than condemn. The Miller Man with his quaint notions of the good life may not be hip, but he flatters us that *we* are because we are ever so slightly more hip than he. Moreover, our sense of superiority is buttressed by the sense that we are spying on our subject, seeing him "offstage" through a hidden camera that produces images like a security camera in a department store.

Like the beer he hawks, the Miller Man is neither fashionable nor remarkable, merely comfortable. Like one's slightly embarrassing uncle who still gets invited to dinner, or the decrepit rump-sprung easy chair we can never quite bring ourselves to toss, Miller Man wins little but our affection. He's like a secondary character on one of the sitcoms that bracket his ads. A stereotypical figure who can be counted on to say the inappropriately funny thing in any social situation, particularly those that are strained. In fact the synergy between ads and the shows they sponsor is a key to their effectiveness. The shows people watch, the characters and values they identify with, are amplified in the ads, which means that viewers will be able to pick up on a fifteen-to-thirty-second commercial almost at once. And the virtual reality of network television, with its countless rapid-fire images, instant plot resolutions, and spectacular effects covering for implausible premises and improbable characters, makes us that much more receptive to the magical associations of advertising.

In sum, advertising can be thought of as something on the order of anti-travel. If the ideal traveler is alert, contemplative, and eager to experience novel situations and to learn from the experience, the ideal (from the advertiser's perspective) viewer/reader of advertising is a passive receptor of fleeting images that circumvent the critical sensibility and go directly to the brain, where they endlessly jostle with one another, forming a powerful network of associational linkages inclining us to experience lustful thoughts at the sight of a Nike swoosh, to smile warmly at the image of a Miller beer, or to imagine that our Benetton sweatshirt makes an important, if vague, political statement to all whom we pass.

That's what advertisers would like us to do. But few of us are that gullible or that inclined to confuse what we consume with who we are. In truth, for all their rhetorical sophistication, there's not a whole lot of empirical evidence that advertising actually works, at least not in the sense that more dollars spent on advertising translate directly into more sales. My fear is that advertising works in far subtler ways to undermine our agency. The dangers of advertisements derive less from their promotion of shallow materialism than from their cumulative effects on our attitudes and priorities and on the degradation of public discourse. Increasingly, the language and logic of advertising has been turned to the service of political ends. Particularly in the realm of foreign affairs, as Jacques Ellul foresaw forty years ago in his groundbreaking work on propaganda, democratic nations market foreign policy changes and wars to their public as if they were a revolutionary detergent or a new drug. But that's a topic for another day and another book.

Conclusion

By way of bringing *Rhetoric: A User's Guide* to its close, it seems appropriate to offer a final word about what is meant by the *use* of rhetoric and how this, the book's final chapter, fulfills the title's promise to make rhetoric useable. "Use" in the context of rhetoric generally refers to two sorts of activity: construing and constructing and their various cognates including interpreting and persuading, reading and writing, perceiving and articulating, analyzing and producing, and so forth. But as earlier noted, there's little to choose between the two activities. To repeat Ann Berthoff's reversible dictum, "How you construe is how you construct." In both cases, you are making meaning, engaging in what rhetoricians call "invention." In the case of persuasion and interpretation, this convergence was most clearly seen in Chapter 3 in the context of a discussion about persuasion in its purest form. Pure persuasion occurs when the agent producing an argument simultaneously becomes a close reader and interpreter of her unfolding argument and follows her text where it takes her ("I find my way by going where I have to go") rather than where some *a priori* design, ulterior motive, or desired response from an audience might lead her. (By the same token, persuasion is most readily distinguished from interpretation at the other end of the continuum when it is at its least pure, when it takes the form of propaganda, and manipulative and deceitful means are used to market unassailable assumptions.)

Perhaps the clearest illustration of the principle that "How you construe is how you construct" can be seen in the earlier discussion of "the rhetorical situation." The debate between the naive realists who would treat the rhetorical situation as there and waiting for us to discover it, and the subjective idealists who would treat it as an invention completely of our own devising, was resolved, it may be recalled, by deeming it a bit of both—discovered *and* invented. Most who persist in seeing this as a contradiction rather than a resolution do so on the grounds that *construction* is a creative activity resulting in something new, while *construing* is a calculative activity (akin to problem or puzzle solving) resulting in the mere conversion of the implicit to the explicit (as in *explication*). Only when both processes are understood as "Acts" in the rhetorical sense, as purposive human motions productive of novelty, does the contradiction disappear. And such an understanding becomes possible as soon as *meaning* is accorded the status of a product, a made thing (*poeisis*) and not some mere epiphenomenon.

All this tail chasing is by way of clarifying what's actually been done in this chapter. One might be excused for thinking that it has been a whole lot more about analyzing than producing, construing than constructing. Much of the chapter has been spent interpreting acts, texts, and circumstances, making sense of cell phone usage, travel, and advertising. No cell phone conversations were actually constructed, no travel narratives written, no goods advertised, and no directions for achieving such ends were offered. What we did was talk about these matters and occasionally "talk about our talk about." And to many, that will sound more like analysis than production. Unless of course one understands the two to be in fact one and the same activity, seen at different moments in a process or from different perspectives. Which I do.

This assumption of equivalence underlies every chapter in the book including this one. It was exemplified in Chapters 3 and 4, through the analysis of the 2003 State of the Union Address, which can be seen with equal justice either as an illustration of how one goes about construing a political speech, as a case study in how one might go about constructing a political speech, or as a demonstration of how one might go about disputing a political speech. The same set of considerations, the same heuristics, would apply in every case. Meanwhile, the principle justifying our equation of the two sorts of "use" in rhetoric can be found back in Chapter 2 in the form of Burke's paradox of substance stating that "the word 'substance,' used to designate what a thing *is*, derives from a word designating something that a thing is *not*" (GOM, 23). Nothing we construct can be fully self-explanatory, its meaning purely intrinsic. As we saw in Chapter 5, even Keats's urn, for all its smug assurances of eternal self-sameness, must become a different thing as its circumstances and audiences change and as it is perceived *in terms of* an ever-changing ensemble of other things and an ever-changing vocabulary. No construction of the urn, or anything else, is possible without construing. The piece of Greek pottery that serves as Keats's model was itself modeled after—understood *in terms of*—other pieces of Greek pottery. And as it turns out, every construction follows a similar logic. Which is why what we have been calling construction is, as others before us have suggested, better understood as *reconstruction*. None of us ever creates anything ab nihilo without first consulting and interpreting a model, a claim, a theory, and so forth. And so to the extent that our rhetorical enterprise can be understood via analogy to the construction industry, we are more properly thought of as humble remodelers and restorers than as grand builders.

There's no way to bring this analysis to a satisfactory halt. Before anything can be constructed, something else must be construed; but what is construed of course must at some point have been constructed. It is a never-ending dialectic process. Every thesis provokes an antithesis from whence a synthesis arises, only to itself become a thesis sure to provoke another antithesis. So by way of rendering all this at least a bit less vertiginous, let us return to one of the metaphors that began this little book, the homely metaphor of conversation.

If rhetoric is to be conceived of as a useful art, its usefulness surely lies in promoting better, richer conversations—conversations capable of forestalling conflict and overcoming indifference, of converting enmity to critical understanding and difference to identification—and in shaping more able conversationalists—conversationalists capable of *both* critical listening and thoughtful speaking. And the endless back-and-forth of conversation is as inviting as the endless back-and-forth of dialectic—that venerable, if slightly menacing engine of German metaphysics—is off-putting. There is no "closure" to good conversations, the best of which long outlive any given cast of conversationalists. Likewise there is no "progress" to a conversation, no inexorable movement toward a higher state and the silence of complete understanding. There is no "good life" apart from this life lying in wait for us at the end of our conversation. Our conversation is not the means to the good life, it *is* the good life. And the usefulness of rhetoric is in turn not an instrumental usefulness, it is an ecological usefulness whose value lies not in securing our success, but in rendering us maximally conscious of the world we live in and better able to evaluate the standards by which success is judged. Which seems quite enough.

BIBLIOGRAPHY

✢

(GOM) Kenneth Burke. *A Grammar of Motives*. Berkeley. University of California Press, 1969.

(LSA) Kenneth Burke. *Language as Symbolic Action*. Berkeley. University of California Press, 1966.

(P&C) Kenneth Burke. *Permanence and Change*. 3d ed. Berkeley. University of California Press, 1984.

(PLF) Kenneth Burke. *The Philosophy of Literary Form*. 1941. New York. Vintage, 1957.

(ROM) Kenneth Burke. *A Rhetoric of Motives*. Berkeley. University of California Press, 1969.

(ROR) Kenneth Burke. *The Rhetoric of Religion*. Berkeley. University of California Press, 1970.

CREDITS

❧

page 66: From "Daddy" from *Ariel* by Sylvia Plath. Copyright © by Ted Hughes. Reprinted by permission of HarperCollins Publishers.

page 205: Copyright 1992 Benetton Group S.p.A. Photo: Gian Luigi Bellini/Globe. Concept: Oliviero Toscani.

INDEX